Stanley M. ~~Hauer~~...
and Peter Ochs, University of Virginia

RADICAL TRADITIONS cuts new lines of inquiry across a confused array of debates concerning the place of theology in modernity and, more generally, the status and role of scriptural faith in contemporary life. Charged with a rejuvenated confidence, spawned in part by the rediscovery of reason as inescapably tradition-constituted, a new generation of theologians and religious scholars is returning to scriptural traditions with the hope of retrieving resources long ignored, depreciated, and in many cases ideologically suppressed by modern habits of thought. RADICAL TRADITIONS assembles a promising matrix of strategies, disciplines, and lines of thought that invites Jewish, Christian, and Islamic theologians back to the word, recovering and articulating modes of scriptural reasoning as that which always underlies modernist reasoning and therefore has the capacity — and authority — to correct it.

Far from despairing over modernity's failings, postcritical theologies rediscover resources for renewal and self-correction within the disciplines of academic study themselves. Postcritical theologies open up the possibility of participating once again in the living relationship that binds together God, text, and community of interpretation. RADICAL TRADITIONS thus advocates a "return to the text," which means a commitment to displaying the richness and wisdom of traditions that are at once text-based, hermeneutical, and oriented to communal practice.

Books in this series offer the opportunity to speak openly with practitioners of other faiths or even with those who profess no (or limited) faith, both academics and nonacademics, about the ways religious traditions address pivotal issues of the day. Unfettered by foundationalist preoccupations, these books represent a call for new paradigms of reason — a thinking and rationality that are more responsive than originative. By embracing a postcritical posture, they are able to speak unapologetically out of scriptural traditions manifest in the practices of believing communities (Jewish, Christian, and others); articulate those practices through disciplines of philosophic, textual, and cultural criticism; and engage intellectual, social, and political practices that for too long have been insulated from theological evaluation. RADICAL TRADITIONS is radical not only in its confidence in non-apologetic theological speech but also in how the practice of such speech challenges the current social and political arrangements of modernity.

Theology, Rhetoric, Manuduction,

or

Reading Scripture Together on the Path to God

Peter M. Candler Jr.

British Library Cataloguing in Publication Data

A Catalogue record for this book is available
from the British Library

0 334 04031 0 / 9780 334 04031 6

1004792026

First published in 2006 in the United States of America by
Wm. B. Eerdmans Publishing Co.
and in the U.K. by
SCM Press
9-17 St Albans Place, London N1 0NX

www.scmpress.co.uk

SCM Press is a division of
SCM-Canterbury Press Ltd

Printed in the United States of America

Ideoque et nos tantam
habentes circumpositam
nobis nubem testium . . .

Contents

Acknowledgments

This book has grown out of a great deal of time spent in cafés, pubs, and living rooms eating, drinking and talking with, but mostly listening to, friends without whom I would be a vastly different person, particularly Gerry Barrett, Conor Cunningham, Michael Hanby, John Hayes, John Montag, Simon Oliver and Natascha Zajac. Their devotion and friendship has made the thought of doing anything but theology unthinkable. I owe a special debt to John Milbank, without whose intellectual generosity and encouragement this project might have never been finished, and to Graham Ward, without whom it might never have begun. To him and to Mary Ward I am grateful for their wisdom, counsel, and incomparable hospitality. I am thankful for the parish churches of Little Saint Mary's, Cambridge, and St. Joseph's, Durham, for being the kinds of communities that, in the most profound sense, make theology possible. I owe an immense debt to my doctoral supervisors, Catherine Pickstock and Janet Soskice, who suffered with me through an earlier incarnation of this project, and who have been my most steadfast advocates and interlocutors.

I am deeply grateful to those who gave their valuable time to read and comment on different drafts of this essay, especially Stanley Hauerwas, Mark D. Jordan, Fergus Kerr, Philipp W. Rosemann, and Denys Turner. I am thankful to Fritz Bauerschmidt, who offered constructive criticism on chapter seven, which appeared previously in *Modern Theology*. I am further grateful to Fritz and Jim Fodor for permission to reprint that essay here in slightly different form. I am especially indebted to Stanley Hauerwas and Peter Ochs, the editors of the *Radical Traditions* series, for their encouragement, enthusiasm, and incisive criticism.

Above all, my greatest debts are to those whom I did not choose, but who first of all chose me: my family. Without the support and unfailing love of my parents, Peter and Shannon, nothing that I have done is imaginable. Likewise, my brother Matt has been a constant support and a careful and enthusiastic reader and interpreter of my writing. They have all been supportive in countless ways, of many of which only I am aware. Finally, I am humbled and continually surprised by my most inspiring reader, my wife, Meredith, who is and has been for me "the light between truth and reason."

Peter M. Candler, Jr.
A Thursday
2005

Introduction

Let the peoples above the heavens, your angels, praise you. They have no need to look up to this firmament and to read so as to know your word. They ever 'see your face' and there, without syllables requiring time to pronounce, they read what your eternal will intends. They read, they choose, they love. They ever read, and what they read never passes away. By choosing and loving they read the immutability of your design. Their codex is never closed, nor is their book ever folded shut. For you yourself are a book to them and you are 'for eternity'.[1]

In a thirteenth-century map of the world discovered in 1830 in the Benedictine Abbey of Ebstorf, the whole of terrestrial creation is pictured, in typical medieval fashion, as a circle, with Jerusalem at its center.[2] The entire image is,

---

1. Augustine, *Confessions*, tr. Henry Chadwick (Oxford: Oxford University Press, 1991), XIII.xv.18.

2. Now known as the Ebstorf *mappamundi*, the map has been tenuously attributed to Gervase of Tilbury (c. 1160-1235). After its discovery in Ebstorf, it was removed to Hanover's Museum of the Historical Society of Lower Saxony. In 1888 it was taken to Berlin for restoration and comprehensively photographed, and later returned to Hanover. During an air raid in 1943, the map was destroyed. See reproductions and historical details in J. B. Harley and David Woodward, eds., *The History of Cartography*. Volume I: *Cartography in Prehistoric, Ancient, and Medieval Europe and the Mediterranean* (Chicago: University of Chicago Press, 1987), pp. 307ff., esp. fig. 18.19. See also Jon R. Stone, "The Medieval Mappaemundi: Toward an Archaeology of Sacred Cartography," *Religion* XXIII (1993), pp. 197-216; David Woodward, "Reality, Symbolism, Time, and Space in Medieval World Maps," *Annals of the Association of American Geographers* LXXV.4 (1985), pp. 510-21.

as it were, superimposed on the body of Christ, whose extremities represent the directions of the compass: the head of Christ in the east, his hands at north and south, and his feet marking the west. Looking at this map, one is forced to orient oneself not according to modern standards of objectivity, but, one might say, as a reader. After all, the map is structured as a complex organization of narratives, with what now seems like bizarre and superfluous information not found on modern maps of the world: architectural structures, animals, human beings, and text.

It quickly becomes apparent to the modern observer that to make sense of the Ebstorf *mappamundi*, it must be *read*. It cannot simply be *seen* and understood; its foreign idiom must somehow be taught, learned and *inhabited*. In turn, it suggests that reading a map such as this and reading a modern atlas bear only an analogical, if not equivocal, relationship to one another. For certainly modern maps must also be "read." But the appearance of the Ebstorf map, with its reorientation of directions — north is not at the top of the map, but on the left — and series of narrative elements and fabulous figures, hints that there is something different about reading this "text" from reading a modern representation of space. It implies not only a different ordering of space, but a different orientation of the reader to the "known." In other words, it suggests a mode of reading which is less the comprehension of a tableau than the performance of a sequence of movements.[3]

Yet it also seems to indicate that to read the world rightly is to read it in Christ, and that the world itself is rendered intelligible only by seeing it as a kind of diaphanous veil which simultaneously hides and discloses the God who creates it. As an exegetical event, the map is "a pattern of signs organized around — and by — the incarnate Word in such a way that all the signs remain signs, all are kept open to the horizon of God, in virtue of their relation to the central acting out in cross and resurrection of God's otherness from the realm of representation."[4] All of creation, it is implied, gathers its meaningfulness from its orientation to Christ the head, the only true agent of knowledge. "For in his hand[s]," the Wisdom of Solomon says, "are both we and our words."[5] As such, the Ebstorf map is a kind of analogy for the way in which Christian theology understands the relationship of human knowledge to divine knowledge, and of reading to *salus*. Moreover, one might say that the Ebstorf map visually glosses the comprehensive claim

---

3. Michel de Certeau, "Spatial Stories," in *The Practice of Everyday Life*, tr. Steven Rendall (Berkeley: University of California Press, 1984), p. 119.

4. Rowan Williams, discussing Augustine's account of Scripture, in "Language, Reality and Desire in Augustine's *De Doctrina*," *Literature & Theology* III.2 (July 1989), p. 147.

5. Wisdom of Solomon 7.16.

over all of Christian discipleship of the command given to St. Augustine in a garden in Milan: *tolle, lege.*[6]

The Christian life, one might argue, is a lifelong training in how to read well, beginning, of course, with the Holy Scriptures, but also extending to how to read the signs around us which together constitute our world. For Augustine, the gerund "reading" is descriptive of the fundamental character of the relationship of creatures to God and his creation. In learning to read the Scriptures, in learning to read the "book of nature," and indeed, in learning to read our own lives, we are led towards God by the orientation of our desire to its proper referent. Because we are creatures of God, we are his readers in the world. Thus Augustine describes the Scriptures as a "firmament" which hangs suspended above the world, like a translucent "skin" that at once conceals and reveals. Reading, for Augustine, is the function not only of mortals but also of angels, who do not need the "firmament" of Scripture because they are able to read God himself as a "book." They read immediately, while we read mediate-ly. They read in an instant, while for us reading takes time.

"Reading," then, describes how creatures relate to and know God, as the product not of immediate apprehension but of time-bound, transient learning, mediated to us by the communication of God through the people gathered around his Word. Reading is thus related to knowing, and therefore also to being. As angelic beings participate in the life of God more fully than do human beings, their reading of God is not mediated through a narrative, but is instantaneous and atemporal, inasmuch as it participates in the eternity of God. For humans, then, participation in the triune life of God is not atemporal but historical and contingent, overlaid, as it were, by the firmament of the Scriptures. Thus Augustine can pray, "Dispel from our eyes the cloud with which you have covered them."[7] In reading, therefore, we come to know God, and in being read, God teaches.

This essay examines the reading of written texts that are designed to teach, that is, to lead us to God. As St. Thomas Aquinas writes in the *De Veritate*, "We are forbidden to call man a teacher in this sense, that we attribute to him the pre-eminence of teaching, which belongs to God. It would be as if we put our hope in the wisdom of men, and did not rather consult divine truth about those things which we hear from man. And this divine truth speaks in us through the impression of its likeness, by means of which we can judge of all things."[8]

---

6. Augustine, *Confessions* VIII.xii.29. For Augustine, the command to "pick up and read" is the particular *form* of Jesus' command to "follow me" (Matthew 19:21). Cf. Augustine's reading of St. Antony's typological figuration of his own conversion there.

7. *Confessions* XIII.xv.17.

8. Thomas Aquinas, *On Truth* [*Quaestiones disputatae de veritate*], 3 vols., tr. Robert W.

If Thomas Aquinas is right, and God alone teaches, then anything we learn of God is not a knowledge superadded to the knowledge of himself which he already possesses, but is rather an analogous kind of knowledge, one which shares in the knowledge God already has of himself. If that is true, then when we read "about" God (for unlike angels we cannot "read" God directly), we learn best when we submit ourselves to the authority of others whom we assume to know better than we do. We give ourselves over to be led by the hand into a more true knowledge of him, one which more perfectly resembles his own.

Hence the concentration in what follows on *pedagogy,* and the ways in which texts guide their readers not towards the merely instrumental goal of a greater accumulation of intellectual data but, in hope, toward the perfect and simple apprehension of God in the beatific vision, that is, the eternal and immediate reading of God himself. Insofar as God's knowledge is one with his being, to participate in God's self-knowledge is at the same time to participate in his being. Thus to grow in knowledge is to grow in being, to come *to be* more truly. As Aquinas says, knowledge exists in part already in the mind potentially; yet it must be, as it were, "activated" by either its own internal principle or from without. This latter he calls "learning by instruction."[9] Thus the causing of knowledge in another is a participation in the teaching activity of God in two ways: one, by analogously "causing" the potential knowledge to be made actual knowledge; and two, by instructing the learner in what he or she did not know before. In both of these ways, the teacher "imitates" God, whose prerogative alone it is to cause knowledge. If texts can be said to teach, then, the reading of them must share in this same mimetic participation in divine knowledge.

In this essay, I hope to illustrate the ways in which the notion of participation in divine self-knowledge is borne out in "learning by instruction" through various textual practices of the Middle Ages. The fundamental claim of this essay is that this notion of participation is embodied in a grammar, in the way in which texts are organized as structures for the manuduction ("leading-by-the-hand") of readers along an itinerary of exit and return from creation to eschatological beatitude. I offer, employing an Augustinian account of rhetoric and grammar, a reading of two medieval texts in particular as paradigmatic instances of just such an itinerary: the *Glossa Ordinaria* and the *Summa*

Mulligan et al. (Indianapolis: Hackett, 1994), vol. II, XI.1 *ad* 1, p. 84. See also Etienne Gilson, *The Christian Philosophy of St. Thomas Aquinas,* tr. L. K. Shook, CSB (Notre Dame: Notre Dame University Press, 1956, 1994), pp. 3-7.

9. *On Truth, resp.*

Theologiae. In these two cases, the metaphors of itinerary and manuduction will be seen to be crucial to the rhetorical persuasion which they conduct.

The corollary to the claim that such a grammar exists is the claim that, in the early modern period, it eventually became displaced by competing rhetorical strategies which privileged mathematical accuracy and a universal method, or *mathesis,*[10] for the arrangement and teaching of knowledge. This latter mode I call a grammar of representation, which instantiated new dualisms, foreign to the texts I discuss here, between reader and text, form and content, subject and object, and so on. What I hope to suggest is that what held all these dualities together before the rise of representation was the doctrine of participation in the Trinity. I will say more in Chapter One about the characteristics of both a grammar of participation and one of representation, but in the meantime, I will attempt to paint a picture of pre-modern reading practices and their relationship to liturgy, and the extent to which the displacement of participation was the result of innovations internal to certain late-medieval and early modern theological traditions.

Throughout the course of this essay, four key concepts will appear which are central to the understanding of these texts in terms of their rhetorical aims. They are 1) *ductus;* 2) *skopos;* 3) *manuductio;* 4) *traditio.* I will treat each of these in more detail in their specific contexts, but introduce them here in a brief sketch of the senses in which I will use them.

This first term, *ductus,* refers to the movement of a particular composition, or the "route" by which a text moves from one place to another. It is a function of both authorial composition and of reading, insofar as when one reads a text, one as it were travels along the *ductus* of the composition. As such, the notion of *ductus* is very much tied to the notion of *skopos,* which refers to the *telos* of the composition. It is, in terms of rhetorical persuasion, that state of being persuaded of something. Thus to reach the *skopos* of the text is to be led along the *ductus,* not simply to a cognition of principles one did not know before, but to reach a "place" of *being* differently.

The third term, *manuductio,* is then linked etymologically to the first, *ductus.* Manuduction suggests the company among whom one travels along the rhetorical route toward the *skopos.* It implies a pedagogical bearing, inasmuch as to course along the itinerary of a text is to be "led by the hand," and to be subject to the guiding of others.

The final term, *traditio,* refers, in a sense, to the diachronic activity of manuduction across a historical multiplicity of texts and interlocutors. It is

---

10. For an account and critique of *mathesis,* see Catherine Pickstock, *After Writing: On the Liturgical Consummation of Philosophy* (Oxford: Blackwell, 1998), pp. 47-74.

related to *manuductio* by virtue of the metaphor of the "hand." For as manuduction is a "leading by the hand," *traditio* is a "handing over," both in the sense of a "passing on" and a yielding of the "rights" to authorial ownership. Each of these terms will surface in much more detail as they pertain to specific textual circumstances and usages, but in brief, and taken together, these four terms illustrate the centrality to a grammar of participation of the notions of motion, pedagogy, and benevolent heteronomy.

If the grammar of participation is descriptive of a pre-modern theologicalliterary procedure, our question now becomes, what did theological writing *before modernity* look like? As much as writing and copying theological manuscripts was an essential part of thirteenth-century monastic or scholastic life, it could hardly be said that it was *de rigueur* for each monk or schoolman to write his own *Summa* or Commentary on the Psalms, in the way that "writing" is the *sine qua non* of modern academic theology. The modern university no doubt owes its origins to the theologians of this period, among whom Thomas Aquinas is popularly recognized for, among other things, inaugurating a tradition of scholarship that represents a break from the monastic form of education. Yet this way of telling the story betrays a host of modern presuppositions, one of which is the way it assumes a particular form of the relationship between reader and text. Much unlike the highly prized silence of our great research libraries, medieval monastic *scriptoria* are saturated with noise.[11] The monk capable of reading without moving his lips and talking to himself is, in this period, considered an oddity.[12] Reading is an activity not only of the eyes, but also of the ears, not to mention of the whole body.[13] The text serves chiefly as an aid to the verbal articulation of words orally, which suggests that at this stage, writing is not only derivative of speech but also simply a record thereof for its further and future vocalization.[14]

11. Cf. Ivan Illich, *In the Vineyard of the Text: A Commentary to Hugh's* Didascalicon (Chicago: University of Chicago Press, 1993), p. 87; Walter J. Ong, S.J., *The Presence of the Word: Some Prolegomena for Cultural and Religious History* (Minneapolis: University of Minnesota Press, 1967), pp. 58, 271. See also Florence Edler de Roover, "The Scriptorium," in James Westfall Thompson, ed., *The Medieval Library* (Chicago: University of Chicago Press, 1939), pp. 594-612.

12. Augustine tells of encountering his master Ambrose reading to himself in silence, which he considers such an oddity that he spends some length speculating as to his reasons for doing so, only to conclude that "Whatever motive he had for his habit, this man had good reason for doing what he did." Augustine, *Confessions* VI.iii.3, pp. 91-92.

13. See Mary Carruthers, "Reading with Attitude, Remembering the Book," in Dolores Warwick Frese and Katherine O'Brien O'Keefe, eds., *The Book and the Body* [Ward-Phillips Lectures in English Language and Literature 14] (Notre Dame: Notre Dame University Press, 1997), pp. 1-33.

14. See Walter J. Ong, S.J., *Orality and Literacy: The Technologizing of the Word* (London:

Even when sufficient literacy is achieved by the medieval monk so as to permit reading privately in one's cell, this form of engagement with the text is never abstracted from a rigorous daily routine of matins, masses, vespers, and so on. *Lectio divina* is, however "private" reading might be, always a matter of reading and interpreting not just communally but liturgically. "*Lectio divina* is always a liturgical act, *coram,* in the face of, someone — God, angels, or anyone within earshot. There was no need, in the time between Benedict and Bernard, to insist on the social responsibility of the reader. It was obvious that his readings would reappear in the comments he would weave into his homily or letters."[15] It is not a possibility for such religious to abstract their reading from the liturgical cycle of daily masses and annual feasts, the use of the entire body, hands, knees, lips, tongue, ears, not to mention the eyes, all of which the reading of such texts requires. This might beg the question of the extent to which the enterprise of modern academic reading is less derivative of the *lectio divina* of the Middle Ages, but rather owes its existence more directly to the silent and lonely reading which is familiar to Descartes. The inviolable privacy of the modern academic, locked up in the impenetrable isolation of his or her centrally-heated room, stands at a dramatic distance from the murmuring holy reading of the cloisters. Yet it is assumed, in modernity, that the situation of the production of "texts" within a liturgical cycle of performance is irrelevant to the *kind* of "texts" which are produced. This assumption betrays a fundamental irony. For it is *only* in the isolation of the stove-heated room that one can even entertain the possibility of the abstraction of pure thought from all material contingencies.

At least in terms of monastic reading arts, something similar could be said about "scholasticism." Though *lectio divina* is chiefly a monastic practice, the skills of reading cultivated in the schools are not altogether different from those taught in the monasteries. The reading of the scholastic is always first an oral performance. In lectures themselves, reading is a function of both the lector and the "reader" — thus in those universities in England which survive from the Middle Ages, to pursue a particular discipline is to "read" it; i.e., to have it read *to* you. The reading done by listening in medieval schools and universities thus elides the arts of grammar and rhetoric, by rendering the *reader* of lectures and the reader of manuscripts an *author* of interpretative commentary and public oration. The live disputations in the universities are evidence of the extent to which medieval "authorship" is bound up with no-

---

Routledge, 1982); William A. Graham, *Beyond the Written Word: Oral Aspects of Scripture in the History of Religion* (Cambridge: Cambridge University Press, 1987).

15. Illich, *In the Vineyard of the Text,* p. 82.

tions of reading and interpretation. To participate in a quodlibetal dispute, for example, requires one to have read well, and to have learned and committed to memory what X said about Y, as that is relevant to the particular debate in question. It also requires the rhetorical skills of composition, by which one must order into a coherent argument all the "texts" stored in one's memory.

Nevertheless, the schools of the twelfth century did introduce new technologies of reading, such as *distinctiones* (which supply the various senses of a given word, and a text for each example), concordances, abbreviation and alphabetization. Texts such as Lombard's *Sentences,* Gratian's *Decretum,* and the *Glossa Ordinaria* are often cited as evidence of the new genres which are aimed at making finding a particular *topos* easier and less tedious. Richard and Mary Rouse have explained the rise to prominence of such books as a response to the failure of memory to retain such a vast array of knowledge, as well as to the need, no longer for reflective *lectio divina,* but for "seeking out specific information" for use in sermons.[16] While such technologies do, as Philipp Rosemann points out, begin to evidence a gradual tension in attitudes toward the page, these *loci classici* of scholastic theology are not, to be sure, yet comprehensive theological "maps."[17] As such, even the collections of *distinctiones* serve a specific purpose, that of aiding the preacher in composing a sermon. The close link, therefore, between grammatical exegesis and rhetorical delivery is maintained. These new technologies of organizing and arranging knowledge do not, however, pretend to be totalities in themselves. For one thing, they are each designed for very specific uses at specific times by specific kinds of readers, and assume a shared idiom with them. In addition, the use of abbreviations in texts such as Gilbert of Poitier's Commentary on the Psalms (as well as in later manuscripts of the *Summa Theologiae*) always points to a prior learned knowledge that requires one to remember that, for example, Ψ points to the penitential Psalms.[18] Thus, far from "containing" knowledge within the "totality" of the book, these texts and their various "finding-devices" point beyond themselves to other texts, past and future, for the continual "discovery" of meaning.

Thus medieval reading, whether "monastic" or "scholastic," is everywhere conditioned by its orientation to *time.* What is central to both arts of

16. Richard H. Rouse and Mary A. Rouse, "*Statim invenire:* Schools, Preachers, and New Attitudes to the Page," in Robert L. Benson and Giles Constable, eds., *Renaissance and Renewal in the Twelfth Century* (Cambridge, Mass.: Harvard University Press, 1982), p. 206.

17. See Philipp W. Rosemann, *Understanding Scholastic Thought with Foucault* (New York: St. Martin's, 1999), Study 3, "Scholastic Intellectual Practices," pp. 59-101.

18. Rosemann, *Understanding Scholastic Thought,* p. 204. See also pp. 63-66 for a reading of abbreviation as a form of negative theology.

reading is the assumption that what one is to learn from reading is never graspable by the immediate gaze. Even to "dip into" a text like the *Glossa* is to be thrown into the midst of a chorus of voices, to be referred back to prior texts, and to realize the necessity for further commentaries and elucidations. To read well, then, one must take time, one must learn to remember, and one must make a certain progression through a text — a progress which is one of gaining knowledge, but also one of drawing nearer to wisdom. In addition, reading is always accompanied by sound, from the tone of one's voice, the musical intonation of a sung Gospel text, even to the acoustical reverb of a chapel or lecture hall. Thus even scholastic academic practices are not separable from liturgy — the quodlibetal disputations take place twice a year, during the seasons of Advent and Lent — but rather, as I argue in the last chapter, derive their intelligibility from the daily participation in the liturgy of the Eucharist.

Drawing chiefly on the work of Mary Carruthers, Michel de Certeau, and Walter Ong, it is my contention, therefore, that the kind of "texts" which we produce is altogether inseparable from the kind of people we are, or from the forms of life which might be said in some sense to constitute us. As such, this contention calls into question the extent to which these texts may properly be called "texts" at all.[19] It is not simply that all our language is bound up with the habits which make such language intelligible, but, more specifically, in the case of the language of Christian theologians until at least the sixteenth century, a grammar is formed which gathers its meaningfulness from its use in the liturgy. The attempted abstraction of this language in the sixteenth century implies a radical shift in the direction of the divorce of a certain "text," the Scriptures, from the way in which it is *used* in the community of people

---

19. That is to say, it is anachronistic to treat the texts of antiquity as written "texts" (or books) first and foremost, insofar as they precede a culture which is fundamentally constituted by, in Michel de Certeau's terms, a "scriptural economy." "In modern Western culture, it is no longer a discourse that plays this role [formerly the role of 'myth'], but rather a transport, in other words a practice: writing. The origin is no longer what is narrated, but rather the multi-form and murmuring activity of producing a text and producing society as a text. 'Progress' is scriptural in type. In very diverse ways, orality is defined by (or as) that from which a 'legitimate' practice — whether in science, politics, or the classroom, etc. — must differentiate itself. The 'oral' is that which does not contribute to progress; reciprocally, the 'scriptural' is that which separates itself from the magical world of voices and traditions." Michel de Certeau, "The Scriptural Economy," in *The Practice of Everyday Life*, p. 134. The implication that I wish to draw out is that the Reformation battle cry of *sola scriptura* by and large inaugurates this economy, but it becomes possible in the sixteenth century only with the help of prior philosophical 'revolutions'. As such, this problematizes the notion of *the* Reformation in general, as well as the concomitant dating of such an event.

whose story it is supposed to tell — indeed, not only from the manner of its presentation but from the voice of its oration or incantation. Due in part to printing, the language of Scripture becomes frozen in textual space, irrespective both of its positioning and contextualizing within the Mass, but also of the sound of its intonation. The shift here is from a story told and performed (with the whole of its body) to a text seen and interpreted.[20]

The historical particulars of the claims of Ong and de Certeau deserve to be more closely scrutinized elsewhere, but nevertheless their arguments prompt us to examine what the craft of reading theological texts might entail in the period before the seismic shift which they both describe takes place. However, I do not wish to challenge the widely held understanding of the Middle Ages as a "culture of the book"; but what I do wish to contest is the way in which this designation often assumes an unquestioned univocity to the notion of "the book" pre- and post-Gutenberg. To be sure, theology is, for the Middle Ages, a "science of the book," but the theology of this period must require of "modernity" an interrogation of what constitutes a "text" or "book" in the first place. Moreover, if one can speak about the "culture of the book," just *what kind of book* is it?

It is perhaps no accident that the Eucharistic controversies of the sixteenth century coincide with the transformation of attitudes toward the page, and indeed of the page itself. If one of the central themes of these debates revolves around the understanding of just what is meant by "in remembrance of me," the newfound lack of a consensus about the precise notion of remembrance is not unrelated to the way in which the page itself, by the middle of the sixteenth century, has ceased to function as a memory-device. The most obvious examples of such devices are the illuminated Gospels and Psalters, Books of Hours and Missals of the Middle Ages. Most of us are familiar with these as "artifacts" of another age — i.e., we see in the Book of Kells or the Lindisfarne Gospels simply a beautifully ornate decoration of a set of texts held by the medieval Christians to be sacred. The painstaking labors devoted to such illustration are often taken as license to read the entire medieval period as a "culture of the book." Of a piece with this presupposition is the implication that the book symbolizes a totality, and of course it is widely assumed that "*the* medieval philosophical project" was concerned chiefly with systematization, with the enclosure of all knowledge within two leather-

20. Cf. de Certeau, "The Scriptural Economy," p. 137: "Before the 'modern' period, that is, until the sixteenth or seventeenth century, this writing (Holy Scripture) speaks. The sacred text is a voice, it teaches (in the original sense of *documentum*), it is the advent of a 'meaning' (*un 'vouloir-dire'*) on the part of God who expects the reader (in reality, the listener) to have a 'desire to hear and understand' (*un 'vouloir-entendre'*) on which access to truth depends."

bound covers.[21] Such a presupposition assumes that such finality was indeed the goal of medieval theology, that the particular "book" in question is nothing less than the encyclopedia.

There were, of course, "encyclopedias" in the Middle Ages (though not in the modern sense), but there were also a whole range of other genres of texts which cannot so easily be classified as attempts to catalog and organize all knowledge in one book. Yet such abstraction of the notion of "the book" is integral to the entire postmodern enterprise of deconstruction, which reads the entire Western metaphysical tradition as a metaphysics of "presence," in which "the book" is the chief archetype of a logocentrism that assumes a totality to all knowledge.[22] As Jacques Derrida writes,

> The idea of the book is the idea of a totality, of the signifier; this totality of the signifier cannot be a totality, unless a totality constituted by the signified preexists it, supervises its inscriptions and its signs, and is independent of it in its ideality. The idea of the book, which always refers to a natural totality, is profoundly alien to the sense of writing. It is the encyclopedic protection of theology and of logocentrism against the disruption of writing, against its aphoristic energy. . . .[23]

Thus Derrida has preferred to speak of "the text" rather than "the book," as the former implies an absence which the latter occludes. But *which book* does Derrida have in mind? The *Encyclopaedia Britannica?* A Latin missal? A printed edition, or a manuscript? Isidore's *Etymologiae?* The *Divine Comedy? Olson's Standard Book of British Birds? Where the Wild Things Are?*[24] These are

21. This assumption governs the critical work of Georges Bataille in his critique of medieval architecture. See Denis Hollier, *Against Architecture: The Writings of Georges Bataille,* tr. Betsy Wing (Cambridge, Mass.: Massachusetts Institute of Technology Press, 1989), pp. 36ff. Hollier argues that for Bataille, the *Summa Theologiae* of Thomas Aquinas is paradigmatic for the way in which, in the medieval episteme, "Time is eliminated" (p. 45). This is a grave misconception; precisely the opposite is the case.

22. There is a long tradition of understanding the book itself as a kind of symbol, as Ernst Robert Curtius has described in *European Literature in the Latin Middle Ages,* tr. Willard R. Trask (Princeton: Princeton University Press, 1953, 1990), pp. 302-47. Curtius has traced this history at least as far as the *Phaedrus,* which is somewhat misleading, for what concerns Plato is not the book as such, but rather the wax tablet or palimpsest. Nonetheless, Curtius' account provides no support for Derrida's univocal usage of "the book." In fact, Curtius writes, "The simile of the book is not logically confined to a single function and a single significance but rather serves to illustrate various facts" (p. 321).

23. Jacques Derrida, *Of Grammatology,* tr. Gayatri Chakravorty Spivak (London: Johns Hopkins University Press, 1976), p. 18.

24. See Ong, *Orality and Literacy,* pp. 132-33: "The printed text is supposed to represent the

only several examples of books of very different kinds, and perhaps the only thing they may be said to have in common is that they are all books in the most basic sense, and that (being Western) they must be read from left to right, top to bottom, front to back. In this sense, the "idea of the book" may make sense only at its most mundane level, as a physical object. The sense in which Derrida uses the book is more applicable to the book closed on the shelf than to the one open in one's hands or on one's desk, not to mention in one's memory.[25] Thus it is the abstraction of "the book" from the practices of reading which lies behind Derrida's critique of logocentrism, an abstraction which itself is ultimately confounded by the peculiar realities of the relationships between books (and at this point it does not matter if one prefers to say "texts") and their readers. For what is at issue is, above all, what kind of books or texts demand what kind of strategies for reading? Moreover, what habits, skills, and indeed virtues are demanded of the reader to make good sense of the text? To each of these questions I will return.

To use Derrida's own words, "I would rather announce the limits and the presuppositions of what seems here to be self-evident and what seems to me to retain the character and validity of evidence."[26] The "evidence" in question here is the "essence" of the book as a univocal symbol for the reification of a metaphysics of presence within a totalizing signifier, which is established by an ontologically prior signified — which for Derrida assumes the status of just the kind of *a priori* evidence which he attempts to overturn. This

---

words of an author in definitive or 'final' form. For print is comfortable only with finality. Once a letterpress forme is closed, locked up, or a photolithographic plate is made, and the sheet printed, the text does not accommodate changes (erasures, insertions) so readily as do written texts. By contrast, manuscripts, with their glosses or marginal comments (which often got worked into the text in subsequent copies), were in dialogue with the world outside their own borders. They remained closer to the give-and-take of oral expression. The readers of manuscripts are less closed off from the author, less absent, than are the readers of those writing for print. The sense of closure or completedness enforced by print is at times grossly physical. A newspaper's pages are normally all filled — certain kinds of printed material are called 'fillers' — just as its lines of type are normally all justified (i.e. all exactly the same width). Print is curiously intolerant of physical incompleteness. It can convey the impression, unintentionally and subtly, but very really, that the material the text deals with is similarly complete or self-consistent."

25. I mention here, not because it is particularly germane to my argument (though not irrelevant), but simply because it is fascinating, Henry Petroski's delightful and engaging *The Book on the Bookshelf* (New York: Alfred A. Knopf, 1999), a chronicle of the history of book storage. Petroski is a civil engineer at Duke University whose literary career is marked by an enthrallment with the origin and development of ordinary objects such as the pencil and the paper clip.

26. Petroski, *The Book on the Bookshelf*, p. 39.

essentialist mythology of the book, which as I have already hinted is problematic, proves untenable once the resonances of "the book" are loosened and elasticized, as is particularly the case in the Christian understanding of the place of the Bible in the life of its community.

Derrida is therefore guilty of a certain "protestantizing" in his notion of the book as a finality, as *one kind* of signifier. The logocentrism which he criticizes is thus allied to the Protestant principle of *sola scriptura*, by means of which the "Word" itself becomes identical with the biblical text, not only in a "spiritual" sense but in a physical one as well. It is perhaps no coincidence that the localization of the Word of God in the page coincides with an analogous suspicion, among the Calvinists in particular,[27] of the localization of the Body of Christ in the Host, a concern which is lucidly articulated, though not shared, by Jean-Luc Marion:

> . . . the transposition of one substance into another (that of the bread and that of the body of Christ) leads one to recognize the traits of a person under the appearances (species) of a substance; the substantial presence therefore fixes and freezes the person in an available, permanent, handy, and delimited thing. Hence the imposture of an idolatry that imagines itself to honor "God" when it heaps praises on his pathetic "canned" substitute (the reservation of the Eucharist), exhibited as an attraction (display of the Holy Sacrament), brandished like a banner (processions), and so on.[28]

Similarly, Walter Ong has expressed related concerns over the localization of the "word-in-space," a trend towards which both Protestantism and Catholicism were heading, by the mid-sixteenth century, owing partly to the transformation of book production thanks to the invention of moveable type. Yet for Ong, the transformation is not simply technological, in the sense that the machinery of manufacturing made the dissemination of texts easier and more widespread. In fact, one might say that this shift is technological in the deepest sense, insofar as it involves not only the apparatuses of production, but, more subtly, the skills of negotiating these new products, the new texts. That is to say, the introduction of new technologies — printing presses, to be sure, but also new genres, new kinds of books (glossaries, concordances, *loci communes,* etc.), and new techniques for organizing them — requires a new *techne*, a new art or craft of reading these texts. Thus the reorganization of typographical space entails a parallel rearrangement of mental space,

27. See Calvin's own treatment in *Institutes of the Christian Religion* IV.xvii, *passim*.

28. Jean-Luc Marion, *God without Being: Hors-Texte,* tr. Thomas A. Carlson (Chicago: University of Chicago Press, 1991), p. 164.

though which comes first is indeterminate. For Ong, however, the shift towards the localization of the word-in-space is due, at least in part, to the place-logics of Rudolf Agricola and Peter Ramus.[29]

Perhaps one might also argue that the Zwinglian understanding of the Eucharist as a simple memorial meal depends on a related, but opposite reaction to localization. For the Reformers, the problem of the word-in-space, or of the Word-in-space, is most worrisome in terms of the limitation of a "spiritual" body to a corporeal locus in the Eucharist. This anxiety towards freezing the body of Christ in the host is expressed lucidly by Calvin, who exhorts that "we must not dream of such a presence of Christ in the Sacrament as the craftsmen of the Roman court have fashioned — as if the body of Christ, by a local presence, were put there to be touched by the hands, to be chewed by the teeth, and to be swallowed by the mouth."[30] Curiously, though, this localization is not problematic for the Reformers in terms of the Scriptures, whereby the Word of God becomes identical with the text of Scripture — not simply the old text of Scripture as such, but with a new technology of Scripture, the gloss-less Bible, the text itself now "liberated" from its interpretive marginal frame, and set down, as it were, on the blank page with nothing else around it, *sola scriptura*.[31]

The notion of communication, from text to reader, from preacher to hearer, from God to human beings, is therefore representative of the scriptural economy which *sola scriptura* (and its concomitant reduction of the significance of the Eucharist) inaugurates, thus emerges as something radically new, and involves a substantial break with the doctrine of the participation in the triune life of God. For it is no accident that the recipients of communion are still called "communicants" and receiving the sacrament "communication." For here, the notion of communication is developed along, and transformed by, specifically and explicitly eucharistic lines. The participation in the Eucharist is communication *par excellence*, and thus subverts any inclination toward a thoroughgoing scriptural economy. One communicates, under this logic, by eating and drinking, not through the immediate confrontation with words on a page. Inasmuch as this communication necessarily presupposes a participation which is social, the participation *of* the body of Christ (the Church) makes sense only insofar as it is a participation *in* the body and

29. See Walter Ong, S.J., *Ramus, Method, and the Decay of Dialogue: From the Art of Discourse to the Art of Reason* (Cambridge, Mass.: Harvard, 1983). I will return to this point.

30. John Calvin, *Institutes of the Christian Religion*, ed. John T. McNeill, tr. Ford Lewis Battles [The Library of Christian Classics; 21] (Philadelphia: Westminster, 1960), IV.xvii.12, p. 1372.

31. On the transformation of the page of Scripture, see Chapter Four, "Memory and the *Glossa Ordinaria.*"

blood of Christ. The account of participation for which I am arguing is therefore at once social and "metaphysical."

At the same time, whereas the development of systematic theology is dependent upon the notion of *sola scriptura,* the maintenance of such a principle
is likewise dependent upon various cultural changes which set the stage for the
Reformation, in particular the invention of moveable type by Johannes
Gutenberg at the middle of the fifteenth century. The invention of the printing
press therefore makes possible the isolation and hypostatization of the biblical
texts as the sole authority for Christian theology, as well as the abstraction of
these texts from the way they are used in Christian worship and in the continuing interpretive tradition. The possibility of *sola scriptura* is thus parasitic
upon the new understanding of the Bible as a physical "thing" whose spatial
limits are quite clearly defined, a thing which is always to hand, easily accessible. Hence the practice of deferring to authority in theology becomes a matter
of making one's theological writing correspond to what is there on the printed
page, whose meaning is allegedly clear and unambiguous. It is evident that *sola
scriptura* is integrally bound to the spatial "metaphysics" of the printed text,
but what is not always so clear is whether the way in which this new mode of
theology is a very nearly complete transformation whose new form may be altogether awkward affects the theology. That is to say, does theology adapt itself
to any mode of exclusively textual presentation without a partial or even thor-
ough reconfiguration of that which is presented? In other words, is the form of
textual teaching irrelevant to its content, or does the form itself *teach?* It was
assumed by the Reformers that the mode of theology's presentation made no
difference to the content of its message, but rather that the printing press af-
forded innumerable possibilities for theology that were altogether functionally
and pragmatically positive, but qualitatively and theologically neutral. The ac-
celerated transmission of texts meant simply that more people could have access to the Bible for themselves (and to theological tracts as well), but that the
content of the texts could remain basically unchanged.

Here it might be objected that there *is* something inescapably textual
about Christianity, insofar as it places centrality upon the texts of canonical
Scripture; in addition, the theological tradition depends upon written texts
(for there is no doubt that the writings of the Church Fathers are still *writings*). Certainly part of the pedagogical project of Christianity consists in the
training of Christians to "read well." However, I suggest that the *implementa-
tion* of *sola scriptura* mitigates against this pedagogy, insofar as the ability to
"read well" may, according to some versions of Protestant theology, effectively
be learned in private, in abstraction from the sense in which this ability can
only be learned by participation in an ecclesial readership.

Inasmuch as the shift in modernity is best described in terms of one from a grammar of participation to a grammar of representation, the primacy of *sola scriptura* always bears the risk of sliding into a grammar of representation in theological speech. This is best seen in the transformation of the liturgy in the Reformed tradition, and the declining centrality of the Eucharist as that which "makes the Church."[32] Already with Calvin, the tendency towards a grammar of representation is discernible in the fact that his Eucharistic theology is everywhere composed in terms of a Word to which one must respond, thereby pushing the participation of the body of believers in the triune life of God himself to the margins. The role of the believer, then, becomes one of *mimesis* of a more "real" event taking place somewhere else, and hence not a "real" participation in the Trinity.[33] The sermon comes to assume the central role in Christian worship, the operative sense now being on the "naked confrontation with the Scriptures"[34] as opposed to the participation of the faithful in the life of God which is performed most acutely in the sacrament of the Eucharist. What Nietzsche saw as this "reductive" tendency in Protestantism,[35] from the hypostatization of the sermon as the paradigmatic form of Christian speech about God to the profound suspicion of the symbolic (as in the reduction of the number of sacraments from seven to three, and then only two) indicates a movement towards literalization in theology and worship, where ecclesial practice and theological speech are to correspond to the letter of the printed text of the Bible.

The shift from a grammar of participation to a grammar of representation is already embodied in the shift within theology itself, as a move from the participative to the representative in the liturgy.[36] That is to say, the grammar of representation which becomes full blown in Enlightenment deistic and theistic discourse is prefigured by the shift toward the generally literalizing tendency of the Reformers to refer all meaning to the letter of Scripture. In the liturgy, this movement is most poignantly represented by the replacement

32. This phenomenon is not exclusive to Protestantism, in that sixteenth-century Roman Catholic theology shares many of these same tendencies, though in respect to "tradition" instead of "scripture." This will be more fully argued later, but for now I use the example of *sola scriptura* to describe a theological shift that is wider than it might at first appear.

33. See Simon Oliver, "The Eucharist before Nature and Culture," *Modern Theology* XV.3 (July 1999), pp. 331-53, esp. 342ff.

34. John Bossy, *Christianity in the West: 1400-1700* (Oxford: Oxford University Press, 1985), p. 97.

35. See, among a multitude of examples, Friedrich Nietzsche, *Daybreak*, tr. R. J. Hollingdale [Texts in German Philosophy] (Cambridge: Cambridge University Press, 1982), pp. 84ff.

36. I will provide a fuller account of a grammar of representation and a grammar of participation in the first chapter.

of the sacrament of the Eucharist (and the broader circumscription of the sacramental itself) with the sermon in the central and focal position in the liturgy.[37] This is evident in the architecture which is characteristic of many Protestant churches, where the pulpit stands in the center of the sanctuary, symbolically blocking off access to the altar, or else standing high above and behind the altar table in a position of absolute governance. In other words, in such churches the procession of the faithful to receive the Eucharistic elements never extends beyond the symbolic sovereignty of the sermon — the sermon always remains beyond, irreproachable, a form of communication whose authority is neither challenged nor even relativized by the Eucharist, whose position of subjection to the pulpit keeps the practice of the sacrament in a role of submission.[38] Here, as is the general rule in Protestantism itself, the sacraments are relativized by the sermon, and not vice versa, as pre-Reformation ecclesial architecture attests.

If this much is true, and if such a shift really does take place, then the claim begins to make sense that a new form of theological literature arises in the sixteenth century which is representative in shape as opposed to participative. The grammar of theological texts prior to the sixteenth century is, by and large, a grammar of participation insofar as it is understood that creatures partake of the divine life of God, by virtue of the plenitude of charity which is the Father, Son, and Holy Spirit. As this is presupposed by theologians such as Augustine and Aquinas, it becomes impossible to separate the writing, reading, and commenting on such theological "texts" as the *Confessions* or the *Summa Theologiae* from the ontological participation of beings in the divine creativity of the Trinity. This act of production (whether in reading or writing) is itself a form of this participation, in that nothing is made by human hands or minds but which shares in the divine activity of creation *ex nihilo.*

Thus in the remainder of this essay, I begin in the first chapter with a kind of genealogy of the construction of philosophical and theological "maps," the

37. To be sure, the Reformers never insisted upon the absolute authority of preaching in the worship of the Church — they rather insisted upon the mutual dependence of preaching and sacrament, and in Calvin's case at least, argued for more frequent celebration of the Eucharist (*cf. Institutes of the Christian Religion* IV.xvii.44). At the same time, the predominance of the preaching role of the clergy over the celebratory role becomes inscribed in the theology of Calvin, who, as a writer, substantially contributes to the invention of the genre of systematic theology, a genre which gathers its power from the Protestant homiletic "science."

38. However, this trend in architecture did not become common practice until the eighteenth century. Wesley's church in the City of London is a perfect example. See Peter G. Cobb, "The Architectural Setting of the Liturgy," in Cheslyn Jones et al., eds., *The Study of Liturgy,* 1st ed. (London: SPCK, 1978), pp. 473-80, esp. p. 477.

origin of which I trace to the exploitation of moveable type and the place-logics of Rudolf Agricola. Following Agricola, Philipp Melanchthon effectively inaugurates the systematic tradition, by organizing his *Loci Communes* according to thirty-six "commonplaces," which for him function as the receptacles for information about various theological subjects. Thus the Protestant principle of *sola scriptura*, which is parasitic upon movable type, contributes to the new understanding of the Bible as a "book" in abstraction from its liturgical usage. That is to say, the Bible becomes present in the life of the church as a physical object, which is identically repeatable in every instance, as opposed to an ongoing story continually performed and re-narrated in the liturgy.[39] Thus *sola scriptura* displaces memory from its central function in the theological imagination, as texts cease to function as aids to the memory, and instead imply the immediate relation of the reader and the page. Moreover, the reification of Scripture into the anti-chronic space of the printed page has its correlate in the Tridentine conception of "tradition." Through the Agricolan *De Locis Theologicis* of Melchior Cano, "tradition" comes to be conceived by analogy to a book, or a set of codified and quantifiably authoritative deposits of revealed truth — thus the introduction of Michel de Certeau's "scriptural economy," the engine of the spatialization of theology, both Protestant and Catholic. Additionally, I outline the elements of both a grammar of representation and its alternative, a grammar of participation, treating the theological presuppositions underlying each, and attempt to lay the groundwork for a reading of selected theological texts as itineraries, which use rhetorical elements to guide the reader towards fuller participation in the Triune life of God.

In Chapter Two, "Itineraries; Or, Theology as Manuduction," I go on to describe the character of an itinerary, and contrast it with the map. Drawing on the work of de Certeau and Pierre Hadot, I suggest that the map is the paradigmatic metaphor for the arrangement of texts and of knowledge in the early modern period, while the itinerary is broadly descriptive of the way in which (for the medieval texts which I discuss) reading a text is an activity, not simply of the transfer of data, but of the authorial "leading by the hand" of the reading soul unto the beatific vision. Through Mary Carruthers' work on memory, I argue that these itineraries aid in the ordering of the memory to its proper object, the Trinity.

In the third chapter, "Augustine and Borrowed Speech," I offer an account of Augustine's understanding of rhetoric, through readings of *Confessions*, *De Doctrina Christiana*, and *De Trinitate*. I suggest that Augustine reorients rhe-

---

39. One might even say that here the Scriptures become present in the church *as the Bible*.

torical *inventio* as a task of both the speaker and the hearer, and moreover, shifts invention to a grammatical category. That is to say, he makes "finding something to say" the task not only of the author, but also of the reader. Moreover, I take the *mise-en-scène* of the conversion of Victorinus in *Confessions* VII as an analogue to the *mise-en-page* of a grammar of participation. Augustine's *Confessions,* then, function as a kind of itinerary, not only of the author's life, but of the destiny of the reader as well. This itinerary is accomplished by the "borrowing" of language, which, as Augustine argues, is the highest form of rhetoric.

This leads to the middle section of the dissertation, in which I attempt to read two texts, the *Glossa Ordinaria* and the *Summa Theologiae,* in terms of the itinerary and memory. In the fourth chapter, "Memory and the *Glossa Ordinaria:* Liturgy and Interpretation," I treat the pre-modern understanding of the relationship between scripture and tradition through the twelfth century *Glossa,* which I read as a kind of iconographic[40] illustration of the mutual indwelling of Christ and the church. Chirographically, the *Glossa* symbolically re-presents the presence of the Scriptures in the living memory of the Church, their 'residence' in the midst of on ongoing community of interpreters. Particularly in the case of the Gospels, the *Glossa* is a chirographical image of the liturgical reading of the Gospel during the Mass, where the lector processes to the center of the congregation and orally makes Christ present among his followers, recalling further the presence of Christ among his disciples. The *Glossa* then becomes a textual figure of the body of Christ itself, wherein the Son of God dwells in their midst, and they in him. This re-enactment of the Scriptures is therefore no mere dramatic spectacle, but rather the performance of the Church's memory as one body. The *Glossa* textually re-enacts this presence of the Word of God among his followers, and among their words, in a kind of textual *anamnesis.* As such, it exhibits the structures of a grammar of participation.

---

40. I use the term "iconography" here in a deliberately unspecific sense. I do not mean to refer specifically to Jean-Luc Marion's account nor to the more conventionally aesthetic sense given to it by Emile Mâle. In using it in this relatively open sense, I am attempting to counter the modern assumption that the way texts are arranged, or the way they *appear,* is irrelevant. Rather, I hope to suggest that there is something to the character of both the *Glossa* and the *Summa,* in the manner in which each is arranged, that is, if not "revelatory," then at least didactic. That is to say, "iconographic" may justly be set over against "typographic," as these two terms represent differing conceptions of epistemic space and of the theological status of vision. In other words, I hope to suggest that these two texts resist reification into mere objects of apprehension by the gaze, and that they in some sense "see" their readers. Whatever ambiguity there is at this point will be clarified in later chapters.

This chapter serves as a kind of preface to the three that follow, which all deal with various aspects of the relation of rhetoric and memory to the theological architectonics of the *Summa Theologiae* of Thomas Aquinas. In the first of these, "The Manuduction of Desire: Will and the Structure of the *Summa Theologiae*," I begin with a critique of Timothy McDermott's one-volume edition of the *Summa,* and the problems inherent in and assumptions underlying such an endeavor. I argue that the peculiar use Thomas makes of the *quaestio* resists any attempt to reify the "responses" of Thomas into self-contained monologues. To do so undermines not only the historical contexts of the work, but much more importantly, it transforms what is essentially an itinerary of the soul's return to God into a panoptic map of the commonplaces of theology.

In the sixth chapter, "Reading as *Manuductio* as *Traditio* as *Reditus*," I further develop the claim made in Chapter Four as to the inseparability of "scripture" and "tradition," through a reading of Thomas' use of *tradere* and *manuductio,* metaphors which he uses to describe the activity of *sacra doctrina.* Thus any talk of "scripture" and "tradition" in Aquinas will prove to be the false imposition of post-Tridentine presuppositions onto a decidedly un-"systematic" text. Following Mark Jordan, I attempt to argue for a reading of the *Summa* as a "curriculum of persuasion." By the end of the *Secunda Pars,* Thomas recommends the religious life as the school of charity par excellence, which illustrates that the rhetorical *skopos* of the text is not simply notional assent to propositions about God, but the devotion to a certain form of life, in which one will be trained more perfectly to know and love, and hence to be.

As the school of charity, the religious life is also preeminently the school of memory. Thus the student of Thomas is "handed over," if he is successful, to another set of *magistri.* The liturgical life of the religious is therefore the training in the proper ordering of the memory. As I argue in the final chapter, "Liturgically Trained Memory," in Question 83 of the *Tertia Pars,* Thomas treats the rite of the Eucharist using decidedly rhetorical tropes, drawn from the Ciceronian tradition, but reoriented, as in Augustine, according to the proper *telos* of desire. The Eucharist, for Aquinas, is the schooling by which we are trained to order the associations of our memory to their proper objects. Since memory is the condition of all thought, as he and Augustine both claim, the Eucharist is the "site" of all theological production, and moreover, pedagogy is itself Eucharistic.

1 Grammars of Participation and Representation

Modern theological writing, both Protestant and Catholic, has in general tended towards the construction of comprehensive, all-consuming "systems" of doctrine. Some systems consume more than others, to be sure, but the drive has been in the direction of the encyclopedic — whether of philosophy, theology, mechanics, or knowledge in general. There are few literal encyclopedias of theology that one reads today, but the mode of reading an encyclopedia and the mode of reading a "systematic theology" like Karl Barth's *Church Dogmatics* are analogously related to one another. That is, one can use the technologies of modern printing — indexes, tables of contents, supplemental volumes — in order to find one's way, to locate what Barth says, for example, on the Virgin Birth. The activity of locating oneself requires the use of aids external to the text itself, such as looking up the particular topic in the index. One thinks of the similar experience of locating oneself on a map. The map itself tells me nothing about where I am; however, with the help of a legend or street index, as well as a grid according to which I may find my particular street, I may locate myself. The map tells me nothing specific about my excursion or my particular location. And thus I always remain "other than" the map. I must first locate myself according to its rules of order. This is the logic of representational correspondence: where I am on the map corresponds to and represents where I already know myself to be: say, where US 61 crosses State Highway 8 in Mississippi.

Therefore, in the first case, the analogy of the map provides a description for what I will call the *grammar of representation*. While I take this term to be broadly descriptive of the linguistic "mode" of modernity, it is by no means exhaustive or foolproof. In employing the term, I hope to illustrate how the move towards representation divorces form from content, and instantiates new dualisms like "scripture" and "tradition," and also participates in the ghettoization of theology as a discrete realm, apart from other autonomous sciences of philosophy, rhetoric, metaphysics, and so forth. In other words, it is the result of a theology that does not understand the way it presents itself to be a theological matter, but as subject to prior, established and universally accepted rules of "method."

The shift toward representation as descriptive of the onset of modernity is located differently, according to whom one asks. Stephen Toulmin, for example, locates the shift towards the purely prosaic in philosophy in the Cartesian "revolution." He writes that "[a]fter the 1630s, the tradition of Modern Philosophy in Western Europe concentrated on formal analysis of chains of written statements, rather than on the circumstantial merits and defects of persuasive utterances. Within that tradition, *formal logic was in, rhetoric was out*."[1] The prioritizing of formal logic[2] over rhetoric is, for Walter Ong, the result of transformations in the curriculum of sixteenth-century Paris, particularly in the arts course, where many of the most influential thinkers of the period were trained, including John Calvin. The elevation of topical logic outlined in the *De Inventione Dialectica* of Rudolf Agricola (1443/4-1485) above the works of Aristotle precipitated the shift, which Toulmin describes, by elevating the new place-logics above rhetoric, and inaugurating a new tradition of logic ordered

1. Stephen Toulmin, *Cosmopolis: The Hidden Agenda of Modernity* (Chicago: University of Chicago Press, 1990), p. 31. See also Mary Poovey's *A History of the Modern Fact: Problems of Knowledge in the Sciences of Wealth and Society* (Chicago: University of Chicago Press, 1998). Poovey's thesis, a Foucauldian genealogy of modern representation, links the origins of "accuracy" and "certifiability" with the publication of double-entry bookkeeping manuals in Britain (by at least 1588) and "mercantile accommodation." She writes, "In implying that the internally coherent systems of writing and exchange constituted signs of honesty and virtue, these two mercantile instruments demonstrated that the idea of system could carry moral connotations whose effects exceeded the referential function of mercantile writing, because one of those effects was the establishment of creditworthiness itself" (p. xvi). See also Alfred W. Crosby, *The Measure of Reality: Quantification and Western Society, 1250-1600* (Cambridge: Cambridge University Press, 1997).

2. "Formal logic is fundamentally an attempt to deal with the activity of the mind in terms of these [composition, implication, definition, division, description, e.g.] and related visualist analogies. It is interested in the 'structure' of our intellectual activity — a notion which cannot even be conceived except by analogy with some sort of spatial diagram. It does not concern itself with 'tone' or other aural-type phenomena [as did classical rhetoric]. For this reason, formal logic is closely connected with mathematics (from the time of the Greeks to that of Alfred North Whitehead) to the extent that modern formal logic is called, somewhat naively, 'mathematical' logic, as though all strictly formal logic were not this sort of thing." Walter J. Ong, S.J., *Ramus, Method, and the Decay of Dialogue: From the Art of Discourse to the Art of Reason* (Cambridge, Mass.: Harvard University Press, 1958, 1983), p. 107.

to a spatial grid. Thus any knowledge, for Agricola (and later Peter Ramus), can be subsumed under the "method," making the strategy of commonplaces a pedagogical theory applicable to any science whatsoever.

Topics had of course been an important feature of classical rhetoric, but Agricola's innovation was the transferal of logic from a rhetorical category to a property of dialectic. But after Agricola's death, the fortune of the *De Inventione Dialectica,* in concert with the new printing technology, effectively freed the book "from the world of discourse and [made] it over into an object, a box with a surface and 'content' like an Agricolan locus."[3] Thus the book itself became a kind of metaphor for the way knowledge itself works: any science is composed of independent units of thought which can be represented by the nominative noun or by the cartographic tableau of images. In other words, the noun is said to "stand for" the object that it represents — hence the rise of labeling, both as a philosophical strategy and as a typographical indexing aid.[4] Thus the proliferation, in sixteenth-century textbooks of logic, of diagrams, charts, and tables illustrating the geometric arrangement of the mind and of knowledge.[5] The triumph of Agricola in the Arts, and, later, Theology Faculties at Paris therefore exhibits a transition towards the grammar of representation, by which words and images literally represent things, truths, ideas, in a mode of strict correspondence.[6]

In Agricola's own words, "speech is a sign of the things that are contained within the speaker's mind" and its "proper function is to display and unfold that which is its task to express."[7] This notion in fact becomes a kind of fundamental commonplace in Protestant and post-Tridentine theologies in the sixteenth century. The visual analogies employed by Agricola in his understanding of the nature and function of speech (signing, containing, displaying, unfolding) will come to dominate the modern production of systematic theologies. That is, whether it be "scripture" or "tradition," it is assumed that these

3. Ong, *Ramus,* p. 311.

4. See Ong, *Ramus,* pp. 310ff. See also Catherine Pickstock, *After Writing: On the Liturgical Consummation of Philosophy* (Oxford: Basil Blackwell, 1997), pp. 89-95.

5. See the reproductions in Ong, *Ramus,* pp. 77-90.

6. "In 1530, the Faculty of Theology at Paris accused the Faculty of Arts of studying Rudolph Agricola more than Aristotle, only to be told by the Arts Faculty that they themselves had better change, since there was nothing more outmoded than the sophistical sort of dialectic which they professed. . . . The Arts Faculty was soon in a position to have its way. As the Faculty of Theology renewed itself out of the new generation of arts students trained in Agricola, the old bastions crumbled. It is then that the 'loci theologici' sprout everywhere, in Protestant and Catholic camps, and signal the arrival, almost always via Paris, of the new Agricolan mind." Ong, *Ramus,* p. 95.

7. Rudolph Agricola, *Three Books Concerning Dialectical Invention,* I.i, in Wayne Rebhorn, ed. and tr., *Renaissance Debates on Rhetoric* (Ithaca, N.Y.: Cornell University Press, 2000), p. 43.

two "things" function on analogy to Agricola's description of the mind: they are "containers" of information, and their purpose is to transmit, in the form of a monologue, this information to the reader. In other words, theology's primary *modus loquendi* becomes that of description and explanation, of displaying and unfolding the content of the ur-text; and our speech (or rather, our writing) is most true when it most accurately represents that content.

The Invention of "Scripture" and of "Tradition": Melanchthon and Cano

This "mapping-out" is demonstrated not only by the transformation of the page itself, but also by the introduction of new genres of writing, which treat, in systematic fashion, the various topics or commonplaces of, in this case, theology. Almost simultaneous with the reformation of the page in the first part of the sixteenth century is the first example of the modern theological map: the *Loci Communes* of Philipp Melanchthon, first published in 1521.[8] In the preface to that work, the author explains that the order of the work will follow the order of the articles of the Apostles', Nicene, and Athanasian creeds. For Melanchthon, the Reformed doctrine which he delineates consists of thirty-six topics, *loci communes,* ranging from God to the sacraments to worldly authority. All of these units are outlined at the end of Melanchthon's preface, wherein he writes, "These are the titles of the principal parts which follow in this book, and I have enumerated them in the beginning so that the reader can observe and consider these titles in sequence and better understand the order and totality of the Christian doctrine."[9]

8. The *Loci Communes Theologici* went through two revisions, in 1535 and 1543, and was translated into German in 1553 by Melanchthon himself. My remarks will refer to the 1555 German edition, translated into English by Clyde L. Manschreck as *Melanchthon on Christian Doctrine:* Loci Communes 1555 (New York: Oxford University Press, 1965), henceforth *Loci Communes.*

9. Melanchthon, *Loci Communes,* p. li. Compared with the actual order of the book, as one can simply glean from a glance at the table of contents, the list in the preface does not correspond exactly; there is some alteration in the order. For example, in the preface, the order of the last seven topics is: Of Christian freedom, of offense, of the kingdom of Christ, of the resurrection of the dead, of trouble and affliction, of prayer, and of worldly authority. By contrast, the actual order of the text concerning the last seven *loci* is: Of the kingdom of Christ, of the resurrection of the dead, of bearing tribulation and the Cross, of prayer, of human precepts in the church, of offense, and of worldly authority. For a general treatment of Melanchthon's *loci,* their order in the successive editions, and their afterlife in Lutheran theology, see Robert Kolb, "The Ordering of the *Loci Communes Theologici:* The Structuring of the Melanchthonian Dogmatic Tradition," *Concordia Journal* XXIII.4 (October 1997), pp. 317-37.

Each of the *loci* is a discrete and individual unit. Though there may be continuity in the work as a whole, and some element of rhetorical *ductus* involved, Melanchthon fully appropriated the Agricolan place-logics as a general method for arranging his material.[10] The influence of Agricola upon Melanchthon is indisputable; in 1539 in Wittenberg he delivered an oration on Agricola's life, in which he described the latter as an "ornament . . . for Germany."[11] Despite his praise for Agricola, Melanchthon seems to make "unexpectedly small use . . . of the detail of his work."[12] Nevertheless, it was the *method* of Agricola which appealed to Melanchthon, whether or not he read Agricola to the letter. As Walter Ong writes, "Agricola is concerned with parking the arguments in his receptacles and making them readily available, Melanchthon with mustering them out."[13]

Significantly, the *Loci Communes* is divided into chapters, each of which treats a separate (though related) subject matter. Each *locus,* then, may consist of one or more "smaller" commonplace questions of theology, which he sets out to answer. For example, in the foreword, Melanchthon states,

> Whoever wishes profitably to teach himself or intelligently to instruct others must first comprehend from beginning to end the principal pieces in a thing, and carefully note how each piece follows the one proceeding — just

10. Melanchthon understood the order of his work to follow the narrative order of Scripture: "God himself has given us the most fitting order in the writings of the prophets and apostles. He puts his doctrine in the form of a story, for Genesis says that God created heaven and earth and then men. Next comes the story of how the first two people, Adam and Eve, fell into sin and death, and of how they were again graciously received. Then is given the twofold doctrine of the law and promise of the future Savior who takes away sin and death" (*Loci Communes,* Foreword, p. xlvi). Each of the "acts" in the narrative therefore contains a theological commonplace, which forms the order of the text. Thus he treats in successive order the *loci* of God, the Trinity, creation, the origin of sin, free will, original sin, law and gospel, and so forth.

11. Philipp Melanchthon, "On the Life of Rudolf Agricola," in *Orations on Philosophy and Education,* ed. Sachiko Kusukawa and tr. Christine F. Salazar (Cambridge: Cambridge University Press, 1999), p. 234. For Melanchthon's debt to Agricola, see Peter Mack, *Renaissance Argument: Valla and Agricola in the Traditions of Rhetoric and Dialectic* (Leiden: Brill, 1993), pp. 320-33. Melanchthon was not alone in his adulation; Erasmus too was both influenced by Agricola's work and not at all reticent in describing him as "the man in all Germany and Italy most worthy of the highest public honour." Quoted in Lisa Jardine, *Erasmus, Man of Letters* (Chichester: Princeton University Press, 1993), p. 93. See especially Chapter 3, "Inventing Rudolf Agricola: Recovery and Transmission of the *De Inventione Dialectica,*" for a lucid account of Agricola's influence and the printing history of his most important work.

12. Mack, *Renaissance Argument,* p. 333.

13. Ong, *Ramus,* p. 237.

as a builder, when he wishes to build a house, must first construct the entire building in his thoughts and himself project a picture.[14]

A reader trained in rhetoric, as Melanchthon was, might recognize in this passage remnants of the classical tradition of oratory, which employed architectural analogies for the construction of an artificial memory, and particularly of Cicero, who, in the *De Oratore*, writes that

> the most complete pictures are formed in our minds of the things that have been conveyed to them and imprinted on them by the senses, but that the keenest of all our senses is the sense of sight, and that consequently perceptions received by the ears or by reflexion can be most easily retained in the mind if they are also conveyed to our minds by the mediation of the eyes, with the result that things not seen and not lying in the field of visual discernment are earmarked by a sort of outline and image and shape so that we keep hold of as it were by an act of sight things that we can scarcely embrace by an act of thought.[15]

Whether Melanchthon is authentically Ciceronian in this account is not a question here; what is novel, though, in Melanchthon's (genuinely Agricolan) account is the fact that the use of topics has now become thoroughly abstracted from the practice of speech and thus of temporal movement. Whereas the topics of a text like the *Summa Theologiae* (and I use the word "topic" with a great deal of caution in this context) are constitutive of an itinerary which is very much a performance of speaking (and even derivative of live disputations), and more particularly a performance of the memory, the topics of Melanchthon are abstract units containing information which is to be imparted to the reader, ultimately for the purpose of teaching others by means of the printed word alone.[16] The analogies are therefore visual ones, and the perception of the whole is like understanding how the pieces of a puzzle fit together, which requires the posture of the map-reader: one stands above and observes the whole and the relationship of its constitutive elements.[17]

---

14. Melanchthon, *Loci Communes*, Foreword, p. xlvi.

15. Cicero, *De Oratore*, tr. H. Rackham, Loeb Classical Library 348 (London: Harvard University Press, 1960), II.lxxxvii.357, p. 469.

16. Melanchthon, *Loci Communes*, Foreword, p. xlvi.

17. "Thus it is very necessary, in every art and teaching, to note all the principal pieces — beginning, middle, and end — and carefully to consider how each and every piece fits with the others, which pieces are necessary, which are false additions, and which are contrary to the right foundation; and the teacher and the hearer must accustom themselves to comprehend this in a

The new genre, though enthusiastically embraced by the Reformers,[18] did not remain an exclusively Protestant prerogative. Though *sola scriptura* remains the archetypal theological strategy of Agricolan-driven spatialization, the reification of the biblical text into an object or deposit of divinely revealed information found its counterpart in the Catholic reification of "tradition" as a similar deposit of doctrine. Both of these competing authorities depended upon a common notion of books as "containers" of truth. Now divorced from the practice of continual interpretation, both "scripture" and "tradition" emerged as two mutually opposed, yet ostensibly "secure," receptacles of a content which would be fixed onto the page. From the pages of both, from the margins of the Vulgate and from the blank space around the commentaries of the fathers, the glosses, literally the *form* of the Christian pedagogical *manuductio* ("leading by the hand"), have been erased. The "tongues" (glosses) or voices of the Church, in whom the biblical text and its interpretation are bound together in eucharistic *anamnesis,* have now been silenced.

---

very orderly totality. For if one is careless about doctrine and omits a few necessary pieces, delusion and error follow in other parts; and if one does not keep the end in view, it is the same as if one undertook a journey and gave no thought to the city to which one desired to go." *Loci Communes, ibid.*

18. See, for example, Martin Chemnitz, "On the Use and Value of Theological Topics" in *Loci Theologici*, vol. I, tr. J. A. O. Preus (St. Louis: Concordia, 1989), pp. 37-47. See p. 37: "The best way to understand this subject is to consider how necessary the church of all ages has judged the use of this kind of writing to be, in which the heavenly doctrine is summarized in an orderly, proper, and clear manner." Further, Chemnitz imagines God Himself as a good Agricolan, since He "showed that He is the best creator of this method, when He wrote the entire doctrine of the Law, that is, His immeasurable wisdom, on two small tablets, so that all the prophets might marvel at the order of His decalog." Finally, the use of topics is essential "so that there be no ambiguous, unclear, difficult, or intricate meanings, but words which can be understood by each individual."

See also Hans-Georg Gadamer, *Truth and Method,* 2nd ed. (New York: Continuum, 1989), p. 175, n.5: "because the theology of the Reformation no longer desired to be an encyclopedic assimilation of dogmatic tradition, but sought to reorganize Christian teaching on the basis of key passages in the Bible *(loci communes)*, it tended toward systematization — a statement that is doubly instructive when we consider the later emergence of the term 'system' in the philosophy of the seventeenth century. There too something new broke into the traditional structure of the total science of Scholasticism: the new natural sciences." I am inclined to agree more or less with Gadamer's assessment, although I contend (as will become more clear) that "encyclopedic" is inadequate as a general description of pre-modern theological texts. It seems more the case that the tendency towards systematization implies the move towards the encyclopedic, and as such would be more characteristic of seventeenth- (and not thirteenth-) century Scholasticism. On the relation between this new hermeneutical principle and the origin of natural science, see Peter Harrison, *The Bible, Protestantism, and the Rise of Natural Science* (Cambridge: Cambridge University Press, 1998).

Instead the "tradition" of the church became, in effect, a second book, alongside the Bible, despite the final attempts of the Council of Trent to resist such implications. The debate over the precise formulation of Trent's decree on the nature of tradition is somewhat controversial, and has been subjected to the scrutiny of generations of scholars. Yet what is certain is that the Council of Trent famously decreed on the eighth of April, 1546, that the truths of the divinely revealed Gospel are "contained in the written books and in the unwritten traditions."[19] The final formulation appears to have been a modified resolution of a dispute among the Fathers of the Council, most of whom had advocated a version of the decree which read "*partly* in the written books and *partly* in the written traditions," the somewhat notorious *partim-partim* formula.[20] That version was rather abruptly abandoned in favor of a more ambiguous statement which stopped short of providing any concrete doctrinal definition of tradition.

Whatever the decree of 8 April 1546 tells us, it does not promulgate a "theory" of tradition.[21] And though the specific reasons for the adoption of the final "*et*" version are unclear, it seems to be the case that, if in fact Trent wished to resist the reification of both Scripture and Tradition into two separate "things" or even "sources," the final version was unsuccessful. Regardless, the final decree of the Council of Trent emphasized the nature of tradition as a source "on which the Church can draw, no less than on Scripture, for the intelligence and communication of revealed truth."[22]

The notion of tradition as a source received its fullest formulation in the *De Locis Theologicis* of the Dominican from Salamanca, Melchior Cano (1509-

19. See H. J. Schroeder, O.P., *The Canons and Decrees of the Council of Trent* (Rockford, Illinois: Tan Books, 1978), p. 17.

20. See Josef Rupert Geiselmann, "Scripture, Tradition, and the Church: An Ecumenical Problem" in Daniel J. Callahan, et al., eds., *Christianity Divided: Protestant and Roman Catholic Theological Issues* (New York: Sheed and Ward, 1961), p. 48: "Only two of them [the Fathers of the Council], the learned General of the Servites, Bonucci, and the Bishop of Chioggia, Jacob Nachianti, well versed in the Bible, protested energetically against this *partim-partim*. Six days later, in the decisive session of April 8, there suddenly appears a modified text. The *partim-partim* has disappeared and been replaced by 'et.' The records of the Council leave us, unfortunately, entirely in the dark about the events which moved the committee charged with the editing of the text to make this decisive change." Geiselmann also notes that the original use of the *partim-partim* comes from a mistranslation of the *De Ecclesiastica Hierarchia* of the Pseudo-Dionysius by Ambrosius Traversari, who renders the Greek *te . . . kai* ("both . . . and") into the Latin *partim-partim* (p. 41).

21. See Geiselmann, "Scripture, Tradition, and the Church," pp. 47-48.

22. Walter J. Burghardt, "The Catholic Concept of Tradition in the Light of Modern Theological Thought," *Proceedings of the Seventeenth Annual Convention of the Catholic Theological Society of America* (1962), pp. 42-75, esp. pp. 46-47.

60). According to Geiselmann, Cano is responsible for the post-Tridentine objectivization of tradition into a container of doctrine, by virtue of his reading of the *partim-partim* back on to Trent's decree.[23] In effect, Cano's treatment, which was published posthumously in 1563, effectively secured the *partim-partim* as the definitive statement of Catholic thought on tradition, in spite of Trent's attempts to resist. In any case, it became impossible for theologians after Trent to imagine tradition in any way other than "by analogy with the written text,"[24] or even more aptly, by analogy with the printed volume.

Cano's commonplaces were a Catholic attempt to counter the Protestant dependency upon "Scripture alone" by delineating, in hierarchical order, the descending *loci* of authority in Christian doctrine. In the first book of the *De Locis*, he describes these *loci* as the authority of: 1) Holy Scripture; 2) Christ and the apostles; 3) the Catholic Church; 4) the Councils; 5) the Roman Church; 6) the saints of old; 7) the Scholastic theologians; 8) natural reason; 9) the philosophers; and 10) human history.[25] Thus Cano conceived of tradition in terms of "seats" of authority, places of incrementally quantifiable reliability. It therefore represents the application of Agricolan topical method to the ranking of authoritative "sites" of argument, and as such, is a mirror image of the transformation of theology that had begun in Philipp Melanchthon. What becomes of Scripture in Melanchthon becomes of tradition in Cano: both are now thought of primarily as sources, containers of doctrine, *instrumenta doctrinae,* from which one can compose an argument, or even a body of teaching which corresponds to the text, whether the text in question is "scripture" or "tradition." For the two have now been so thoroughly divorced that it is impossible for either Protestants or Catholics, in this period, to imagine their "sources" as anything but "books." No longer is tradition simply the activity of interpreting and performing the Christian story; it becomes an independent totality, a body (*corpus* or *corpse?*) of knowledge separate from the practice of interpretation. Tradition now becomes *a thing to be interpreted* rather than the act of interpretation itself.

Thus the grammar of representation, though largely a Protestant invention, became, by the middle of the sixteenth century, the arbitrary terrain for the construction of theological systems. The new genres of theology, it was as-

23. Geiselmann, "Scripture, Tradition, and the Church," pp. 42-48. Geiselmann's claim, though widely accepted, is challenged by George Tavard in "Tradition in Early Post-Tridentine Theology," *Theological Studies* XXIII.3 (1962), pp. 377-405. I am indebted to John F. Montag, S.J., for discussions on Cano.

24. Walter Ong, S.J., *The Presence of the Word: Some Prolegomena for Cultural and Religious History* (New Haven: Yale University Press, 1967), p. 277.

25. Melchior Cano, *De Locis Theologicis, Opera* I (Rome: Forzani et Soc., 1890), I.iii, pp. 5-6.

sumed, were ultimately neither Protestant nor Catholic, but neutral applications of a single method in different ways.

Strategy and the Grammar of Representation

The *modus loquendi*, therefore, becomes the object of a "method," a transferable "strategy" for constructing a system.[26] As a strategy, first, it removes temporality from dialectic. It displaces the historical and the contingent from argument (and from contemplation) in favor of a putatively absolute "autonomous place,"[27] which is independent of all temporal, human operations. Second, it is, in de Certeau's words, a "mastery of places through sight." The visual priority of place-logics, and of maps, "makes possible a panoptic practice proceeding from a place whence the eye can transform foreign forces into objects that can be observed and measured, and thus control and 'include' them within its scope of vision."[28] Third, as a strategy it transforms "the uncertainties of history into readable spaces."[29] This ability depends upon a certain power of knowledge to "elaborate theoretical places (systems and totalizing discourses) capable of articulating an ensemble of physical places in which forces are distributed."[30]

A grammar of representation, then, is strategic; it seeks to confirm and validate itself by a "proof," by the correspondence of discourse to a given text, a *datum*. That is, the discourse most truly and accurately "represents" when its content accords with prior knowledge — i.e., with "data" — knowledge which is, in this case, not the product of continuing and unfinished exegesis, but the result of a simple encounter, of an *observation* by means of which the reader "takes in" the text. Here the mode is chiefly visual — one "sees" this to be the case, because it is there in the text, it is there on the page, for all to see. Nothing prior is therefore required, no training is demanded of the reader in order to make sense of the text, for the construction of the latter operates on the assumption that any "reasonable" agent, who reads the language in question, may come to an understanding based on the incontrovertibility of the "evidence" in favor of the argument. This mode may of course be oral, but if

---

26. See Michel de Certeau's distinction between "strategies" and "tactics" in "'Making Do': Uses and Tactics" in *The Practice of Everyday Life*, tr. Steven Rendall (Berkeley: University of California Press, 1984), pp. 29-42.

27. de Certeau, "'Making Do,'" p. 36.

28. de Certeau, "'Making Do,'" p. 36.

29. de Certeau, "'Making Do,'" p. 36.

30. de Certeau, "'Making Do,'" p. 38.

so it is an orality that listens and does not respond or dispute; it simply hears, and whatever "interpreting" it does is performed in the inviolable privacy of the mind. Either way, the *modus loquendi* here is chiefly monological. Thus under the aegis of "reason," "hermeneutics" becomes a universalized technique for making sense of any book, a general method of reading which can be applied to any text whatsoever.

But more than a philosophical or theological *episteme*, representation also implies a strategy for the organization of knowledge. It is not simply a new approach — it is a new approach instantiated in and instantiating a new rhetorical method, a new grammar. Representation is, for Foucault, a seventeenth-century innovation which substitutes analysis, a universal technique, for "the hierarchy of analogies."[31] Signs now signify within a language which we already know, which we already speak. It is no longer the case that our respective traditions make intelligible, by practice, the interpretation of analogical relations. Rather, we are, for Foucault as for Hans-Georg Gadamer, in possession of a universal "procedure," a single "hermeneutics" applicable to any readable text.[32] Again, it transforms the contingencies of time into manipulable, readable spaces.[33] For Gadamer, this *mathesis* "is not differentiated even by the way the ideas are transmitted — whether in writing or orally, in a foreign language or in one's own."[34] Thus the grammar of representation is strategic, insofar as, in de Certeau's first sense, it involves a "mastery of time through the foundation of an autonomous place."[35] It assumes that there is no relation between the form of presentation and its content. All that matters is the argument, and the validity of this argument is, as we said, supported by the references to prior textual authorities. Making sense of the argument, then, requires little more than an ability to read a language in the most rudimentary sense. And this reading is ahistorical, as it removes temporality from both the composition and the act of interpretation. One is not required first to find oneself situated within an ongoing process of agreement and disagreement, qualification and rebuttal, stopping here and starting again there, all of which is never finally resolved nor fully realized. In the grammar of representation, one sign may be resolved by citing another one, no longer by reference to a potentially endless catena of references which are never secured by the textual fixity of the printed letter.

31. See Michel Foucault, *The Order of Things: An Archaeology of the Human Sciences* (New York: Random House, 1970), pp. 54-55.

32. See Hans-Georg Gadamer, *Truth and Method*, 2nd ed., tr. and rev. Joel Weinsheimer and Donald G. Marshall (New York: Continuum, 1975, 1989), p. 179.

33. Gadamer, *Truth and Method*, p. 179.

34. Gadamer, *Truth and Method*, p. 179.

35. de Certeau, "'Making Do,'" p. 36.

The model here is that of the printed book, as opposed first of all to the manuscript, and more particularly to the glossed manuscript. For both are types of texts, but differ fundamentally in the way they organize the knowledge they are said to "contain," and even more, in the way they (insofar as inanimate objects may be said to do so) assume differently whether one can speak meaningfully of the book or the page as "containing" anything to begin with. In the case of the printed book, which I take it serves as the metaphor for all modern theories of the "medieval idea of the book" (which as we have seen is tautological), one can speak of the freezing of content, of the codification of dogma within specifically delimited parameters. The front and back covers of the bound and printed volume become the metaphors for the fixity and totality of knowledge that Derrida rightly derides. Whereas the printed volume cannot be amended except by another printed edition, the manuscript assumes itself not to be a totality, precisely because the text itself is never finished. The whole tradition of glossing texts — not just the Scriptures but also the writings of Boethius, and later the Lombard, among others — flatly contradicts the notion that the medieval idea of the book is "the idea of a totality." It is more correct to say, as Gerard Loughlin does, that it is more "the idea of its impossibility: of a text that promises and defers self-present meaning, that involves its readers in an endless process of interpretation."[36]

The printed text, then, as opposed to the glossed manuscript, is the *mise-en-page* of the grammar of representation.[37] Temporality, history, and mem-

---

36. Gerard Loughlin, *Telling God's Story: Bible, Church and Narrative Theology* (Cambridge: Cambridge University Press, 1996), p. 101. Loughlin examines narrativist theologians such as Hans Frei and George Lindbeck, and particularly their "chief conceit," namely that "the Bible is an all-consuming text" (p. 97). He links this notion with the medievals via the work of Jesse Gellrich (who follows Derrida) and E. R. Curtius, and attributes the origins of the encyclopedia to this conception of the book. Such a conception, while not entirely wrong, is rather too general in its assumption of the univocity of "book-ness." In other words, whatever that quality of book-ness is in which all books participate, it is not the idea of a totality. But, as Loughlin says, the book is impossible because it can never be completed, particularly in the case of the Bible. It seems worth noting here that "totality" need not imply "finality" or "closure" (as it does not for Loughlin, but does for Derrida). For Derrida this impossibility is a warrant for nihilism, but for Loughlin, this incompleteness is made intelligible only by the Eucharist.

37. To be sure, there are many kinds of printed books. To be more specific, and to attempt to resist the ahistorical generalization which I have attributed to Derrida and others, the printed, glossless Bible might serve as a better metaphor. For an even more particular example, one might look at the early Gutenberg versions and the early European vernacular Bibles. See the reproductions in S. L. Greenslade, ed., *The Cambridge History of the Bible*, Volume III: *The West from the Reformation to the Present Day* (Cambridge: Cambridge University Press, 1963), plates 1-5 and 7. However, perhaps the most significant and poignant symbol of what I am describing

ory have all been literally wiped from the margins, leaving the impression that all that remains for the reader is to make sense of the argument set before him on the page. As such, then, the *mise-en-page* represents the panoptical apparatus of representation. This new logic abstracts dialectic from speech, and assumes the priority of visual analogies over aural ones — a shift which, as Ong argues, depends upon the invention of printing as the technological innovation which instantiates, very subtly, a reorganization of the human sensorium, whereby the mind is now, after moveable type, understood to learn by the visual "reception" of data imprinted on the page.[38] Thus for Catherine Pickstock, "the appearance of knowledge in the impersonal arena of a printed page, in contrast to the individual and erratic scribal 'hands' of the past, precipitated the notion of a pseudo-eternity of 'given' reality unaffected by the human being who enacts its representation."[39]

Printing necessarily involved a reduction on many levels, especially in the types of books which could affordably be produced. Glossed Bibles were notoriously difficult to arrange, considering the fact that they involved at least two different sets of type, one in the middle and one in the margins. The problem of interlinear glosses made the situation even more problematic. A text such as the *editio princeps* of the *Glossa Ordinaria* (1480), and later, the magnificent *Complutensian Polygot* (1520)[40] represent both the zenith of printing achievement and the tension inherent in printed texts.[41] These two volumes are masterpieces of typography, and represent the kind of youthful ambition characteristic of early printers and scholars with respect to their new technology. Yet they are also transitional pieces, in a way. The printed edition of the *Glossa*, it might be argued, ensured its death because it at-

---

is the edition of the Psalms published by Johannes Grunenberg at the request of Martin Luther in Wittenberg in 1513. See Chapter Four, "Memory and the *Glossa Ordinaria*."

38. See Ong, *The Presence of the Word* and *Orality and Literacy: The Technologization of the Word* (London: Routledge, 1982).

39. Catherine Pickstock, *After Writing*, p. 50. See her critique of spatialization on pp. 47-100.

40. See Basil Hall, "The Trilingual College of San Ildefonso and the Making of the Complutensian Polyglot Bible," in G. J. Cuming, ed., *Studies in Church History V: The Church and Academic Learning* (Leiden: Brill, 1969), pp. 114-46.

41. For reproductions of these two, see Margaret T. Gibson, ed., *The Bible in the Latin West*, The Medieval Book 1 (Notre Dame: Notre Dame University Press, 1993), plates 16 and 27, pp. 56-57 and 84-85. By way of comparison, see also plate 14, pp. 52-53, which is a reproduction of an English *incipit* to the Pauline epistles from the middle of the twelfth century. The tension is evident between the inherent incompleteness of the glossed manuscript and the fixity inherent in print. The printed version inherits a medieval form, and reproduces it faithfully, but by freezing the marginalia it renders a new product altogether. Only now can one speak of the codification of both "scripture" and "tradition."

tempted an impossibility: the identical repetition of a text which by its very nature prohibited against this. The "erratic" character of the marginal and interlinear annotations and glosses in manuscripts such as the glossed Bible can in practice be reproduced in print, but to reduce them to a codified set of "authoritative" interpretations defies the capacity of the glosses to resist reification, insofar as the act of reading and commenting on Scripture is never finished, and there is never quite enough space in the margins or in between the lines to say all that needs to be said.

Finally, the terms "participation" and "representation" do not, as such, describe two mutually opposed philosophical *loci*. One might more comfortably set "repetition" over against "representation" as philosophical *aporiai*. By "participation" I refer to an ontological principle by which creatures "are" by analogy to the way in which God "is," but also the notion that *sacra doctrina* is a kind of *scientia* which participates in God's knowledge of himself, and is therefore not something superadded to God. If this is true, then it must become embodied not only in the way in which one thinks about God, but also in the particular textual form in which such thought is made present to the reader, and in the form of Christian pedagogy which understands its task not to be the mere impartation of information about God, but a real leading into the Trinity. Thus to know, under this mode, is an ontological endeavor — one comes to know more truly only by "being" more perfectly, and therefore by loving more rightly.

Representation, on the other hand, is not precisely the philosophical antithesis to participation; in fact, there is a sense in which "representation," rightly understood as methectic, is a theological prerogative that all of creation shows forth, in its being, the divine glory. Nevertheless, it is genuinely opposed to it, since it assumes God to be a kind of object which can be depicted. Representation assumes a neutral and unequivocal register across which descriptions can be ferried from a code or tableau of knowledge to the mind, regardless of either the temporal identity of the mind or the temporality of texts themselves, which print is supposed to have overcome. Representation, then, is a matter of immediate apprehension by virtue of an exterior sign, and is removed from the variables of time and human communities. As such, representation is the fundamental philosophical and theological strategy of modernity.

Thus "participation" can be asymmetrically set against "representation" as the two terms denote two distinct grammars, each of which is embedded in a theology of knowledge itself. As grammatical approaches underwritten by differing theological understandings, they are instantiated in differing organizing principles and rhetorical structures as well as goals. For in the first instance, a grammar of participation seeks, through its peculiar arrangement of textual material, to communicate, that is, to "bring into common," by drawing the reader into a prior community of interpretation and by attempting to lead the reader to a goal which is both textual and ontological. For this reason, it will be shown that the common practice of concluding a theological writing in the Middle Ages with a discussion of the beatific vision is not a result of a simple logical order, but of a cosmological order which situates the immediate vision of God at the end because it is the ultimate goal of all knowing, and the reader, it is hoped, by persuasion and pursuit will come to share in it herself.

Tactics and the Grammar of Participation

The glossed manuscript, then, as opposed to the printed book, is as it were the archetype of a grammar of participation. On one level, the glossed manuscript can neither be an exclusively oral object, insofar as it is written, nor a merely visual construct, as the immediate object of the gaze. Rather, it synthesizes the oral and the visual in terms of its arrangement as both a cue for speech and an iconographic theological statement. Glossed manuscripts must be read aloud, and though they can be read in private, one never has an unmediated relationship to a "pure" text. There is no truth which is not already mediated, through the "scribal hands of the past." Textually, the glossed manuscript images the historical determinacy of meaning through memory — through a "tradition" of interpretation which is inseparable from the text itself. To read a text like the *Glossa Ordinaria*, then, one must be inscripted into an ongoing conversation with other readers. There is no access to the text itself, either visually or otherwise, save through its commentary.

Moreover, the *mise-en-page* of the glossed text images a relationship of the reader to this community of interpretation. It suggests that reading itself is "liturgical," that the antiphonal *sic et non* of text and interpretation requires the anamnesic orientation of memory through learned texts towards its goal in God. In the terms of the *Glossa*, the scriptural text re-members its commentaries, and the commentaries in turn situate the text within an "itinerary of return"[42] to an eschatological "origin." Thus, in contrast with representation, which attempts the freezing of space as a kind of pseudo-eternity, participation assumes the centrality of memory, not as a simple recollection of stored data, but as the orientation of the itinerary towards a destination by way of the "remembrance of God," or, in terms of textual mechanisms, the rejection of the autonomy of the paragraph for the necessarily historical *quaestio*.

---

42. Henri de Lubac, *Theology in History*, tr. Anne Englund Nash (San Francisco: Ignatius, 1996), p. 151. De Lubac is here referring specifically to the *Summa Theologiae*. The term is apropos here, and I will have occasion to employ it in de Lubac's more precise sense in Chapter Five.

This forces the reader to relinquish his authorial rights as a reader and be thus confronted with the imperative of accounting for the "*ways* of using" the text and its interpretation, as opposed to the simple and direct encounter with "*what* is used."[43] Over against the autonomy of the paragraph, a grammar of participation recognizes the priority of the sequence of questions and responses. As de Certeau writes, the itinerary or the "trajectory" suggests

> a temporal movement through space, that is, the unity of a diachronic *succession* of points through which it passes, and not the *figure* that these points form on a space that is supposed to be synchronic or achronic. Indeed, "representation" is insufficient, precisely because a trajectory is drawn, and time and movement are thus reduced to a line that can be seized as a whole by the eye and read in a single moment, as one projects onto a map the path taken by someone walking through a city.[44]

Similarly, Pierre Hadot has argued that, against many modern readings, ancient philosophy understood itself as a kind of school for the development of the whole person. "It is ancient philosophy itself that the ancients thought of as a spiritual exercise."[45] Texts were composed primarily for the schools which produced and were produced by them. "Understanding a work of antiquity requires placing it in the group from which it emanates, in the tradition of its dogmas, its literary genre, and requires understanding its goals."[46] But this is more than an obligatory appeal to the banalities of context. To make sense of a text of ancient philosophy, then, one is required to be in possession of a different set of reading habits and skills. To read an ancient text like a modern one, and to expect from it all the requisite elements of systematic coherence, is to overlook, and fundamentally to reject as insignificant, the basic character of these writings as derivative of oral performance.[47]

43. de Certeau, "'Making Do,'" p. 35.

44. de Certeau, "'Making Do,'" p. 35.

45. Pierre Hadot, *Philosophy as a Way of Life: Spiritual Exercises from Socrates to Foucault,* ed. Arnold Davidson, tr. Michael Chase (Oxford: Basil Blackwell, 1995), p. 126.

46. Hadot, *Philosophy as a Way of Life,* p. 64.

47. Hadot, *Philosophy as a Way of Life,* p. 62: "More than other literature, philosophical works are linked to oral transmission because ancient philosophy itself is above all oral in character. Doubtless there are occasions when someone was converted by reading a book, but one would then hasten to the philosopher to hear him speak, question him, and carry on discussions with him and other disciples in a community that always serves as a place of discussion. In matters of philosophical teaching, writing is only an aid to memory, a last resort that will never replace the living word."

Further, "true education is always oral because only the spoken word makes dialogue possi-

For Hadot, as for de Certeau, the metaphor of the itinerary is central for the understanding of how texts function in classical philosophical pedagogy:

> Above all, the work, even if it is apparently theoretical and systematic, is written not so much to inform the reader of a doctrinal content but to form him, to make him traverse a certain itinerary in the course of which he will make spiritual progress. This procedure is clear in the works of Plotinus and Augustine, in which all the detours, starts and stops, and digressions of the work are formative elements.[48]

Such "detours, starts and stops, and digressions" may be said to be those rhetorical elements of a composition which are designed so as to lead the reader to a certain *skopos,* or destination. What Hadot has in mind with regard to the texts of ancient philosophical schools is eminently the case with the medieval theological texts which I will be discussing. For Hadot, Christianity took to describing itself as a "philosophy" from Justin Martyr onwards, precisely because, as he argues, "philosophy itself was already, above all else, a way of being and a style of life."[49] Thus some theological writings, insofar as they were constitutive of a "school," were understood as aiding the reader in the cultivation of the "remembrance of God."

Memory, then, in Hadot's account, is not only the technical skill of recollection by rote of learned formulae, but also the artful activity of the mind that orders thought to God. This requires the "fundamental attitude of the monk," *prosoche,* which "consists in paying attention to the beauty of our souls, by constantly renewing the examination of our conscience and our knowledge of ourselves."[50] Thus the notion of *memento mori*, "remember your death," orients memory toward the future, and directs the will to the proper object of thought and action. Likewise, "remembrance of God" consists not in the recollection of some object, but points towards the teleological consummation of thought and desire in God, who is the proper object of such.[51]

Hadot's thesis is instructive for the reading of some texts of medieval theology against the modern tendency to treat them as systematic, totalizing maps of thought. One must therefore situate texts such as the *Glossa*

---

ble, that is, it makes it possible for the disciple to discover the truth himself amid the interplay of questions and answers and also for the master to adapt his teaching to the needs of the disciple."

48. Hadot, *Philosophy as a Way of Life*, p. 64.

49. Hadot, *Philosophy as a Way of Life*, p. 130.

50. Hadot, *Philosophy as a Way of Life*, p. 131.

51. See also Mary Carruthers, *The Craft of Thought* (Cambridge: Cambridge University Press, 1998), pp. 66-69.

Ordinaria and the *Summa Theologiae* within their particular schools of production, but, more importantly, one cannot abstract these texts from the training in reading which the liturgy inculcates, or from the liturgically conditioned character of their grammar and composite languages. For if the *Glossa* and the *Summa* are texts of the medieval schools, they are not merely "academic" textbooks in our sense, insofar as medieval academic theological exercises occur in the context of the daily offices of the liturgy.

The grammar of participation therefore resembles a "tactic" more than it does a "strategy." For de Certeau, a tactic is "a calculated action determined by the absence of a proper locus." Moreover, it "must play on and with a terrain imposed on it and organized by the law of a foreign power."[52] A tactic lacks its own "place," its own panoptic view of the whole, and, finally, is "determined by the *absence of power* just as a strategy is organized by the postulation of power."[53] Tactics, therefore, take advantage of opportunities offered by the powerful, and exploit these by a kind of guileful legerdemain.[54]

While the question of power is an extremely important one as regards the question of the construction of theological systems and texts and the grammar which I am attempting to describe, and while it does employ the provisions of power to its own advantage, it is not so subversive as de Certeau suggests. Whereas tactics assume the existence of a prior strategy according to which it must adapt itself, theology cannot be wholly tactical insofar as it assumes itself to address itself to everything that is. Thus inasmuch as theology refers all things to God as their source and end, it seems that it does contain an element of the strategic as well as an element of the tactical. However, theology can never assume the status of political sovereignty — rather it must call into question the legitimacy of such absolutist strategies, while tactically subverting them, not by the imposition of a finally authoritative dictum, but from within. That is to say, theology makes use of languages foreign to itself in order to undo them, to expose them as improperly ordered and internally incomplete, but also to order and to perfect them, to consummate them. This will be seen to be the case in the texts which I will examine, as they represent not a self-enclosed totality, but a kind of iconographic grammar of the fundamentally "borrowed" character of theological language.

However, this language is not borrowed from the powerful; it is borrowed, paradoxically, from itself. Thus theological vocabularies are borrowed not from an original "site," but from an ongoing participation in a political body,

---

52. de Certeau, "'Making Do,'" p. 37.
53. de Certeau, "'Making Do,'" p. 38.
54. de Certeau, "'Making Do,'" p. 37.

the worshiping church. The claim is therefore that truth is not a possession of the church, but that, nevertheless, what the traditions of holy teaching hand over is true. It is not the case that the church "has" the truth; rather, it "hands on" the truth because its existence is a sacramental participation, though imperfect, in Truth. The distinction is subtle, though crucial. Though the language of theology is, as it were, derived from the language of the scriptures as these are learned in the liturgy, even the liturgy itself is not a *site* from which power is exercised. Rather it is the performance of a vocabulary, and an interpretive enactment in the form of a re-narration. In this sense, a grammar of participation distinguishes itself from one of representation by virtue of the role of *time*.

Whereas the former is necessarily historical, the latter attempts to remove itself from temporal contingencies. Just as strategies "reduce temporal relations to spatial ones," "[t]actics are procedures that gain validity in relation to the pertinence they lend to time," and "pin their hopes . . . on a clever utilization of time, of the opportunities it presents and also of the play it introduces into the foundations of power."[55] A grammar of participation, therefore, though not precisely tactical in de Certeau's sense, makes use of tactics in the sense that it is never finished, but always underway. As an "art of the weak,"[56] it can never assume its work to be done, but ever incomplete and ever in need of further commentary.

This is, I argue, embodied in the way such texts are arranged. While the printed page images an incontrovertible absoluteness to the words stamped upon it, the glossed manuscript in principle can never be finished. There is always blank space to be filled in with commentary, but it is blank space already determined visually by the prior comments in between which further comments may be inserted. It is not a blank space pure and simple (as an empty margin is), but a space that is conditioned by a participation in a historically prior fellowship of interpretation, not by the sheer imposition of an inviolable and individual will onto a silent page.

Thus a *mise-en-page*, or even a grammatical structure, can be iconographically instructive for a theology of knowledge itself. How a page is organized theologically suggests something about how the mind itself is teleologically organized, and thus demands sets of tactics for reading diverse texts. That is, there is no single *mathesis* of reading which is applicable to any text whatsoever — rather, readers must, as it were, "move across lands belonging to someone else, like nomads poaching their way across fields they did not write, de-

55. de Certeau, "'Making Do,'" pp. 38-9.
56. de Certeau, "'Making Do,'" p. 37.

spoiling the wealth of Egypt to enjoy it themselves."[57] Yet, this poaching need not be treated with the kind of cynicism with which de Certeau sometimes treats it. Particularly in view of the texts I will be discussing, a benevolent form of poaching is precisely the tactic of the author, and the recommended act of the reader.

57. Michel de Certeau, "Reading as Poaching," in *The Practice of Everyday Life*, p. 174.

2 Itineraries; Or, Theology as Manuduction

In its first activity, therefore — the actual retention of all temporal things, past, present and future — the memory is an image of eternity, whose indivisible presence extends to all times. From its second activity, it is evident that memory is informed not only from outside by sensible images, but also from above by receiving and holding within itself simple forms which cannot enter through the doors of the senses by means of sensible images. From the third activity, we hold that the memory has an unchangeable light present to itself in which it remembers immutable truths. And so from the activities of the memory, we see that the soul itself is an image of God and a likeness so present to itself and having God so present that the soul actually grasps him and potentially is capable of possessing him and of being a partaker in him.[1]

If one were to be asked by a traveler how to get from one place to another, from the Covent Garden tube station to the National Gallery, for example, one might have two basic options: 1) the drawing of a map, or the production of a *London A-to-Z;* or 2) the narrative description of how one comes to the National Gallery by marking a journey according to various signs and markers along the way. That is to say, the latter description could look something like this: "Coming out of the tube station onto Long Acre, turn to the left. After a few minutes' walk you will come to the intersection of several smaller roads with St. Martin's Lane. Turn to the left there, and you will know you are

---

1. St. Bonaventure, *The Soul's Journey into God,* in Ewert Cousins, tr., *Bonaventure: The Soul's Journey into God, The Tree of Life, The Life of St. Francis,* Classics of Western Spirituality (Mahwah, N.J.: Paulist, 1978), III.2, pp. 80-81.

on the right path if you can see the hexagonal steeple of St. Martin-in-the-Fields. Once you arrive at the latter, to your right will be a large plaza full of camera-toting tourists and opportunistic pigeons. Avoid these, and cross St. Martin's Lane, which will now be full of black cabs operated by impatient cabbies, irritated at the congestion and the throngs of foreigners clogging the pedestrian walkways. The long building facing the square to the south (or towards Big Ben, which is just visible through Whitehall) with a small grey dome atop the entrance is the National Gallery."

In a place like central London, it is not entirely clear which would be the simpler option. Each requires distinct mental operations: the former requires that one first locate oneself on the map itself, and the latter requires an exertion of the memory. The relationship between these two, the itinerary and the map, is, as Michel de Certeau says, a relation "between two symbolic and anthropological languages of space."[2] The map is a spatial depiction of a place, a "totalizing stage on which elements of diverse origin are brought together to form the tableau of a 'state' of geographical knowledge, [which] pushes away into its prehistory or into its posterity, as if into the wings, the operations of which it is the result or the necessary condition. It remains alone on the stage. The tour describers have disappeared."[3]

According to de Certeau, the development of cartography from the fifteenth to the seventeenth centuries demonstrates a move towards accuracy of description and representation, whereas before that period, maps typically included "only the rectilinear marking out of itineraries (performative indications chiefly concerning pilgrimages), along with the stops one was to make (cities which one was to pass through, spend the night in, pray at, etc.) and distances calculated in hours or in days, that is, in terms of the time it would take to cover them on foot."[4] Gradually these "tour describers" fall out of the picture, literally, and the map becomes a kind of panoptic image of the whole of a place.[5]

2. Michel de Certeau, "Spatial Stories," in *The Practice of Everyday Life,* tr. Steven Rendall (Berkeley: University of California Press, 1984), p. 119.

3. de Certeau, "Spatial Stories," p. 121.

4. de Certeau, "Spatial Stories," p. 120.

5. "Between the fifteenth and the seventeenth centuries, the map became more autonomous. No doubt the proliferation of the 'narrative' figures that have long been its stock-in-trade (ships, animals, and characters of all kinds) still had the function of indicating the operations — travelling, military, architectural, political or commercial — that make possible the fabrication of a geographical plan. Far from being 'illustrations,' iconic glosses on the text, these figurations, like fragments of stories, mark on the map the historical operations from which it resulted. Thus the sailing ship painted on the sea indicates the maritime expedition that made it possible to represent the coastlines. It is equivalent to a describer of the 'tour' type. But the map gradually wins out over these figures; it colonizes space; it eliminates little by little the pictural

To return to our London narrator, then, what the itinerary requires, as the map does not, is a performance of the memory. In order for the traveler to get from Covent Garden to the National Gallery, she must in some way reenact the narrative which she has heard. Thus as the narration of the journey resides in the memory, the traveler performs the operations which make the narration intelligible, and by doing so, traces a "route" through a series of mnemonic signs (Long Acre, a hexagonal steeple, throngs of tourists, pigeons, etc.). Through the sequence of these way-markers, the traveler is directed, in memory, towards her goal, and in doing so, becomes to some extent identical with the narrated itinerary. As she performs the itinerary from memory, she becomes coextensive and coterminous with it, and is led towards the destination of her route by enacting her memory.

Medieval rhetoricians (who, in many cases, were theologians) often employed the concepts of *ductus* and *skopos* to refer precisely to the process of memorial performance and its *telos. Ductus* signifies the flow and movement of a composition, "the movement within and through a work's various parts. Indeed, *ductus* insists upon movement, the con*duct* of a thinking mind on its way through a composition."[6] *Skopos,* on the other hand, is the goal to which the *ductus* of a composition leads. In the case of our London traveler, the National Gallery is the *skopos* of the narrative of her guide, who through a very particular *ductus,* leads her to her destination. The *skopos* of the composition (the narration of the itinerary) thus becomes identical with the actual destination of the tourist, once the itinerary is performed completely.

The disappearance of de Certeau's "tour describers" is not limited to the field of cartography, however. Indeed, compositions of all sorts have come to privilege the straightforward and the readily intelligible. Thanks to shifts in the understanding of rhetoric from the fifteenth and seventeenth centuries, knowledge has, according to Walter Ong, become spatialized, mapped out, and legible. But the problem here is not space itself, but the habits of thought and imagination which make, by virtue of memorial performance, such space the result of a practiced itinerary, the intelligible scene of rhetorical opera-

---

figurations of the practices that produce it"; de Certeau, "Spatial Stories," p. 121. For an account of the often deliberate political "silencing" of early modern maps, see J. B. Harley, "Silences and Secrecy: The Hidden Agenda of Cartography in Early Modern Europe," *Imago Mundi* XL (1988), pp. 57-76.

6. Mary Carruthers, *The Craft of Thought: Meditation, Rhetoric, and the Making of Images, 400-1200* (Cambridge: Cambridge University Press, 1998), p. 77. For a discussion of *ductus* in the context of medieval music, see Nancy van Deusen, *Theology and Music at the Early University: The Case of Robert Grosseteste and Anonymous IV,* Brill Studies in Intellectual History 57 (Leiden: Brill, 1994), pp. 37-53.

tions, or the route of the reader from one "place" towards, through compositional *ductus,* a *skopos.* Perhaps the difficulty is that in the modern period, the space which one traverses in the well-trained memory becomes transferred to the blank page, which ultimately cannot hold it. The itinerary of the soul becomes usurped by the autonomy of the map or the page, and thus "spatialized" to the exclusion of the reader.

Through a reading of two medieval theological texts, which each have a peculiar *ductus* but a common *skopos,* I hope to show that the itinerary of the soul is the function of a pedagogy of manuduction, by which the reader is not merely given information but led into God. I will argue that particularly in the case of the *Glossa Ordinaria* and Thomas Aquinas' *Summa Theologiae,* the reader is not simply provided with a deposit of doctrine independent of an interpretative community, nor a "summary map" of all of theology. Rather, both of these texts have a specific rhetorical purpose, and their authors and their interlocutors act as the reader's guides along the way, her manuductors, towards their common *skopos,* namely, the beatific vision.

For example (to invoke a text which I will not treat in detail here), to read well Bonaventure's account of the "soul's journey into God" in his *Itinerarium Mentis in Deum* is, in some sense, to traverse the route of the "reading soul" toward its true home in the Trinity. Though reading does not effect *salus,* the latter is at least intimated by the manuduction of knowledge into participation in God's self-knowledge. Thus to read the *Itinerarium* is not simply to learn more about God, but to be led toward God — an activity which, like all knowledge, is unfinished and mediated. To put it yet another way, manuduction is the *form* of *theosis.*

Likewise, for Thomas, the celebrated "*exitus-reditus*" pattern of the *Summa Theologiae* is not simply a clever Neoplatonic rhetorical device on the part of its author. Rather, the framework of exit and return, the *ductus* of the work, is meant to lead the reader to its goal, the vision of the blessed. This is a case of "remembering heaven" which, as Mary Carruthers rightly suggests, is "preeminently a moral activity rather than what we think of as intellectual or rational."[7] Thomas therefore draws the reader toward the "memory of heaven," where the soul learns the proper object of its desire, and indeed, gets a glimpse of it. Thus the process of "reading" the soul's return to God is also, analogously,

---

7. Carruthers, *The Craft of Thought,* p. 68. Carruthers' accentuation of the ethical character of memory is an important emphasis, but it seems her stress away from its intellectual and rational aspect is an unnecessary conclusion. It does not seem to me that one should have to make a choice between being *either* moral or intellectual and not both at the same time. Carruthers seems to me not to take seriously enough the theological character of memory, which a closer reading of Augustine would help to modify.

the process of that return itself. In other words, "reading" is not something other than the activity of rightly ordering our desire towards its proper object.

Like the narration of our London guide, these texts are kinds of itineraries. By the arduous act of reading the reader is given a route, with indicative markers and signs, towards a destination. By the process of reading, or the memorial performance of the itinerary, the reader becomes in a sense identical with the text, though in a rhetorical sense and not (obviously) a physical one. And though the "tour guide" is not physically present, he is nevertheless the manuductor in memory, insofar as to trace the route is to recall the voice of the one who has narrated it. And as rhetorical activities, itineraries are also acts of meditation and devotion, ways "marked out by the schemes and tropes of Scripture. Like sites plotted on a map, these functioned as the stations of the way, to be stopped at and stayed in before continuing; or they could serve as route indicators, 'this way' or 'slow down' or 'skim this quickly' or 'note well.'"[8] This is not to say, however, that the activity of reading a text is exhaustive of the activity of return. On the contrary, texts such as these, understood as itineraries of manuduction, represent moments in the larger *reditus* to God which is descriptive of the Christian life as a whole. To read them as itineraries, then, is not to suggest that texts *effect* that return — lest one fall prey to the very kind of Cartesian reading which I suggest these works undermine — but rather that they contribute to the larger pedagogy of Christianity as an art of reading well. In other words, the route to *salus* is not *contained* by the text, but, as it were, furnished by it. As I will show later on, the extent to which a text like the *Glossa* or the *Summa Theologiae* (two quite different texts, to be sure) can be read well is made possible and intelligible by the practices of reading (oral, communal, and public) and the concomitant arts which accompany them (memory, composition, and delivery).

In the case of Bonaventure, a theologian who delights in symbolic associations, the *Itinerarium* is a seven-part account of the soul's ascent into God through contemplation. It is of course clear that the text has a hexameral design, whereby we reach, with the seventh chapter, the soul's rest in the "internal Jerusalem."[9] And the journey for Bonaventure begins with the first words of Genesis: *In principio.*[10] Thus the narration of Bonaventure's itinerary recounts the whole of the biblical story, from the first creation of light, a central metaphor in his account of illumination, to the final Amen, the Sabbath in which the soul at last comes to rest in the Trinity.

8. Carruthers, *The Craft of Thought*, p. 116.
9. Bonaventure, *The Soul's Journey into God*, p. 111.
10. Bonaventure, *The Soul's Journey into God*, p. 53.

The trope of "steps" or "rungs" in a ladder is, of course, a favorite one among medieval theologians (an obvious example is John Climacus' *The Ladder of Divine Ascent*).[11] It captures well the concept of rhetorical *ductus,* but particularly in terms of an ascent from things lower to things higher.[12] Thus reading the account of the soul's itinerary necessarily makes of the reader a co-traveler along that very journey. Thus it is no "mere" metaphor Bonaventure employs when he describes the first six chapters of his work as "like the six steps of the true Solomon's throne, by which we arrive at peace, where the true man of peace rests in a peaceful mind as in the interior Jerusalem."[13]

As in the passage I cited at the very beginning of this chapter, for Bonaventure the memory is the activity by means of which we are made capable of participation in God. From the activity of memory, he says, "we see that the soul itself is an image of God and a likeness so present to itself and having God so present that the soul actually grasps him and potentially "is capable of possessing him and of being a partaker in him."[14] Thus the reader, as she performs this itinerary through the "things" in her memory, by arriving at the perception of the source of the soul's true rest, does not merely perceive a representation of divine beatitude, but comprehends that "the soul itself is an image of God," and therefore becomes capable of wisdom, by the analogical participation in Wisdom itself. Therefore what is "learned" in memory is not a deposit of immutable data about the "supreme Being" inscribed upon the mind but rather an absorption into the imperishable unity of God, who is ultimately the object of all language. The soul learns that there is nothing outside the Trinity, even the soul itself, which exists only by participation in God's being, and comes to wisdom only by participation in God's wisdom — which, of course, for Bonaventure, as for Aquinas, amounts to the same thing.

The route to this wisdom, therefore, is the peculiar *ductus* of these theological texts: for Bonaventure it is the seven steps toward restfulness; for Aquinas it is the "architecture" of exit and return, and within it, the *sic et non* of

---

11. John Climacus, *The Ladder of Divine Ascent,* tr. Colm Luibheid and Norman Russell (Mahwah, N.J.: Paulist, 1982).

12. Cf. Carruthers, *The Craft of Thought,* p. 60: "The trope of 'steps' or 'stages' was commonly applied to the affective, emotional 'route' that a meditator was to take in the course of such composition, from 'fear' to 'joy' — perhaps even that inarticulate, sensory joy that Augustine characterized as the earthly memory of the vision of God. These 'routes', emotional and rational, are always characterized as routes through the things in one's memory."

13. Bonaventure, *The Soul's Journey into God,* p. 110. See also Augustine's account of memory in *The Trinity* IX-XV, *passim.*

14. Bonaventure, *The Soul's Journey into God,* p. 80.

each *quaestio,* which begins with God in the *Prima Pars,* "descends" through the human vices and virtues in the *Secunda Pars,* and ascends to the Incarnation and the Vision of Blessedness in the *Tertia Pars.*[15] As Chenu writes, in Thomas' discussion of the Incarnation, Christ is the "way" of our return to God. Notice the echoes of rhetorical *ductus:* Christ as the "way," or *via,* indeed, *ductus.* Christ conducts us towards the rest of the blessed, yet again, as we saw in Bonaventure, this is no mere "account" of how the soul makes that return. It is an itinerary of the soul's return to God, and as such, the reader of the *Summa* is meant to be led towards that "memory of heaven" to which we alluded earlier. This is what John of Saint Thomas calls the "golden circuit of theology."[16]

As in Bonaventure, the reader is led towards that wisdom which is begotten of the Father. As Aquinas himself says, "Now men are called the children of God in so far as they participate in the likeness of the only-begotten and natural Son of God, according to Rom. viii. 29, *Whom he foreknew . . . to be made conformable to the image of His Son,* Who is Wisdom Begotten. Hence by participating in the gift of wisdom, man attains to the sonship of God."[17] Wisdom, like the seventh chapter of Bonaventure's *Itinerarium,* is that Sabbath, the "seventh beatitude" wherein the soul finds rest in union with Begotten Wisdom, Jesus Christ. Here ontological participation in God's Being is related, of course, to participation in Christ the redeemer of humanity, the "Wisdom" of God. Moreover, this participation in God is fully trinitarian insofar as the form of our participation in God is made possible by the Holy Spirit, from whom we "receive the likeness of the natural Son, who is Begotten Wisdom."[18]

The soul arrives at this "seventh beatitude" by ascent towards the *skopos* of

15. Cf. Marie-Dominique Chenu's classic discussion of the framework of *exitus et reditus* in his *Toward Understanding St. Thomas,* tr. Albert M. Landry, O.P., and Dominic Hughes, O.P. (Chicago: Regnery, 1964), pp. 304-18.

16. Therefore, as may be seen from the prologue of the second question of Part I, St. Thomas divides the entire teaching of his *Summa Theologiae* according to the threefold causality of God, that is to say, of God as the effecting principle, of God as the beatifying end, of God as the repairing savior. And thus, proceeding from God as he is in himself and in his being, proceeding through God as he effects, and finalizes, and saves, there is a return to God to be enjoyed in himself through the ultimate glory of the resurrection, *which is evidently to complete the golden circuit of theology, which the divine* Summa *of Saint Thomas follows out.* John of Saint Thomas, *Cursus theologicus in Summam D. Thomae* (Paris, 1883), I, 191, quoted in Chenu, *Toward Understanding St. Thomas,* p. 305 n.9.

17. Thomas Aquinas, *Summa Theologiae,* tr. Fathers of the English Dominican Province (Allen, Texas: Christian Classics, 1948), IIaIIae.xlv.6, *resp.*

18. *Summa Theologiae* IIaIIae.xlv.6, *ad* 1.

the Wisdom of God, along the *ductus* of theology, as it reads Thomas' itinerary, performing the mnemonic task of "ordering" its "house," assigning to the "things" in one's memory their proper reference, their proper *intentio*. The *Summa* accomplishes this by recalling from memory the *auctores* of Christian memory: Augustine, Pseudo-Dionysius, Jerome, "the Philosopher," "the Apostle," and so on, and invoking them along the way, in an ongoing "conversation" which has a particular destination. One might imagine the *Summa* as such a conversation between these figures, which takes place "on the way to Emmaus,"[19] with the goal as the celestial feast of the saints. The reader is a participant on this journey, and by "overhearing" the conversation between Aquinas and his interlocutors, performs this same itinerary from the *in principio* to the final Amen. This image may appear trite and sentimental, but for the mnemotechnical pedagogy in which Aquinas and his students would have been trained, it is an example of precisely the kind of rhetorical *inventio* which would have been the goal of such texts. The object is not to transfer data from the page to the reading mind, but rather for the reader to engage in an imaginative performance of the text in the memory, which is not to say, in "recall," but in that activity which orders the mind towards its proper object, namely the wisdom which is the Son of God himself. Moreover, the milieu of this reading is eminently social and not individual. In fact, Aquinas urges that the most appropriate context for learning to read and remember well is the religious life.[20] Therefore reading, the ascent towards understanding and wisdom, cannot be separated from the very participation of the soul in the Trinity, in whom alone it can be at all, and in whom it receives the gift of sonship. Adoption as children of God, therefore, is not simply "announced" or "imputed," but enacted and performed, through grace, which enables the proper ordering of the human memory towards its true source and end, the Triune God.

Something similar to this might be said of another of Thomas' works, namely the *Catena Aurea*, his collection of sayings of the Fathers on the four Gospels, particularly as regards its "conversational" character. Thomas' *Catena* is one of a host of related texts which became popular from the twelfth century onwards. These, like the *Sententiae* of Peter Lombard and the *Decretum* of Gratian, are often referred to as the "standard textbooks" for their particular disciplines (in this case theology and canon law), and are typically understood as simply a collection of glosses by authorities on the Scriptures, on ecclesiasti-

19. An image borrowed from Nicholas Lash. See his *Theology on the Way to Emmaus* (London: SCM, 1986).
20. See Chapter Six, "Reading as *Manuductio* as *Traditio* as *Reditus*."

cal documents, or on other authorities themselves. As a genre, they are not as-signed much creativity on the part of their authors or compilers, and are treated as systematic "maps" of the whole of theology, as in the case of the Lombard. The accusation of the literary aridity of such texts is found in Janet Coleman, who describes them as "structurally nothing more than mosaics of such collected authorities."[21] Such ambivalence might be forgivable were it not the case that this claim comes in a section entitled "The Bible and the Art of Memory." For even mosaics are more than collections of colored fragments.

By contrast, Mary Carruthers argues that "no format shows better [the medieval book's] compositional, cogitational, *catena* characteristic than the lay-out of the glossed books, which developed during the course of the twelfth century in France, particularly in Paris."[22] This is particularly true in the case of the *Glossa Ordinaria* (indeed of all glossed Bibles, whose history goes back at least to the eighth century). Far from being a "map" of biblical exegesis, both patristic and early medieval, the reading of a text like the *Glossa* requires a certain kind of memory training that is not required of modern biblical readers. However, there is a certain sense in which the layout of the page itself tells a story, as it were, which at first glance is more like a map than an itinerary, but which after investigation emerges as a sophisticated set of routes through the Scriptures. Moreover, there is also a characteristic of visual appearance which is less cartographic than *iconographic*. The page presents an image of Christ and his Church: the Word of God resides "in the center," surrounded by a "cloud of witnesses," in the form of an ongoing community of authorities, or interpreters, who are both determined by the narrative in the center, and give a kind of definition to the biblical text. This image (one hesitates to use the word "icon," though it is perhaps not inappropriate) is therefore a liturgical one, in the sense that it is made intelligible by the read-ing of the gospel in the liturgy, and also in the sense in which reading the *Glossa* is a kind of "liturgical" activity. There is the back-and-forth motion from text to gloss, aided by memorial cues which act somewhat like tour guides, directing us toward further associative meanings and away from oth-ers, which is part of a larger procession through the Scriptures as a whole. "In a properly designed memory, just as on these pages, the verses of the source will be like a line with many hooks on it, and as one pulls in one part of it, all the fish will come along. To pull in one text is to pull all the commentary, as

21. Janet Coleman, *Medieval Readers and Writers, 1350-1400* (New York: Columbia Univer-sity Press, 1981), p. 172.

22. Mary Carruthers, *The Book of Memory: A Study of Memory in Medieval Culture* (Cam-bridge: Cambridge University Press, 1990), pp. 214-15.

well as other texts concording with it. Source, glosses, citations, punctuation, and decoration are all married up together in a single memorial image which constitutes 'the text'; one cannot meaningfully talk for long about one of these strands in isolation from the others, for that is not how they were perceived."[23]

In brief, the *Glossa* provides a kind of image of textual *anamnesis,* wherein the Word of God (Scripture) dwells in the midst of the Body of Christ (the ongoing community of interpreters and performers of the Word), as in the Eucharist, where the performance of Christ's memory, in his real presence in the Host, re-members the Christian community, making it truly "one body." The practice of ascent is inherent in the text of the *Glossa* inasmuch as, through the imaginative exegesis of the reader, with the help of guides along the way, one "remembers" the text and learns to orient it toward the ultimate goal of exegesis, namely, the beatific vision. That is to say, the practice of reading the *Glossa* is the practice of the fourfold mode of reading, whereby the soul, through the prayerful work of memory, ascends to the level of "spiritual" truth, where one is made capable of receiving the vision of God himself. This, however, is not to ghettoize biblical reading within the realm of the purely "spiritual" or immaterial, for reading is ultimately a physical and communal task, where there can be no purely private belief about the "meaning" of Scripture. For first of all, the ability rightly to read the biblical texts is an art learned not through the strenuous exercise of a solitary mind, but rather from the use of the Scriptures in the liturgy, not to mention the larger liturgical apparatus of high medieval culture, which must include art, architecture, political relations, the mechanics of local commerce, and so forth.[24] When one understands that the whole network of memorial "background," cue, *ductus, skopos,* etc. (which are so much a part of the texts in question), is the result of a training in reading arts which is thoroughly "embodied," it becomes clear that the ascent to the anagogical sense of Scripture, through the other three senses, is not the process of the soul's escape from matter, but the practice of the proper ordering of both soul and body as one creature towards the Trinity.

These texts suggest what a "grammar of participation" might look like. For here theology is not understood as the probative demonstration of the truth of the Christian faith, of God's existence, or of the resurrection of the

23. Carruthers, *The Book of Memory,* p. 217.

24. See Johan Huizinga, *The Autumn of the Middle Ages,* tr. Rodney J. Payton and Ulrich Mammitzsch (Chicago: University of Chicago, 1996); Eamon Duffy, *The Stripping of the Altars: Traditional Religion in England, 1400-1580* (New Haven: Yale University Press, 1992); John Bossy, *Christianity in the West: 1400-1700* (Oxford: Oxford University Press, 1985).

body, but primarily as the practice of the proper ordering of one's will (and here the full force of *intentio* as both a rhetorical and a moral category is most strongly exhibited) toward its object. The practice of reading, therefore, is the "art" of conforming one's will to the likeness of Christ, by virtue of the "baptism" of understanding, which is transformed into wisdom, indeed the very wisdom of God himself, the Son of God. Thus the soul is drawn into fuller participation in the mystery of the Trinity by the remembrance of Christ in reading, a practice which is informed above all by the Church's understanding of its own participation in the triune God in the Eucharist. As the soul "reads" the itinerary of its return to God, it in some sense performs that return — never finally of course, for there is always an apophatic moment inherent in the soul's understanding, but "through a glass darkly," which, though it is a dim vision, is nevertheless a vision. If the soul sees but darkly, nevertheless it still sees.

Before turning to the Glossa itself, in the next chapter I will show that according to St. Augustine, training in Christian teaching requires the benevolent "borrowing" of a grammar on the part of the reader. In fact, the notion that one can read without "poaching" will be shown by Augustine to be not merely a benign illusion, but a self-destructive, even unchristian one as well. Augustine suggests that rhetoric properly becomes itself by becoming its "other," by becoming the remembered speech of the Church's confession of faith. Thus rhetoric will be consummated in doxology. By reading a particular *mise-en-scène* — that of the conversion of Victorinus — I hope to provide a narrative analogue for the *mise-en-page* of a grammar of participation.

3 Augustine and Borrowed Speech

What language shall I borrow to thank thee, dearest friend,
For this thy dying sorrow, thy pity without end?[1]

In the modern period, with the help of Agricolan-Ramist developments in theological and philosophical textual apparatuses, "orthodoxy" has come to suggest a kind of correspondence to a codified deposit of teaching which is typically reducible to a set of propositions about the world and its author. The rightness of a belief, therefore, consists, for modernity, in the ability of a belief to "get at" or correspond to its object or at least to its reified formulation. For in this sense, the "object" of belief may be as much a *proposition* as, if not more than, God himself.

For Saint Augustine, by contrast, "orthodoxy" might be seen as no less a matter of right belief than of *rightly-ordered praise*. For in Augustinian terms, *doxa* may mean "opinion" or "belief," but it may also refer to the praise or glory which is attributed to others. Indeed, the ease with which we are able to separate the notion of belief from the activity of desire or worship betrays how deeply we may be stuck in a philosophical quagmire of peculiarly modern making. Belief, for Augustine, might be more or less convertible with "praise," insofar as what one thinks is "right" or "correct" only when the intellect is ordered towards its proper object, its origin and end, namely the Triune God. In this sense then, I will be suggesting a certain kind of interpretation of the *lex orandi, lex credendi* principle (attributed to Celestine I) which does

---

1. James Waddell Alexander, "O Sacred Head, Sore Wounded," *The Hymnal 1982* (New York: Church Publishing, 1985), 168.

not privilege one over against the other, but sees them in a relationship of mutuality and reciprocity.

"Our hearts are restless until they find their rest in thee." The same might be said for our *minds* — in fact there is a certain case to be made for translating *corda* as "memory," but more on that in a moment. To be sure, the extent to which this famous passage from the beginning of the *Confessions* has been enlisted to underwrite a pietistic diremption of "heart" and "mind" (privileging, of course, the former) is itself symptomatic of a kind of epistemic reversal. For this claim, that our "hearts" (by which Augustine means not some codifiable, but nevertheless hidden, emotional or psychological space, but surely the whole of our being) "are restless" until they find their rest in God, is the principle by which the entire narrative structure of the *Confessions* (if not the structure of all theology more generally) is governed. After all, what is this story, if not one of the return of the author to "the source whence we have our being," a story whose telling is at the same time continuous with that very return to God? This is as true for Augustine the author as it is for the reader — the *account* of the return to God, our true rest, is co-extensive with the return itself. The narrative *reditus* is not just rehearsed; it is *performed*. The gradual return of the soul to its source is coextensive with an intensification of knowledge of that source — these two activities presuppose one another, and in that sense are not really two separate activities at all. Thus to read Augustine's account is to begin to take part in that circuit of exit from and return to God.

Therefore the grammar of the *Confessions* may be read as (what I will call) a *grammar of participation* in the sense that the writing and the reading of this "text" are themselves part of an activity which is a participation, not only in the story of the Church, but in the very life of the Holy Trinity. The very structure of the *Confessions* is a kind of story in its own right, which is ultimately indivisible from the "content" of the narrative. There is no possibility of an abstraction of the "form" from the "content" of the *Confessions*, for the telling of this story, inasmuch as it is "creative," is only so by the participation of creatures in the continuing act of creation. In other words, the same story put in a different structural apparatus, a different genre or a different style, would be a very different story indeed — not just on an aesthetic level but in terms of the kind of readers it might produce. For as it is (and if it is not too much of a presumption to claim that) Augustine has in mind not just the transferal of autobiographical information to the reader, but her transformation. Augustine, it seems, hopes for his readers to repeat, non-identically, his own itinerary, and it is by the performative reading of the *Confessions* that the reader is con-ducted to the vision of God. For even in Augustine's own literary repetition of his life, he too repeats it *differently* — and most importantly, as prayer.

So what is ultimately at stake here is the role and function of rhetoric in theological discourse. In our own day "rhetoric" is a generally pejorative term; often accompanied by the modifier "mere," it frequently denotes a political strategy of obfuscation, or the posturing of "empty words." For Augustine, of course, this is not so. Granted, it *can be* the case, but only when rhetoric serves its own ends, and is not subordinated to theology. Professionally trained in rhetoric in late-fourth-century Carthage, Augustine would come to write what has often been described by modern authors as a preachers' manual, which indeed the *De Doctrina Christiana* is. But more than a mere appropriation of Ciceronian rhetoric to the needs of clergy, the *De Doctrina* represents, among other things, the re-orientation of rhetoric to its properly theological ends. As Richard McKeon writes, "This rhetorical language has, however, been adapted to the statement of a theology: discovery has been qualified as discovery of 'what should be understood' and statement as 'what has been understood,' with the result that the classification of signs and their uses is dependent, as it had not been in rhetoric, on the classification of things."[2] That is to say, words are not taken simply to name objects, but they point to the ends towards which they are ordered. They are "signs which are useful less to designate things than to express truths and persuade minds."[3]

Persuasion, then, represents the chief aim of rhetoric for Augustine, though the art of eloquence is too often admired for its own sake.[4] At one point in the *Confessions*, he refers to the conversion of the learned (and quite aged) Victorinus:[5]

> Finally the hour came for him to make the profession of faith which is expressed in set form. At Rome these words are memorized and then by custom recited from an elevated place before the baptized believers by those who want to come to your grace. Simplicianus used to say that the presbyters offered him the opportunity of affirming the creed in private, as was

2. Richard McKeon, "Rhetoric in the Middle Ages" in *Rhetoric: Essays in Invention and Discovery* (Woodbridge, Connecticut: Oxbow, 1987), p. 128.

3. McKeon, "Rhetoric in the Middle Ages," p. 130.

4. See *Confessions* I.iv.7; V.vi.10; V.xiv.24.

5. Augustine had first encountered Victorinus as a translator of "some books of the Platonists" and "one time rhetor in the city of Rome" (*Confessions* VIII.ii.3, p. 135). Augustine reports that he "was extremely learned and most expert in all the liberal disciplines. He had read and assessed many philosophers' ideas, and was tutor to numerous noble senators. To mark the distinguished quality of his teaching he was offered and accepted a statue in the Roman forum, an honour which the citizens of this world think supreme," *Confessions* I.iv.7; V.vi.10; V.xiv.24.

their custom to offer to people who felt embarrassed and afraid. But he preferred to make profession of his salvation before the holy congregation. *For there was no salvation in the rhetoric which he had taught; yet his profession of that had been public.* How much less should he be afraid in proclaiming your word, when he used to feel no fear in using his own words before crowds of frenzied pagans. When he mounted the steps to affirm the confession of faith, there was a murmur of delighted talk as all the people who knew him spoke his name to one another. And who there did not know him? A suppressed sound came from the lips of all as they rejoiced, 'Victorinus, Victorinus!' As soon as they saw him, they suddenly murmured in exaltation and equally suddenly were silent in concentration to hear him. He proclaimed his unfeigned faith with ringing assurance. All of them wanted to clasp him to their hearts, and the hands with which they embraced him were their love and their joy.[6]

This is a remarkable tale, particularly as it foreshadows Augustine's own narrative of conversion from the vanity of pagan eloquence to the true rhetoric of Catholic Christianity. One might read this as a kind of allegory of the conversion of pagan rhetoric unto the Christian gospel, however "historical" the account of Victorinus may be.

For here Augustine sets before the reader two alternative models of speech. On the one hand, the classical Ciceronian art of oratory that he learned as a young man in Carthage prizes innovation, cleverness, and the grand style. The great speaker is one who can elicit a response of thundering applause. Yet the *telos* of this kind of speech is "delight in human vanity," the corrupt turning-in on oneself of the will. For Augustine, this is a "damnable and conceited purpose" which results only in self-destruction and the cultivation of self-deception among one's hearers. Finally, there "was no salvation in the rhetoric which he had taught";[7] however, there is, for Augustine, a rhetoric which truly delivers, and it does so because it persuades and leads its hearers to the proper object of their speech.

Thus Victorinus, the great Roman rhetor, forsakes this art of deceit for the rhetoric of the Gospel, which, like pagan rhetoric, requires a well-trained memory. However, the memory of the Church is collective, as opposed to the individualistic character of classical memory-arts. Whereas one can, in the classical model, learn on one's own what one needs to recall for the delivery of a speech, in the Christian community, memory is a function of the whole

---

6. *Confessions* VIII.ii.5, pp. 136-37.

7. Augustine surely uses "he" here in a double sense, to refer to both Victorinus and to himself.

body. The confession of faith, which Victorinus makes publicly in full view of the body of Christ from atop a dais, is constitutive of the identity of this body, in some sense causes it to be. The implication here is that the truth of Christianity consists in the "borrowed" character of its language and not in the proud conceit of cleverness. In fact Augustine emphasizes Victorinus' *refusal* to succumb to the temptation, out of embarrassment or fear, to make his affirmation in private, though he could in practice have done so. Fear of crowds is not a problem for Victorinus, for his profession of pagan rhetoric had been quite public. Rather, for Augustine, it is as if the rhetoric he had taught before, in public, only now comes to a full realization, as if his own professional rhetoric suffered for not being public *enough,* as much as it always concealed a secret desire, never made public, for self-adulation. A public confession therefore is not seen as a potential embarrassment for Victorinus; on the contrary, he has all the more reason not to be fearful now, precisely because the words are no longer his own ("How much less should he be afraid in proclaiming your words, when he used to feel no fear in using his own words before crowds of frenzied pagans"[8]). Thus for Augustine, to speak most truthfully is to borrow one's words from others, and therefore to *be* most perfectly is to imitate. For this reason, the narration of the story of Victorinus, like all good theological speech, results in the action of *mimesis:* upon hearing the story, Augustine "was ardent to follow his example" *(exarsi ad imitandum).*[9]

This rhetoric is therefore liturgical — confessions have a "set form" and are "affirmed," words are "memorized" and "recited," and so forth. Victorinus' conversion, therefore, takes place within the liturgically performed language of the "holy congregation," within a prior political body. Moreover, the *telos* of Christian speech is not mere fleeting delight in the aesthetics of appearance, but in the simultaneity of the three aims of rhetoric: teaching, delighting, and moving.[10] Now, perhaps more than ever before, Victorinus is at the top of his rhetorical powers, but for a different reason. For the aim of the speaker, which for Augustine is to become the object of an operation — "to be listened to with understanding, with pleasure, and with obedience"[11] — is as it were consummated here in the donative character of Victorinus' confession of faith. The words are not his own (although his "unfeigned faith and ringing assurance" are — at least partly), and neither is their effect.

---

8. *Confessions* VIII.ii.5, p. 137.

9. *Confessions* VIII.v.10, p. 139.

10. Cicero, *Orator* XXI.69: *Erit igitur eloquens — hunc enim auctore Antonio quaerimus — is qui in foro causisque civilibus ita dicet, ut probet, ut delectet, ut flectat. Probare necessitatis est, delectare suavitatis, flectere victoriae.*

11. Augustine, *De Doctrina Christiana* IV.87, p. 235.

Rather, by "borrowing" the church's vocabulary in his confession, he is "handed over" (in the sense of *tradere*) both to the people of God and to God himself. His speech, precisely by virtue of its *not* being exactly his own, comes to partake of God's own utterance, by the gracious participation of the Holy Spirit, who is the true agent of true speech about God. As Augustine writes in the *De Doctrina Christiana*, "If the Holy Spirit speaks in those who are delivered *(traduntur)* to their persecutors for Christ's sake, why should he not also speak in those who deliver *(tradunt)* Christ to their pupils?"[12] Here Augustine is playing on the Latin *tradere*, "to hand over," which he uses to refer both to the transmission of theological teaching (which is the concern of the *DDC*), and to the handing over, in the literal sense, of captives to their captors, and in the allegorical sense, of converts to the body of Christ.[13] Thus the same word is used for a rhetorical trope (delivery) and a conversion of faith — the implication being that in this particular form of speech the rhetorical objective of persuasion finds its most perfect realization in the conversion of the soul to God, the only proper object of persuasion.

Victorinus surely serves as an example of this act of *traditio,* of handing over to the church, as well as the object of the rhetorical delivery of Christ to the pupil. For as Augustine tells the story, the rhetorical delivery of Christ to *incipientes* is the effective production of true delight. That is to say, Christian rhetoric — in this case, the confession of faith made by Victorinus in the midst of the *ecclesia* — supersedes secular rhetoric by uniting the delight of the hearers with a political reality, which may be said to be the function of a motion *(flectere, movere).* In other words, it unites rhetorically inspired delight to delight itself. Hence the reaction of the crowd to Victorinus' confession is one of delight — from the murmuring recognition of the famous orator to the silent attention to his words to the joyful reception of him into their midst. Thus the teaching of the church, its *doctrina,* instantiates, in a way that eloquence whose chief aim is delight does not, new relationships of *caritas:* "All of them wanted to clasp him to their hearts, and the hands with which they embraced him were their love and their joy." Delight is not posterior to the establishment of fellowship; rather the community is itself delight because it shares in the work of God himself.[14]

This might be well illustrated by the use Augustine makes of the word

---

12. Augustine, *De Doctrina Christiana* IV.89, p. 237.

13. This double-entendre will appear again in Thomas Aquinas. See my treatment of *tradere* in the *Summa Theologiae* in Chapter Six, "Reading as *Manuductio* as *Traditio* as *Reditus.*"

14. Compare *De Doctrina Christiana* IV.76, p. 231: "It is not the aim of the eloquence or the intention of the speaker that the truths or the eloquence should in themselves produce delight; but the truths themselves, as they are revealed, do produce delight by virtue of being true."

flectere, which had been a kind of commonplace in rhetorical theory since Cicero. Augustine cites the latter as "a man of eloquence" in *De Doctrina Christiana* IV, to the effect that "the eloquent should speak in such a way as to instruct, delight, and move their listeners."[15] The reference to Cicero is almost verbatim (the sole exception being that Augustine has *doceat* where Cicero has *probet* — no doubt due to the emphasis on *doctrina*): *ut doceat, ut delectet, ut flectat. Flectere* here serves as one of the three principal aims of rhetoric, and is more or less convertible with *persuadare* or *movere.* To persuade, for Augustine, is not to convince one of a theory of right action, but is synonymous with the movement of the will toward its proper object. To be persuaded truly is not simply to consent that this or that is the case; rather, to be persuaded is to be made active — even to move, as Aquinas might say, from a state of potency to one of actuality. Persuasion, *flectere,* performs this in the hearer, who Augustine says "must be delighted, so that he can be gripped and made to listen, and moved so that he can be impelled to action" *(Sicut est autem ut teneatur ad audiendum delectandus auditor, ita flectendus ut moveatur ad agendum).*[16] In other words, persuading and moving amount to the same thing, just as being persuaded constitutes an action of movement, or of being moved.[17]

This theme is developed much more thoroughly in the *De Doctrina Christiana,* where Augustine writes that "when advocating something to be acted on the Christian orator should not only teach his listeners so as to impart instruction, and delight them so as to hold their attention, but also move them *(flectere)* so as to conquer their minds."[18] Good theological teaching thus leads one to wisdom, to the prudential ordering of knowledge and habits towards their proper ends. Eloquence, then, serves wisdom, and not vice versa. What distinguishes Christian discourse from all other secular modes of speech is that the former truly leads to *salus,* as God is the source and end of anything that one can say, whereas the latter leads to artificial pleasure for its own sake. Good speech is thus inseparable from a good life — and "good life" is not to be understood in simple moralistic dimensions, but as referring to a life like that of Victorinus — it is, as Wittgenstein might have said, less a matter of definition than of family resemblance. Hence Augustine writes that "We should therefore acknowledge that our canonical authors and teachers

---

15. Augustine, *De Doctrina Christiana* IV.74, p. 229.

16. Augustine, *De Doctrina Christiana* IV.75, p. 229.

17. Cf. Augustine, *De Doctrina Christiana* IV.79, p. 233: "But when one is giving instruction about something that must be acted on, and one's aim is to produce this action, it is futile to persuade *(persuadetur)* people of the truth of what is being said, and futile to give delight by the style one uses, if the learning process does not result in action."

18. Augustine, *De Doctrina Christiana* IV.79, p. 233.

are eloquent, and not just wise, with a kind of eloquence appropriate to the kind of persons they were."[19]

Nevertheless, Augustine does not specifically say that his treatment of the Christian art of oratory is designed for preachers alone, nor, for that matter, for exclusively oral genres; rather, his description of rhetoric is as true for written texts as for spoken ones. This is the case partly because for Augustine, writing always serves speech, as letters and treatises are intended to be read aloud. But on another level, it is because all discourse about God, whether written or spoken, consists of words which point beyond themselves to their origin and end. "But since we are discussing the discourse of the man whom we wish to be a teacher of those things by which we are freed from eternal ills and attain eternal well-being, wherever they may be raised — whether in public or in private, whether with one person or several, whether with friends or opponents, whether in continuous speech or in debate, whether in treatises or in books, whether in letters of great length or extreme brevity — they are important."[20]

As Rita Copeland has suggested, Augustine reorients the rhetorical *inventio* of Cicero as a function of *textual* interpretation, thus uniting the art of grammar with the art of eloquence.[21] Reading, then, becomes the site of theological production in terms of interpretive invention. "Making meaning" then becomes a responsibility of the reader, and not just of the original author.[22] In this way, to read a text emerges as an act of participation in the creative character of authorial intention, an act which is never completed by the author alone, but must be continually finished by the community of interpretation which a text produces. However, this does not represent a privileging of the visual, as understood as the mere noetic "reception" of data on the page. The transfer of the *modus inveniendi* to the *modus interpretandi*[23] implies a theological reorganization of the aims of rhetoric as inseparable from the aims of grammatical interpretation, or what Copeland calls "hermeneutics."[24] "But if hermeneutics

19. Augustine, *De Doctrina Christiana* IV.60, pp. 221-23.

20. Augustine, *De Doctrina Christiana* IV.102, p. 243.

21. Rita Copeland, *Rhetoric, Hermeneutics, and Translation in the Middle Ages: Academic Traditions and Vernacular Texts*, Cambridge Studies in Medieval Literature 11 (Cambridge: Cambridge University Press, 1991), pp. 154ff.

22. This is not to say that the reader is therefore entitled to make any meaning whatsoever, but is rather limited by the community's collective interpretation. In other words, the temptation to construct self-present meaning from the text on the power of one's own ability is moderated by the guiding interpretive principle of "that which builds up charity."

23. Copeland, *Rhetoric, Hermeneutics, and Translation*, p. 156.

24. Copeland, *Rhetoric, Hermeneutics, and Translation*, p. 154.

could take on the function and character of rhetoric," she writes, "it is also the case that rhetoric, and specifically rhetorical invention, could be redefined as a hermeneutical procedure."[25]

Not only are grammatical structures built into the arrangement of orations, as the latter operate as interpretations of texts (particularly in the case of the sermon), but rhetorical structures are inscribed into the texts themselves. So just as texts can no longer be read in abstraction from the rhetorical function of persuasion, neither can oral performances be divorced from the practice of exegesis and *ekphrasis*. The effect of Augustine's conflation of rhetoric with grammar is to orient both to the ends of persuasion, of a leading of the reader to a certain destination. In other words, both rhetoric and grammar have the same *telos*, namely, the beatific vision.

The teaching of Christianity therefore represents a comprehensive "curriculum of persuasion,"[26] which is not designed simply to convince that such-and-such is the case, but to transform character and to reorder our loves to the proper object of desire. In this sense, Nicholas Lash's claim that Christianity is like a school "whose pedagogy has the twofold purpose of weaning us from our idolatry and purifying our desire"[27] is most apposite, particularly with respect to the understanding of Christian teaching that Augustine outlines in the *De Doctrina Christiana*. Accordingly, to be a pupil in this school is to participate in a political body, the church. To enter into this pedagogy is to entrust oneself to a language which is not one's own, yet which transforms one's language and orders it to God. It renders *everything* important, as Augustine says, because Christian teaching refers all things to their creator. For that reason *doctrina Christiana* alone is just speech; hence Augustine's link between persuasion and justice, both in language and in social order.[28]

25. Copeland, *Rhetoric, Hermeneutics, and Translation*, p. 154.

26. The term is Mark D. Jordan's. He uses it in the context of Thomas Aquinas, but I think it is equally applicable to Augustine. See his "The Competition of Authoritative Languages and Aquinas's Theological Rhetoric," *Medieval Philosophy and Theology* IV (1994), pp. 71-90.

27. Nicholas Lash, *The Beginning and the End of 'Religion'* (Cambridge: Cambridge University Press, 1996), p. 27. See also p. 21: "The modern dissociation of memory from argument, of narrative from reason, made us forget how deeply all understanding and imagination is shaped by memory, coloured by circumstance, constituted by tradition."

28. Augustine, *De Doctrina Christiana* IV.97, p. 241: "But in our situation, since we must relate everything, especially what we say to congregations from our position of authority, to the well-being of human beings not in this temporary life but in eternity, where there is the added danger of eternal perdition, all matters that we speak of are important, so much so that not even what a Christian teacher says about acquiring or losing sums of money should be thought of as a small matter, whether the amount is big or little. For justice, which we must certainly observe even in small financial transactions, is not a small matter."

Participation, then, is not simply a principle of social relations, but of a metaphysical order. To participate in the body of Christ as a pupil, or as a "reader," is thus to become part of a kind of pilgrim city whose origin and destiny is transcendent. One's allegiance to this body, effected by the sacramental rite of initiation in baptismal confession (as in the case of Victorinus) and sustained by the unceasing "production" of the church in the Eucharist, cannot be divorced from the training in theological teaching, whether as a student or as a teacher. To participate, therefore, in the ecclesial reality of the church, is not a separate activity from participation in the pedagogy of Christianity, nor is it apart from the participation of the body of Christ in the Trinity. As such, pedagogy, like liturgy, aims at the reordering of knowledge and desire, through the participation in the ritualized activity of reading and inscription into the continuing narrative community of interpreters that is the church.

To that end, this understanding of knowledge as participation in the triune self-understanding of God must show itself in the form teaching takes. That is to say, it must not remain an abstract principle of knowledge in general, but must become the instantiation of a particular way of speaking, of a *grammar.* Central to this grammar is the role of memory, which, far from being a matter of developing a *techne* for the retention of material, represents "in its own little way some sort of likeness in this image of trinity to the Father, however immeasurably inadequate the likeness may be."[29]

Memory is, for Augustine, ultimately a question of desire, of the right *intentio* or affection towards that which one remembers.[30] The well-trained memory is one in which good use is made of the "things" in one's memory. "A character," he says, "is only to be praised for loving passionately when what it loves deserves to be passionately loved."[31] He describes the threefold character of disposition, learning and practice *(usus)* which correspond to the threefold division of memory, understanding and will (which further corresponds to the three rhetorical functions: delighting, teaching, moving). As is typical in his treatment in *De Trinitate*, the third term is a combination of the first two. Thus the practice of a person's memory, or its "use," consists

---

29. Augustine, *The Trinity* XV.vi.43, p. 428.

30. *The Trinity* XI.ii.7, p. 309: "The more vehement the fear or the desire, the deeper is the impression made on the attention, either by the body you perceive with the senses in the place near you, or by the image of the body you are thinking about which is contained in the memory." Further, "the same attention of the will is to the coupling of the image of a body in the memory to the sight of the one thinking about it, which is the form grasped by the conscious attention as it goes back to the memory."

31. *The Trinity* X.iv.17, p. 298.

in the "use the will now makes of what the memory and understanding hold, whether it refers them to something else or whether it takes delight in them as ends in themselves."[32] Therefore, to remember well is to will rightly, to have the proper kind of learned disposition towards that which one remembers.

Rhetorical *inventio,* which in some sense is the task of the preacher performatively exegeting the text as *enarratio,* is therefore impossible without memory, as Augustine argues in Book XI of *De Trinitate.* Perception and therefore memory of sensible bodies are the condition of all thought, since one cannot compose anything except from that which it already knows and has experienced through the senses. The thinking attention then orders the memory by the activity of will, which "fastens memory to sense and the thinking attention to memory."[33] Thinking, as the willed ordering of those things "held in the storerooms of memory,"[34] constitutes the imaginative composition of a rhetorical scene through the proper disposition of desire towards those objects in the memory. "So I remember it as I have seen it, but I think of it moving as I wish or standing still where I wish, or coming from where I wish or going where I wish. It is easy for me to think of it square though I remember it round, and of any color at all, though I have never seen a green sun and therefore do not remember it."[35] Yet there is no escaping memory. Just as one can imagine a green sun, there is no conception of "green" that is not already sensed and experienced in observation of some green object, and then, as it were, stored in the memory.

To remember well, for Augustine, is therefore to love rightly. For this reason he concludes *De Trinitate* with a discussion of the role of memory in contemplation. As he says in the final chapter of the final book, "the love which joins together the sight settled in memory and the sight of thought that is formed from it, as parent and offspring, would not know what to love rightly unless it had some knowledge of desiring things, which it could not have without memory or understanding."[36]

Love remembers, and love understands. "My love too, when it remembers and understands what it ought to go for and what to avoid, remembers with my memory, not its own; and with my understanding, not its own, it understands whatever it understandingly loves."[37] Love joins that which is "already

32. *The Trinity* X.iv.17, p. 298.
33. Augustine, *The Trinity* XI.iii.15, p. 315.
34. Augustine, *The Trinity* XI.iii.12, p. 313.
35. Augustine, *The Trinity* XI.iii.13, p. 314.
36. Augustine, *The Trinity* XV.vi.41, p. 427.
37. Augustine, *The Trinity* XV.vi.42, p. 428.

lurking, but hidden, in memory"[38] to the ends to which it is to be put. Thus memory is no longer a simple recollection of a knowledge previously learned, but rather becomes part of the *vestigium trinitatis* in the human being, whereby love joins together as parent and offspring the sensible images in the mind and orders them to their proper use. Thus the "erotic" character of *anamnesis* — as in the Pseudo-Dionysius — is effecting a union, bringing things together; it is an image of the Trinity because it tends towards the inseparable and the coinherent, and away from the separate and the divided.

It is therefore not as a mere afterthought that Augustine concludes this discussion of memory, will, and understanding with a discussion of the eschatological immediacy of vision, wherein the intellect will come to participate fully and without remainder in the perfect unity of intelligence and love in God. As with Aquinas much later, Augustine is imminently concerned here with the ends of Christian education. The teaching of Christianity, as he understands it, orders all things to God, and, though it does so in an imperfect and ever incomplete fashion, nevertheless participates in the real understanding of the Trinity. As much as this constitutes a real knowledge, God alone is its true agent (hence the discussion of the "innermost word which does not belong to any language"[39]). Again like Aquinas, the aim of this pedagogy is beatific vision:

> But when the sight comes that is promised us *face to face* (1 Cor. 13:12), we shall see this trinity that is not only incorporeal but also supremely inseparable and truly unchangeable much more clearly and definitely than we now see its image which we ourselves are. However, those who do see through this mirror and in this puzzle, as much as it is granted to see in this life, are not those who merely observe in their own minds what we have discussed and suggested, but those who see it precisely as an image, so that they can in some fashion refer what they see to that of which it is an image, and also see that *other by inference through its image which they see by observation, since they cannot see it face to face.* For the apostle did not say "We now see in a mirror," but *We see by a mirror* (1 Cor 13:12).[40]

As a kind of counterimage to the tale of Victorinus' conversion, Augustine treats his own desire for conversion in terms of a public confession. Yet in Book X of the *Confessions*, his confession of faith is made public through *writing*, albeit in a form which is both grammatical and rhetorical. This be-

38. Augustine, *The Trinity* XV.vi.40, p. 427.
39. Augustine, *The Trinity* XV.vi.40, p. 427.
40. Augustine, *The Trinity* XV.vi.44, p. 429.

comes a matter of "doing the truth," by means of which one "comes to the light."[41] The truth is therefore not a static proposition to be believed, but an activity of the memory, understanding, and will, which is here enacted in a text. Augustine therefore understands his confession as an act of doing the truth, and submits his own narrative to the conditions of a text to be read. "This I desire to do, in my heart before you in confession, but before many witnesses with my pen."[42]

Volo eam facere in corde meo coram te in confessione. Note well that the term for heart *(cor, corda)*, here as in the very first lines of the book, is the root of the term for recollection, *recordari*.[43] "Memory" and "heart" are often used as synonyms in classical and medieval writings; their equivalence was supported by Jerome, and there is good reason to suppose that Augustine shared that assumption. For Augustine began the *Confessions* with the prayer, "You stir man to take pleasure in praising you, because you have made us for yourself, and our heart [*cor nostrum*] is restless until it rests in you."[44] It is perhaps not too much of a stretch to gloss this by saying that "our memory is restless until it rests in you."

Read as an itinerary of Augustine's soul's return to God, then, the desire for confession expressed at the beginning of Book X represents the proverbial closing of the circle which was opened at the very introit of the *Confessions*. The question he posed in Book I ("Who will enable me to find rest in you?"[45]) thus approaches an answer by the beginning of Book X. The implication here is that it is the Triune God, who, through the mediation of Christ's body in the church, enables Augustine to find true rest. This is effected (both rhetori-

41. Augustine, *Confessions* X.i.1, p. 179, quoting John 3:21.

42. Augustine, *Confessions* X.i.1, p. 179.

43. See Mary Carruthers, *The Book of Memory: A Study of Memory in Medieval Culture* (Cambridge: Cambridge University Press, 1990), p. 49: "'Memory' as 'heart' was encoded in the common Latin verb *recordari*, meaning 'to recollect.' Varro, the second-century BC grammarian, says that the etymology of the verb is from *revocare* 'to call back' and *cor* 'heart.' The Latin verb evolved into the Italian *ricordarsi*, and clearly influenced the early use in English of 'heart' for 'memory.' Chaucer often uses the phrase 'by heart' as we still use it, and while he was perhaps echoing the medieval French phrase 'par coeur,' there are also much earlier uses of the metaphor in English. The Middle English Dictionary records an early twelfth century example of 'herte' to mean 'memory'; there is an Old English use of 'heart' to mean 'the place where thoughts occur,' *cogitationes*. Since the common Old English verb meaning 'to remember' was made from the noun *mynde*, 'mind,' it seems probable that the metaphorical extension to memory of the English word *heorte* was made on the direct analogy of the Latin metaphor in *recordari* and its derivatives. Certainly, the existence of *recordari* in Latin is the justification for Jerome's assertion that, in the appropriate Biblical contexts, *cor* is a common metaphor for *memory*."

44. Augustine, *Confessions* I.i.1, p. 5.

45. *Confessions* I.v.5, p. 5.

cally and ontologically) by a return to the source and end of his being, as in the case of Victorinus, through the providence of the vocabulary of confession of faith. Just as he had begun his literary account with a desire for the memory's restfulness, ten books later, he has discovered that true rest begins in the memory ordered towards God as the proper object of our love. He speaks of this return to rest as an ascent into the mysterious and "vast palaces of memory."[46] "Hidden there is whatever we think about," yet there are corridors and chambers that are difficult to find, and which make remembering an effort of the will. "Memory's huge cavern, with its mysterious, secret, and indescribable nooks and crannies, receives all these perceptions, to be recalled when needed and reconsidered."[47] The memory, therefore, is a vestige of the Trinity, and through the peripatetic recollection of the mind, the soul comes to see in itself the impression of its creator. Thus it is through memory, for Augustine, that the soul begins to find its true rest.

Through the activity of the memory, one is confronted with the fact that that which is most intimate to itself, the soul, is not its own, and that the power of ontological self-determination is unmasked as a vapid illusion: "This power of memory is great, very great, my God. It is a vast and infinite profundity. Who has plumbed its bottom? This power is that of my mind and is a natural endowment, but *I myself cannot grasp the totality of what I am.*"[48] The practice of memory, therefore, leads to an understanding of the soul's excess, whereby it transcends its own intelligibility precisely because it partakes of the divine and because it is an image of God.

What follows, then, in the remaining three books of the *Confessions*, is no mere afterthought, as some have argued.[49] Instead, from what we have seen so far, we are in a position now to understand Books XI-XIII as the actual activity of the memory doing its work, as the plumbing of its unfathomable and mysterious depths. Yet the locus of this activity is not only the individual mind, but the collective memory of the church. The content of that recollection is not the boyhood adventures of Augustine; it is rather the story of God's way with the world. Thus he begins Book XI with a retelling of the account of creation in Genesis, and concludes in Book XIII with a discussion of the eternal Sabbath. That is to say, Augustine now formally situates his own

---

46. *Confessions* X.viii.12, p. 185.

47. *Confessions* X.viii.13, p. 186.

48. *Confessions* X.viii.15, p. 187, italics mine.

49. For a survey of criticism of the literary structure of the *Confessions*, see Kenneth B. Steinhauser, "The Literary Unity of the *Confessions*" in Joanne McWilliam, ed., *Augustine: From Rhetor to Theologian* (Waterloo, Ontario: Wilfrid Laurier University Press, 1992), pp. 15-30.

personal narrative within a larger story, that which the church tells — moreover, that story in whose telling and performing the church is itself *enacted*.

To return to the story of Victorinus: before his conversion he had confided privately in Simplicianus, telling him that he was already a Christian. Simplicianus was suspicious of this claim, particularly since his faith was not yet a public matter.[50] Regarding his friend's skepticism, Victorinus famously joked, "Then do walls make Christians?" As it turns out, Simplicianus' and Augustine's answer to this is to be found in Victorinus' repudiation of the falsity of the pagan rites and submitting his name for baptism in the church of Rome. Therefore in a certain sense it is precisely walls that make Christians — in this sense the walls of the church's "vast palaces of memory";[51] and for Augustine those walls surely contain the whole world.

Turning from the story of his own itinerary, he now offers an alternative narrative, a new history, but in doing so he does not *depart* from the earlier story. Rather he *completes* it. The itinerary of the self comes to be recounted through the peregrination of the church in the world, from creation of the world to its consummation in God, at whose center is the Incarnation. This new narrative constitutes the exploration of the hidden and secret corridors of the memory of the church, the story which is told through the quotidian offices and sacraments of the church's liturgy. In this sense, then, Augustine suggests, one's memory is consummated only by being taken up into the anamnesic memory of the church, which is made capable of re-membering the disparate parts of the biblical stories into a coherent tale of God's grace.

Therefore, the final books of the *Confessions* trace an itinerary from origin to end, from creation to beatitude — a second itinerary but not an *other* one. Augustine concludes his narrative with the seventh day of creation, type and figure of our future repose in God. One may find restfulness, though not complete rest (which is only realized eschatologically), in the participation in these daily mysteries, through which God works in the church. "But you, God, one and good, have never ceased to do good. Of your gift we have some good works, though not everlasting. After them we hope to rest in your great sanctification. But you, the Good, in need of no other good, are ever at rest since you yourself are your own rest."[52]

It is through the reading of this text, as its author understands it, that the soul may be led to this repose. Thus the displacement of the authorial voice (developed later in the *De Doctrina Christiana*) is already manifest in the

50. *Confessions* VIII.ii.4, p. 136.
51. *Confessions* X.viii.12, p. 185.
52. *Confessions* XIII.xxxviii.53, p. 304.

Confessions, where the rhetorical function of invention is transferred from the author to the reader. The latter is implicated in the renarration of the story of the church, as it is truly catholic, and therefore involves all people. In this sense he is attempting to persuade, both rhetorically and grammatically, as author and as provider of the cues for the memory and imagination. What he writes in *On Free Choice of the Will* could be as true for the audience of the *Confessions:*

> if only they would consider themselves and understand that they would owe thanks to God even if he had willed to make them lower than they are. Then the very bone and marrow of their conscience would cry out, "I said, 'O Lord, have mercy upon me; heal my soul, for I have sinned against you.'" Thus they would be led in the secure paths of divine mercy along the road to wisdom, not becoming conceited when they made new discoveries or disheartened when they failed to do so. Their new knowledge would simply prepare them to see more, and their ignorance would make them more patient in seeking the truth.[53]

Insofar as the *Confessions* is a text originally meant to be read aloud and listened to, the one who reads the text aloud assumes the voice of Augustine. As Thomas Martin has shown, "the pervasiveness of the first person singular throughout the narrative, when read aloud, cannot help but reverberate back upon the one speaking."[54] Moreover, Augustine's frequent interchanging of "I" and "we" further suggests that his voice becomes the voice of the reader, who reads on behalf of the listening community. The resonances with prayer are of course intentional. The ancient reader of the *Confessions* therefore transforms, by the act of vocalized reading, the text from a narrative about the tawdry and pious life of a bishop into a prayer in the "borrowed" voice of Augustine. The language of Augustine is therefore lent to the community, in the same way that Victorinus borrows the language for his confession of faith from the church. The prayer of the saint becomes the prayer of the church, as, for example, he writes in Book IV: "Our good is life with you for ever, and because we turned away from that, we became twisted. Let us now return to you that we may not be overturned." Thus more than simply an account of the re-

---

53. Augustine, *On Free Choice of the Will,* tr. Thomas Williams (Indianapolis: Hackett, 1993), III.2, p. 74. See also the discussion in Peter Brown, *Augustine of Hippo,* 2nd ed. (Berkeley: University of California Press, 1967, 2000), pp. 170f.

54. Thomas F. Martin, O.S.A., "Augustine's *Confessions* as Pedagogy: Exercises in Transformation," in Kim Paffenroth and Kevin L. Hughes, eds., *Augustine and Liberal Education* (Aldershot: Ashgate, 2000), p. 40.

turn of the author to his creator, the *Confessions* becomes a prayer for that return on behalf of his readers. Moreover, it is the drawing-in of his readership,
to whom Augustine loans his own voice, into that same itinerary of return,
which has as its final goal beatific vision.

"I inquired what wickedness is," Augustine writes in Book VII of the *Confessions*, "and I did not find a substance but a perversity of will twisted away
(detortae) from the highest substance, you O God, towards inferior things, rejecting its own inner life and swelling with external matter."[55] Augustine's
word for this movement of the will, *detorquere*, suggests a visceral kind of
bending away from the will's proper object. It is in some ways synonymous
with *flectere*, which also implies a kind of bending. Of course Augustine uses
the latter in the classical Ciceronian manner, as a rhetorical function, but he
also uses it in two other related ways. The first is a citation of Philippians 2:10,
where Paul writes that "at the name of Jesus every knee should bow" *(ut in
nomine Iesu omne genu flectat)*. Paul emphazises that it is not the sight of Jesus
that persuades, but the utterance of his *name*. Interestingly, here is the juxta-
position of the invocation of the name of Jesus — certainly a rhetorical act —
and the rhetorical response of movement.

The second instance of *flectere* is in the final book of the *Confessions*,
where the image from Philippians is reversed. He writes,

> Against this background the able reader can grasp your apostle's meaning
> when he is saying that "love is diffused in our hearts by the Holy Spirit who
> is given to us" (Rom. 5:5). Teaching *(docentem)* us concerning the things of
> the Spirit he demonstrates that the way of charity is "supereminent" (1 Cor.
> 12:1). Moreover, he bows the knee for us *(flectentem genua pro nobis ad te)*
> that we may know "the supereminent knowledge of the love of Christ"
> (Eph. 3:14, 19).[56]

Whereas in the letter to the Philippians, Paul speaks of knees bending at the
name of Jesus, here Augustine (with triple reference to Paul) reads the Holy
Spirit as himself genuflecting to the church. Once again the familiar rhetorical motifs appear: *docere, flectere,* and the diffusion of *caritas* in the church
which is redolent of *delectare*.[57] The ascending motion of persuasion therefore corresponds to the descent of the Holy Spirit, the bending of the will
back towards God and away from the self alone. Thus the whole motion of
the *Confessions* is one of bending — of the life of Augustine back to God and

---

55. Augustine, *Confessions*, VII.xvi.22, p. 126.
56. Augustine, *Confessions* XIII.vii.8, pp. 276-77.
57. Cf. the discussion of the conversion of Victorinus, above, pp. 54ff.

of the reader as well. The distortions of *detorquere* therefore find their counterpart in the *flectere* of the will, by the agency of the Spirit, back to himself. The corrupt turning inward is now made right by the turning back towards the Trinity. Finally, rhetoric is seen to be properly rhetorical when it becomes doxology. Moreover, for Augustine, rhetoric is consummated in a form of discourse in which different voices utter the same words, words which they did not themselves invent but which are lent to them. The highest form of speech is thus borrowed speech, and the highest form of rhetoric is liturgy.

This Augustinian vision of the "true" rhetoric of Catholic Christianity is exhibited, as I argue in the next chapter, in the construction and logic of the medieval glossed Bible, the most comprehensive example of which is the twelfth-century *Glossa Ordinaria*. As a *mise-en-page*, the *Glossa* provides an analogue for the *mise-en-scène* described in Book VII of the *Confessions*, by which is pictured the consummation of rhetoric in liturgy. The *Glossa*, then, provides both an iconographic and programmatic route to wisdom, as the function of rhetorical manuduction of interpretation. The character of the *Glossa* will be shown to be "liturgical" in constitution, in its gathering of voices around the "table" of the Word of God, and in its character as an itinerary towards *theoria*. Finally, I will suggest that this is most poignantly illustrated in the *Glossa* to the third of the "three books of Solomon," the Song of Songs.

4 Memory and the *Glossa Ordinaria:* Liturgy and Interpretation

Since at least the middle of the sixteenth century, biblical exegesis has taken as axiomatic the distinction between "scripture" and "tradition." During the Council of Trent, the relationship between these two is, for the first time in the modern period, clearly defined.[1] It might even be argued that the very writing of such a declaration is in itself curious, not to say ironic, insofar as a written document is, at Trent, used not only to shore up the authority of other written documents, but also to make certain just which writings outside those of the canonical scriptures are to be given credence. The *writing* of Trent's declaration on scripture and tradition is ironic for this reason: it is an attempt to counter the absolute dependence of the Protestants upon a written text in itself, while at the very same time, declaring the relative authority of scripture *in writing.*[2]

---

1. For example, from the Fourth Session of the Council of Trent, 8 April 1546: "Further-more, to check unbridled spirits, it decrees that no one relying on his own judgment shall, in matters of faith and morals pertaining to the edification of Christian doctrine, distorting the Holy Scriptures in accordance with his own conceptions, presume to interpret them contrary to that sense which holy mother Church, to whom it belongs to judge of their true sense and inter-pretation, has held and holds, or even contrary to the unanimous teaching of the Fathers, even though such interpretations should never at any time be published." See H. J. Schroeder, O.P., tr., *The Canons and Decrees of the Council of Trent* (Rockford, Illinois: TAN, 1978), p. 18. There is a further theological point here to be made regarding whether "holy mother Church" is identi-cal with the Roman Curia, or the interpretive tradition of the *auctoritates* in the *Glossa Ordinaria.* I do not wish to press this point here, but suffice it to say that, as far as I can tell, the shoring up of the authority of the Roman Church to interpret the Scriptures is of a piece with the Protestant principle of *sola scriptura* — both are bound up within the same "scriptural economy" (see n. 12).

2. The real turning point in Trent's decree on the canonical Scriptures (though not original to it) is in the fact that books come to be understood as "containers" of truth. "It also clearly

Thus the only way around *sola scriptura*,[3] for Trent, is to proclaim the necessity of an interpretive tradition of the scriptures, but to do so within an already hypostasized economy of writing. The declarations of the "counter-Reformation" therefore cannot fully escape what Michel de Certeau calls the "scriptural economy," as inaugurated by the Reformation.

Though de Certeau argues that it is only in the seventeenth century that this shift occurs towards what we might call a "grammar of representation," its seeds are arguably sown earlier, with the theological priority which the early Reformers place upon the "Word of God" as a physical text, which in turn establishes the conditions of possibility for a Catholic response to *sola scriptura*. Similarly, Hans-Georg Gadamer argues that the impetus for Romantic hermeneutics is found in the sixteenth century's new, humanistically inspired tendency to treat the Scriptures through a universal methodological principle. In fact, for Gadamer, the Reformers' principle of *scriptura sui ipsius interpres* ("Scripture interprets itself") is itself a reaction to Tridentine hermeneutical prerogatives on tradition.[4] In this sense, the unity of the biblical text is only a rear-guard action against the initial reaction of Trent against what it saw as an interpretive practice unmoored from traditions of interpretation. In truth, Trent's effects and tendencies were equally bound up in the prior economy of representation which neither *sola scriptura* nor its Catholic opposite simply *effected*. Instead, both are instances of an already enacted cultural shift, whose relation to which is not one of either simple cause or simple effect, but much more complex. However, my aim here is not to argue the specifics of when this shift took place, nor is it to demonstrate the relationship of the claim of *sola scriptura* to modernity in general. These points are not merely peripheral to the larger project, though, and they must be borne

---

perceives that these truths and rules are contained in the written books and in the unwritten traditions, which, received by the Apostles from the mouth of Christ himself, or from the Apostles themselves, the Holy Ghost dictating, have come down to us, transmitted as it were from hand to hand." Schroeder, *Canons and Decrees*, p. 17. See also Walter J. Ong, S.J., *The Presence of the Word: Some Prolegomena for Cultural and Religious History* (New Haven: Yale University Press, 1967), pp. 275-76.

3. I must thank Dr. David Steinmetz for pointing out to me that no theologian in the sixteenth century is known to have used the phrase "*sola scriptura*," and that the status of this claim as central to Luther's theology is not at all uncontroversial. However, regardless of whether the early Reformers used the term, I employ it here with the understanding that it does name a real shift in the understanding of texts and their relationship to their readers. Whether or not it was used in this period is ultimately not relevant insofar as the term is used as descriptive of what happens at this point in the history of texts.

4. Hans-Georg Gadamer, *Truth and Method*, 2nd ed. (New York: Continuum, 1989), pp. 174ff.

out in more detail elsewhere. I mention Trent to direct us back to the high Middle Ages, which I think will make clear just how peculiar is such a text as the *Glossa Ordinaria.*

Though the *Glossa Ordinaria* refers to a specific set of manuscripts, I will be using the term to refer to the salient features of a whole genre of texts in the medieval Latin biblical tradition.[5] Taken together, these texts share some common characteristics. All of them consist of two major parts: first, the text of scripture itself; and second, the commentaries of Church Fathers and other ecclesiastical and theological luminaries. Though the *Glossa Ordinaria* is a product of the middle of the twelfth century, its basic structure is older, and was in place centuries earlier. Since at least 850, Carolingians had been glossing Bibles with much the same format. As Margaret Gibson writes, "virtually all the principles of its physical production were well understood in the ninth century, and continued in practice through the tenth and eleventh."[6] By the first third of the ninth century, "[t]ext and gloss seem already to have been envisaged as a single unit."[7]

Scholarship on the *Glossa Ordinaria* has tended to be the exclusive domain of paleographers and medieval historians and not of theologians, except those with a historical interest in the period. Apart from the work of a handful of scholars such as Beryl Smalley, Margaret T. Gibson, and Henri de Lubac, there is little sustained theological treatment of the *Glossa,* and

5. "Every schoolboy knows that the *Glossa Ordinaria* is in two parts: the marginal gloss was written by Walafrid Strabo in the early ninth century, while the interlinear annotation is the work of Anselm of Laon in the later eleventh. Every schoolboy also knows that this is wrong. Since the late 1920s the *Glossa Ordinaria* has been identified as one of the achievements of the twelfth-century Renaissance, first planned on the hilltop at Laon and subsequently completed by a miracle of teamwork among the masters of Auxerre, Laon, and Paris. The date is broadly set at c. 1080-1130, but . . . the manuscripts belong to the next generation, c. 1140-1170. This is a text with a brief, intense flowering, and a long reputation thereafter. In a less romantic metaphor, the twelfth century glossed Bible may be regarded as the hinge, the *Wendepunkt,* between the old exegesis and the new. The traditional exegesis of the Fathers and their Carolingian editors reaches its summation in the mid-twelfth century Gloss." Margaret T. Gibson, "The Place of the *Glossa Ordinaria* in Medieval Exegesis," in Mark D. Jordan, ed., *Ad Litteram: Medieval Texts and Their Readers* (Notre Dame: Notre Dame University Press, 1992), p. 5. See also Karlfried Froehlich, "Walafrid Strabo and the *Glossa Ordinaria:* The Making of a Myth," *Studia Patristica* XXIII (1969), pp. 192-96.

6. Margaret T. Gibson, "The Twelfth-Century Glossed Bible," *Studia Patristica* XXIII (1969), p. 236.

7. Gibson, "The Twelfth-Century Glossed Bible," p. 234. In terms of substance, "[i]t cannot be said that the twelfth-century *Gloss* is more learned, more profound or linguistically more sophisticated than Otfrid's marginalia in the ninth century or the anonymous annotation that was prepared for Otto III at Reichenau *c.* 1000" (p. 239).

even in those three authors it receives little treatment as a genre in itself.[8] Smalley's accounts of the *Glossa* are the most extensive and well known, but it has been nearly half a century since any scholar has devoted much more than a passing nod to it.[9] Lubac's use of the *Glossa* is of course vast, and his work relies on the *Glossa* at a textual- or source-critical level, so to speak, and does not, again, specifically treat the *Glossa* as a peculiar kind of text in itself. The following account does not pretend to fill this void; however, I do wish to offer a theological reading of this text and its form which, I hope, will illustrate precisely how radical the shift is, in the early modern period, from a "grammar of participation" to a "grammar of representation."

As de Certeau writes,

> before the "modern" period, that is, until the sixteenth or seventeenth century, this writing (Holy Scripture) speaks. The sacred text is a voice, it teaches (the original sense of *documentum*), it is the advent of a "meaning" *(un "vouloir-dire")* on the part of a God who expects the reader (in reality, the listener) to have a "desire to hear and understand" *(un "vouloir-entendre")* on which access to truth depends.[10]

8. This situation has changed somewhat since Smalley's time, however, particularly with the publication (in 1997) of the *Glossa Ordinaria* to the Song of Songs, in English and Latin, in the *Corpus Christianorum: Continuatio Mediaevalis*. In recent years, the stature of the *Glossa* seems to have risen such that it has been accorded an entire chapter (written by Jenny Swanson) in the recently published *The Medieval Theologians*, edited by G. R. Evans (Oxford: Basil Blackwell, 2000). See also Evans' *The Language and Logic of the Bible: The Earlier Middle Ages* (Cambridge: Cambridge University Press, 1984), ch. 3, pp. 37-50.

9. That being said, however, the recent work of E. Ann Matter is, to my knowledge, the only example of the kind of theoretical critique of the *Glossa* that is lacking in both Smalley and Lubac. See Beryl Smalley, *The Study of the Bible in the Middle Ages* (Notre Dame: Notre Dame University Press, 1964); "Glossa Ordinaria," *Theologische Realenzyklopädie*, Volume XIII (Berlin: Walter de Gruyter, 1984), pp. 452-57; Henri de Lubac, *Medieval Exegesis*, Volume One: *The Four Senses of Scripture* (Grand Rapids: Eerdmans, 1997); E. Ann Matter, "The Bible in the Center: The *Glossa Ordinaria*," in W. Caferro et al., eds., *The Unbounded Community: Papers in Christian Ecumenism in Honor of Jaroslav Pelikan* (New York: Garland, 1996), pp. 33-42; "The Church Fathers and the *Glossa Ordinaria*," in I. Backus, ed., *The Reception of the Church Fathers in the West*, Vol. I (New York: Brill, 1997), pp. 83-111. Jenny Swanson's recent chapter in *The Medieval Theologians* (n. 8 above) pays considerable debts to the work of Smalley and Gibson, but similarly lacks any sustained theological treatment of the *Glossa*. This situation is certainly not helped by the fact that the *New Catholic Encyclopedia's* entry on the "Glossa Ordinaria" makes the very slightest mention of the *Glossa* to the Bible (a mere one sentence), preferring instead to concentrate on the (later) development of the *glossa* in canon law. See the *New Catholic Encyclopedia*, Vol. V (New York: McGraw-Hill, 1967), pp. 515-16.

10. Michel de Certeau, "The Scriptural Economy," in *The Practice of Everyday Life*, tr. Steven Rendall (Berkeley: University of California Press, 1984), p. 137.

In the modern period, it is popular to speak of texts — particularly those books one finds in the "Inspirational" section of one's local bookstore — as "speaking to" us. Yet for us this has only a metaphorical meaning. Books do not literally "speak" to us any more than films sit down with us and chat over a cup of coffee. We are incapable of imagining a book "speaking" to us as anything more than a bizarre synaesthetic, perhaps even "mystical," phenomenon. However, if de Certeau is right, for medievals, texts, particularly the Holy Scriptures, *literally* speak to their readers. It is only in the modern period that the page is silenced, rendered a deaf and dumb space which is capable only of presenting decipherable images and codes to the eyes. The blank page is, as de Certeau writes, "a space of its own [which] delimits a place of production for the subject. It is a place where the ambiguities of the world have been exorcised. It assumes the withdrawal and the distance of a subject in relation to an area of activities."[11] As such the text on the page becomes separable from the author, and therefore from the reader as well. What is read is ultimately a product which can be consumed, ingested, and spat out, or a commodity which can be exchanged and identically reproduced *ad infinitum*. The text becomes inert, a physical object whose spatial limits are clearly visible and tangible. The Scriptures in particular become a portable object which can be described and even drawn, like a place which can be mapped, but unlike a story which can only be told and performed.

Sola scriptura, then, must be understood not as an abstract theological principle, but must be situated within the textual history of the Bible, which includes the history of the Bible as a printed book. The "*sola*" in *sola scriptura* must be defined in reference to what it leaves out, what it attempts to silence, or at least relativize. The received wisdom on the Reformation tells us that the Reformers wanted to protect the Scriptures against their abuse by Roman "papists" and clerics, and thus emphasized the sole authority for theology of the canonical Scriptures, and that this movement began on the thirty-first of October, 1517, on the front porch of a parish church in Wittenberg. While this is not necessarily untrue, *sola scriptura* has a particular textual force to it when understood within the context of the medieval tradition of the *Glossa Ordinaria*.

One turning point in the history of books and their readers (and indeed from the medieval to the modern) may be found several years before Luther's celebrated posting of the ninety-five theses. In the winter semester of 1513-14, in preparation for his first lectures on the Psalms, Luther, as Gerald Bruns writes,

11. de Certeau, "The Scriptural Economy," p. 134.

wanted each of his students to have a copy of the scriptural text to consult. [He] therefore instructed Johannes Grunenberg, the printer for the university, to produce an edition of the Psalter with wide margins and lots of white space between the lines. Here the students would reproduce Luther's own glosses and commentary, and perhaps (who knows?) they would have room for their own exegetical reflections as well. At all events Luther produced for his students something like a modern, as opposed to a medieval, text of the Bible — its modernity consisting precisely in the white space around the text.[12]

Bruns is exactly right, I think, to point to this seemingly insignificant incident in the history of printed Bibles as a kind of transitional moment into the modern. Luther's wiping the margins clean of their patristic comments and glosses creates a new space on the page, a space in front of which, as de Certeau says, "every child is already put in the position of the industrialist, the urban planner, or the Cartesian philosopher — the position of having to manage a space that is his own and distinct from all others and in which he can exercise his own will."[13] Thus one can locate an originary locus of de Certeau's "scriptural economy" in Luther's Grunenberg Psalter of 1513.

Thus if *sola scriptura* is to have any meaning, it must refer to this moment — the clearing of the margins of all exegetical accretions, so that the text is freed from its interpretive moorings and loosed upon the reader. One is no longer burdened with sorting out the relationship of the text in the middle to

12. Gerald Bruns, *Hermeneutics Ancient and Modern* (New Haven: Yale University Press, 1992), pp. 139-40. While it would not have been unusual for a medieval glossator, or even a copyist, to insert his own commentary in the margins or between the lines of a glossed Bible, Bruns is right to say that the modernity of Luther's Grunenberg Psalter is precisely in the white space itself — in the very lack of interlinear or marginal spaces already determined by other glosses. See also Hilton C. Oswald's introduction to these lectures in *Luther's Works*, Vol. 10: *First Lectures on the Psalms I* (St. Louis: Concordia, 1974), pp. ix-xii. Luther's own marked copy of Grunenberg's edition, now known as the Wolfenbüttel Psalter, has survived, and is kept in the Herzog August Bibliothek in Wolfenbüttel, Lower Saxony. For biographical details on Grunenberg, and on his relationship to Luther, see Maria Grossmann, "Wittenberg Printing, Early Sixteenth Century," *Sixteenth Century Essays and Studies* I (1970), pp. 53-74.

13. de Certeau, "The Scriptural Economy," p. 134. In the case of Luther's Grunenberg Psalter, the blank space is not uninterrupted — it still has margins which are defined by the biblical text in the center. Nonetheless, it is clear that what is at issue here is not writing itself (if understood as the "pure" act of inscribing one's will onto a blank page), but interpreting an already received text by inscribing onto that blank space a will that is, in some sense, in conversation with the biblical text. In any event, there is no writing which is not somehow interpretation, and what is essential here is the extent to which one's interpretation can be abstracted historically from all its antecedents. We are left, finally, with nothing but ourselves and the text alone.

the texts in the margins, or of the relation of "scripture" to "tradition" but is left with the scripture all by itself, *sola scriptura.*

Of a piece with this is, of course, the hermeneutical principle of the Reformers, *scriptura sui ipsius interpres,* "Scripture interprets itself." The text of scripture on its own, now "liberated" from its "imprisonment" within the glosses, is sufficient to provide the reader with the interpretive tools she needs to make sense of any given passage, when read in the larger biblical context. Thus the page itself may not be sufficient to the fullness of its meaning, but for the Protestants, the book as a whole is. Where the Council of Trent risks confusing matters is in suggesting that it is not Scripture *alone* which is the sole necessary authority for faith and doctrine, and in setting "tradition" alongside "Scripture" as two separate and distinct "things." The teachings of the Church become codified just as the canonical books of Scripture become codified.[14] Once the two are separated *as texts,* it becomes impossible to imagine them in any other way, i.e., than as texts.

Thus to impose a Tridentine understanding of the relationship between "Scripture" and "tradition" onto a text such as the *Glossa Ordinaria* proves altogether baffling. For during the period of the *Glossa's* development, it makes little sense to speak of the Bible exclusively as a physical object. For though the Middle Ages continues to be understood as a "culture of the book," this designation obscures the sense in which the "book" as a metaphor is itself polysemous and flexible. That is to say, if the Middle Ages is a "culture of the book," precisely what kind of book is it with which medievals are particularly taken? After the invention of moveable type, the sense of "the book" becomes attenuated to refer to sheets of paper bound together within a leather cover, a physical object which can be bought or sold, carried in one's pocket, read at home, opened and read at will. There are, of course, senses in which some medieval books can be described in this way as well, but for the early Middle Ages at least, the cost and scale of book production, the mechanisms and logic of medieval libraries, among other factors, make it difficult to speak of the "book" in the Middle Ages as a metaphor in the same sense in which we speak of books in the age of print. In other words, there is no univocal sense of "the book" as signifying *one particular type of object* which can be transferred to an age which knows nothing of our technology of printing. That having been said, what is of particular interest in this case is the extent to which Christians are called "a people of the book,"[15] or Christianity a "religion of the book" — which begs the question, what *kind* of book?

14. See also Chapter Six below.
15. See, for example, Ong, *The Presence of the Word,* p. 14.

Thus what is at stake in the *Glossa* is not the relationship between two sets of texts, but the relationship of the biblical story to the people which it creates, or of the body of Christ to the narrative which it performs. First of all, there is the question of the way in which the Scriptures are present in the life of the Church. In the early and high Middle Ages, the Scriptures are present not primarily as a physical object, but rather preeminently in the memory. The Scriptures, as they are read, and importantly, heard,[16] by the congregation over the course of the liturgical year, are assigned to certain times in the calendar, and over the course of a year the Scriptures in their entirety may be read at least three times. In monastic communities the whole of the Psalter is read aloud each week, and over the course of a year, the average monk would have heard each Psalm at least fifty-two times.

These texts are not simply memorized by rote — they are all read not solely in the privacy of the monk's cell, but also among the worshiping community, and in the context of the liturgy. With the lectionary, readings are assigned their appropriate place in the calendar — as, for example, the birth narratives of Jesus are read at Christmas, obviously, and, less obviously, the account of the Transfiguration is read on the last Sunday before Lent. Thus when the Christian reads Scripture, it is, first of all, read *to* him or her. Second, it is associated with a peculiar time or activity in the life of the Church.[17] The "meaning" of the Scriptures is therefore diachronic and synchronic — it reaches across the historical life of the body of Christ and looks forward to the eschatological fulfillment of that meaning, and it makes sense within the liturgy of the Church as it is performed daily. When the monastic learns a passage of Scripture, it is always within the context of the larger narrative of the body of Christ, and future recall of those passages points to other layers of signification. Reading privately, then, always points back, or forward, to public reading. The only sense that a text might have in one's cell is one which points to something already learned in the liturgy.

16. In the Middle Ages, these two activities are not separated. To attend a lecture is to "read" a text, i.e., to have it read aloud by a lector — a sense of the word "read" which remains in use in English universities, when we still say one "reads" (as opposed to "studies") Anglo-Saxon, for example, as well as in the title given to a "Reader" in a particular discipline.

17. Particular texts are also associated with different sounds: "Strict rules were given for the distinctive accent to be used for different kinds of books: the literally mono-tonous *cantus lectionis* for the glosses; the *tonus prophetiae, epistolae, evangelii* by which anyone, without understanding a word, would know that the Old Testament, St. Paul, or the Gospel, respectively, was being read. The more solemn parts of the liturgy had and still have their distinguishing musical characteristics corresponding to the season in which they are read. The Latin of the time was the product of the choir as much as of the scriptorium." Ivan Illich, *In the Vineyard of the Text: A Commentary to Hugh's* Didascalicon (Chicago: University of Chicago Press, 1993), p. 69.

Therefore the memory of the church in the Middle Ages is one which is trained liturgically. By reading and being read to aloud, at appointed times within the church calendar, one learns not only the words of Scripture but what they mean, to what they refer, when they are used, who is speaking them, and how to associate and interpret them. The texts, as they are read over and over again, are non-identically repeated, insofar as they are not frozen on the page, but are continually voiced.[18] As such the words are never exactly the same twice — because they are always read differently by the lector, they will be read differently by the hearer. Thus what is to be negotiated in terms of the relationship between the reader and the text is not simply the words themselves and the reading subject, but this *and* the entire network of bodily movements, sounds, smells with which these readings are associated, as well as the time of day and season in which they are read. This is a long way from the modern practice of pietistic private and silent reading, by which the memory is trained not liturgically but solipsistically. For modern literary criticism, the relationship between the reader and the page is the only relationship there is. Of course the subject arrives at the text with all sorts of presuppositions, as the writer does at the blank page. But ultimately the text and the reader are two isolated individuals — the reader may remember the text, but the text will always forget the reader.

It is this remembering, however, that is the peculiar and distinctly theological characteristic of the *Glossa Ordinaria*. The *Glossa* is a textual form of Eucharistic *anamnesis* — the remembrance of Christ in the Eucharist which is no mere recall, but an intensely political act, by which the body of Christ is re-membered and re-made into one body. The character of the *Glossa* is fundamentally *anamnesic* — it unites the text of the Scriptures and the commentaries of the Church into one text, and makes them one body. The narrative of Scripture remains central, of course, and in doing so, gives definition to the space in which the glosses are written. The scriptural text in the center gathers the commentary around itself. The glosses are meaningless without the "Bible in the center,"[19] and "the *Glossa* does not exist, as a coherent text, in isolation from the Bible text it glosses."[20] As it appears on the page, the biblical

18. On the notion of non-identical repetition, see Søren Kierkegaard, *Repetition,* in *Fear and Trembling; Repetition,* ed. Howard V. and Edna H. Hong (Princeton: Princeton University Press, 1983), pp. 125-232; also Catherine Pickstock, *After Writing: On the Liturgical Consummation of Philosophy* (Oxford: Basil Blackwell, 1997).

19. E. Ann Matter, "The Bible in the Center: The *Glossa Ordinaria*," in W. Caferro et al., eds., *The Unbounded Community: Papers in Christian Ecumenism in Honor of Jaroslav Pelikan* (New York: Garland, 1996), pp. 33-42.

20. Matter, "The Bible in the Center," p. 40.

story creates the space within which the interpretive tradition is inscribed. But here the scriptural text does not gather other texts so much as it gathers other voices, sometimes identified, sometimes not.[21] I say voices and not texts, because the character of the *Glossa Ordinaria* is essentially dialogical. It presents an ongoing conversation between the Scriptures and its readers, between the people it forms and the story which is its form. As such, though it is a text chiefly intended for use in the schools, it is text which is both the product of and organized according to a liturgically trained memory.[22]

The difference in the treatment of the Scriptures from the Middle Ages to the Reformation involves a shift in the understanding of the way in which the Scriptures are *present* in the liturgy. For the Reformers, the Bible is chiefly present among the community of believers *as a book,* whose spatial limits are clearly defined. After printing, the Bible becomes an identically repeatable text, with the inevitable implication that its single sense is univocal for both the pew in the front and the pew in the back.[23] This premise lies behind a transition from the mode of language which characterizes theological teaching from the early period of the church to the high Middle Ages. That is, the "presence of the Word of God" (until the Reformation, owing in part to the invention of moveable type) as a complex amalgamation of the oral and aural, the visual and the corporeal, depends upon and emerges from an ontology of participation in the divine life of the Trinity which becomes lost when the "Word" is transformed into some "thing" primarily legible, visible, and transportable, but whose meaning remains fixed.[24]

---

21. To be sure, the scriptural text in the center with commentary on all four sides is one of a number of different typographical arrangements of glossed Bibles. For an account of variant types, see C. F. R. De Hamel, *Glossed Books of the Bible and the Origins of the Paris Booktrade* (Woodbridge, Suffolk: D. S. Brewer, 1984), esp. Ch. 2, "The Layout of the Pages," pp. 14-27.

22. I will develop this theme, with specific reference to Thomas Aquinas, in Chapter Seven.

23. See Pickstock, *After Writing.* Pickstock contends that "during the period of early modernity, with Ramism and later, Cartesianism, which were encouraged by the facility of printing and its identical repetitions, and by the breakdown of the traditional religious order, space becomes a pseudo-eternity which, unlike genuine eternity, is fully comprehensible to the human gaze, and yet supposedly secure from the ravages of time"(p. 48). Luther's invention of the "pew Bible" is therefore most significant in this sense — the localization of the Word in a limited spatial frame, whose meaning is infinitely transportable and identically repeatable. As such it is important that he stresses the *sensus literalis* of the text of Scripture as paramount. In so doing, the reading of the Bible becomes spatialized and the memory ultimately transformed into "a matter of simple retrieval of objects, merely a kind of stocktaking or enumeration, thus vastly reducing the reach of memory presumed by the traditional mnemonic treatises of earlier rhetorics" (*After Writing*, p. 54).

24. Cf. Ong, *The Presence of the Word,* p. 269: "Under these conditions the Bible was present to people largely in what we can style an oral mode. Some medieval theologians may have fa-

In the liturgy of the Mass, the physical text of Scripture is present during the reading of the Gospel, and there in a very peculiar fashion. The "Word of God" is present in the liturgy first as voice, and only secondarily as text; or it might perhaps be better to say it is present as *voiced text*.[25] That is to say, it is present as a written text only so as to be read aloud. However, the Gospel procession is also a visible act, by means of which the Gospel book symbolizes the Word of God, without "containing" it in any crude locational sense, and the coming of his kingdom in the midst of his people. When the deacon or celebrant proceeds into the nave holding aloft the "book," he performs an activity which is the climax of the gradual drawing near of God into the midst of the *ecclesia*.[26]

---

vored theories of exact verbal inspiration of the Scriptures, but whatever theological doctrine may have breathed through the schools, the culture as a whole assimilated the biblical word not verbatim but . . . thematically and formulaicly, tribally rather than individually." Though Ong's thrust seems here to be more anthropological than theological, his argument does seem to bear out Mary Carruthers' discussion of tropes and "backgrounds" in the mnemotechnical arts in *The Craft of Thought* (Cambridge: Cambridge University Press, 1998). However, the fact that medievals remember "thematically and formulaicly" does not necessarily mean that they do *not* remember verbatim. We have here not a choice between *either* memorization by *topos or* memorization verbatim, but some kind of combination of the two.

25. The reflections that follow have in mind primarily the lections in the synaxis, which do not yet culminate in the "eating of the Word" in the Eucharist, which demands further and more radical revision of the way in which we may call this "Word" "present." See Gerard Loughlin, *Telling God's Story: Bible, Church, and Narrative Theology* (Cambridge: Cambridge University Press, 1996), pp. 223-45.

26. I realize that this is a much later Anglican development, but I think it makes little substantial difference to my argument if the Gospel is read in between the aisles, at the choir screen, or at the ambo (as in the Roman rite), as is typically the case in this period. What is important (and a particular stress of the medieval Ambrosian and Gallican rites) is that the Gospel is carried in procession to the ambo or nave, symbolizing this drawing-near and indwelling of Christ. Whichever shape the liturgy takes, the reading of the Gospel represents the climax of this drawing-near, whether the emphasis be on the Incarnation (as in the case of the reading in the middle of the nave) or on the height of the teaching, its transcendence of all "worldly philosophies" (as in the case of the ambo). "The old Expositio of the sixth century Gallican Mass interprets the procession with the Gospel book as the triumph of Christ, who now ascends his throne [the ambo] to proclaim the gifts of life (*dona vitae*, pp. 14f. in Quasten edition). The acclamation 'Glory to you, O Lord' (*Gloria tibi, Domini*), which occurs for the first time in this Expositio, expresses the conviction of Christ's presence in the Gospel, as does also the later and still widespread 'Praise to you, O Christ' (*Laus tibi, Christe*)." Josef A. Jungmann, S.J., *The Mass: An Historical, Theological, and Pastoral Survey,* tr. Julian Fernandes, S.J. (Collegeville, Minn.: The Liturgical Press, 1976), p. 177. See his more extended discussion in *The Mass of the Roman Rite: Its Origins and Development,* 2 vols., tr. Francis Brunner (Allen, Texas: Christian Classics, 1986, 1949), vol. I, pp. 412-19, 442-55. See Anne Walters Robertson, "From Office to Mass: The Antiphons of Vespers and Lauds and the Antiphons before the Gospel in Northern France," in

From the first Old Testament reading to the Psalm and Epistle to the reading of the Gospel, the Incarnation (whose real climax is not the reading of the Gospel but the real presence of Christ in the Host) is re-enacted, the procession of the Word from the distant to the very near. Indeed, the Gospel is proclaimed in the midst of the congregation, and repeats the presence of Christ among his disciples. The location of the "reading" is important to its meaning — the Gospel lection is the culmination of the story of Emmanuel, God with us (but here this still only foreshadows the eucharistic presence). For here the Word of God is present as voice, dynamic in its musical intonation yet fleeting in its presence. The vocalized re-enactment of the presence of Christ among his disciples soon yields to silence, and the return of the priestly procession towards the altar symbolizes the return of Christ to the right hand of the Father, and the temporary character of the dwelling-among-us, yet at the same time foreshadowing, again, the permanence of the presence of Christ in the world in his Church, and creation's return to its eschatological home in God.

It seems clear from these observations that this performance of the Word of God resists the fixity of the word in space, against any idolatrous tendency to freeze the presence of Christ locally, and against any false permanence which might arise from the abstraction of the Gospel from its proclamation among the midst of the faithful. There is nothing, that is, in the readings of the Gospel, or even in the Eucharist itself, which *guarantees* or *secures* the presence of Christ in this community. Rather, the Church, like the Word of God in the biblical narrative, is always coming into existence by virtue of its daily liturgical performance. Thus liturgical reading sustains a kind of tension between fulfillment and postponement, as a kind of "positive but not fetishizable arrival."[27] As such, each reading looks forward to the next reading for its continual realization of meaning.

Thus the text of Scripture becomes, in the Mass, a part of the congregation and in some sense, identical with it, insofar as it is read aloud and learned by hearing, and thus performed as an act of the memory. In the same way, the text of Scripture becomes a part of its interpretation (and vice versa) and inseparable from it, while nevertheless remaining in the center and distinct. Thus the Scriptures become embedded within a kind of liturgy of interpretation, a diachronic and ultimately open-ended performance of the memory.

Margot E. Fassler and Rebecca A. Balzer, eds., *The Divine Office in the Latin Middle Ages: Methodology and Source Studies, Regional Developments, Hagiography* (Oxford: Oxford University Press, 2000), pp. 300-23.

27. John Milbank and Catherine Pickstock, *Truth in Aquinas,* ch. 4, "Truth and Language" (London: Routledge, 2000), p. 92.

As many examples of medieval *Glossae* attest, the only limitation to the extent of commentary is the space on the page, and in many cases even the glosses themselves bear further glosses by later commentators, often penciled in the margins or between the lines.

The location of the text of Jerome's Vulgate in the center of the page creates the space for the gloss — but equally, the location of the gloss around the entire margin of the Vulgate centers it within the interpretive tradition. This mutual interplay of chirographical positioning therefore suggests that the Scriptures have meaning only within this continuing liturgy of interpretation, and that the interpretation equally derives its meaning from the formative character of the Bible as the story of the people of God. As such, the interpretation is seen as simply a continuation of this narrative. The *Glossa Ordinaria* therefore provides a kind of textual image of the indivisibility of "Scripture" and "tradition," while yet maintaining the distinction between them. As Erwin Panofsky has argued, there is, in medieval architecture, the same kind of interplay between historical motifs in cathedral architecture as there is in Peter Abelard's *Sic et non* — the new elements are themselves glosses on the old, a 'yes' and a 'no' to what has come before.[28] Likewise, the architecture of the *Glossa* is similarly conversational in that it is a textual instance of the church's interpretive performance of its own narrative. Moreover, it is fundamentally liturgical in the sense that it defies the possibility of closure of meaning.

From what I have said so far, it might be fair to ask whether the *Glossa Ordinaria* does not itself represent a transition from what one might call an "oral" economy of the text to a "visual" one. In other words, does the iconographic character of the *Glossa* make it, in effect, what de Certeau calls a "tableau of a state of . . . knowledge" or even a "totalizing stage"?[29] On this reading, the *Glossa merely* pictures the Church — and one might not necessarily have to read or understand the content of the text in order to grasp this aspect of its signification, but simply recognize the order and arrangement of the texts within the text to understand the way these texts (or "authorities") are related to one another. That is to say, it is less the content of the glosses, or even their specific relationship to particular texts of Scripture, and to one another, that is important, than the *idea* of the glossed text. Or to put it another way, there is not an art of reading which is peculiar to the *Glossa*, but merely an art of seeing or gazing.

To borrow de Certeau's distinction, it would appear, on this reading, that

---

28. Erwin Panofsky, *Gothic Architecture and Scholasticism* (New York: Meridian, 1957).

29. Michel de Certeau, "Spatial Stories," in *The Practice of Everyday Life*, p. 121.

the *Glossa* resembles a "map" more so than it does an "itinerary." However, the curious achievement (if not "genius") of the *Glossa* lies in the fact that it simultaneously *does* image or picture the theological reality of the Church, and of the presence of Christ in its continuing performance and interpretation of the Gospel, as well as narrate a route or set of routes through the text, towards a certain *skopos*. It is both iconographic and programmatic: it both pictures and must be read.

As in other theological texts of the period (for example, Bonaventure's *Itinerarium Mentis in Deum* and, much earlier, John Climacus' *Ladder of Divine Ascent*), the operative metaphor for the reading of the text itself is that of ascent. While perhaps a vaguely "Neoplatonic" theme in these writings, it would be misleading to construe this as simply an assimilation of Christian "mystical" writings to Platonic (or even Gnostic) paradigms of ascent, or as nothing more than a rhetorical device. Rather, the role of ascent serves a specifically theological end in the literature of the monastic schools. It is a trope of monastic rhetoric and memory-training by means of which the reader is led onwards, through practice, to that "intellectual" vision of God, or *theoria*. As Mary Carruthers recognizes, this is "the goal, the *skopos*, of all human seeings."[30] The route to divine *theoria*, or beatific vision, is performed through the memory of Christ and his Church. The *Glossa Ordinaria*, then, in its context within medieval mnemotechnical arts and monastic practice, emerges as not merely a "map" of the biblical story, but a route for the ascent of the soul to the vision of God. As I show in what follows, this is illustrated in the *Glossa* to the most popular book of Scripture among medieval exegetes, the Song of Songs.

It would seem that the Bible as a whole does not narrate a coherent itinerary from beginning to end, insofar as modern biblical scholarship has emphasized the relative "disunity" of the Scriptures as a collection of various and diverse texts by equally various authors — an idea that was not the major preoccupation of medieval exegetes. For the compiler of the *Glossa Ordinaria*, the trope of ascent is an obvious one for the reading of the text, as is the textual unity of, if not the entire Scriptures in this case, at least the "three books of Solomon." However, what unites these three texts, which are all of course attributed by the glossator to Solomon, is not their authorship, nor even their subject matter, but rather the "like order" of their "philosophical affiliations."[31] That is, the three books of Solomon, Proverbs, Ecclesiastes, and the

---

30. Carruthers, *The Craft of Thought*, p. 172. See also her treatment of Bernard of Clairvaux's sermon *De conversione*, pp. 94-99.

31. *Prothemata* v, p. 77: *Simile ordine etiam philosophi institutiones suas ponunt.*

Song of Songs, together represent a coherent route towards *theoria*, through the sciences of ethics and natural history. "[F]irst they teach ethics, then they teach natural history, and they lead *(perducunt)* the man whom they see to have benefited from these to theoretical wisdom."[32] Here the glossator, whom we have good reason to believe is Anselm of Laon, refers to a tradition going back to Origen,[33] who had argued that the three books of Solomon taught three respective *scientiae:*

> The branches of learning by means of which men generally attain to knowledge of things are the three which the Greeks called Ethics, Physics, and Enoptics; these we may respectively call moral, natural, and inspective. . . . That study is called moral, on the other hand, which inculcates a seemly manner of life and gives a grounding in habits that incline to virtue. The study called natural is that in which the nature of each single thing is considered; so that nothing in life may be done which is contrary to nature, but everything is assigned to the uses for which the Creator brought it into being. The study called inspective is that by which we go beyond things seen and contemplate somewhat of things divine and heavenly, beholding them with the mind alone, for they are beyond the range of bodily sight.[34]

For this reason, Origen maintains that the Song of Songs is not milk for babes, but strong meat for those who have learnt "how to hear love's language."[35] Thus reading the Song is the result of a training in the Christian grammar of charity, by means of which the mind is freed from the imprisonment of the letter of the text so that it may love properly, and indeed, speak properly of love. Origen describes this itinerary of the reader thusly:

> This book comes last that a man may come to it when his manner of life has been purified, and he has learnt to know the difference between things corruptible and things incorruptible; so that nothing in the metaphors used to

32. *Prothemata* v, p. 77: *Primum ethicam docent, postea phisicam, et quem his profecisse uident ad theoricam usque perducunt.*

33. Origen's presence in the *Glossa* is strongly felt: "The *Glossa Ordinaria* is quite filled to the brim with Origen. In the absence of a critical edition, it is not possible to see the exact measure of its borrowings. But the general effect is not in doubt. *The Gloss of Exodus*, attributed with a fair bit of probability to Gilbert the Universal, is an almost uninterrupted string of citations or adaptations of Origen, and Gilbert makes no bones about it." Henri de Lubac, *Medieval Exegesis*, vol. I, tr. Mark Sebanc (Grand Rapids: Eerdmans, 1998), p. 168.

34. Origen, *Commentary on the Song of Songs*, Prologue 3, tr. R. P. Lawson, *Ancient Christian Writers* 26 (New York: Newman, 1957), pp. 39-40.

35. Origen, *Commentary*, Prologue 1, p. 22.

describe and represent the love of the Bride for her celestial Bridegroom —
that is, of the perfect soul for the Word of God — may cause him to stum-
ble. For, when the soul has completed these studies, by means of which it is
cleansed in all its actions and habits and is led to discriminate between natural things, it is competent to proceed to dogmatic and mystical matters,
and in this way advances to the contemplation of the Godhead with pure
and spiritual love.[36]

This is the route towards what he calls "inspective science," the ascent towards *theoria,* or that knowledge which beholds the divine, in some fashion,
as it really is, even if only dimly.[37] This is for Origen the *skopos* of the text —
that goal towards which the whole movement of the Song of Songs leads.[38]

The *ductus,* or that movement of the text towards the *skopos,* of the Song
as a whole, for Origen at least, is bound up with the structure of the Song as a
drama, and more particularly as a dialogue. Though in this case the dialogue
is between several characters, as opposed to only two, it is the form of the dialogue itself which Origen finds particularly "inspired." For the dialogue as a
genre is a kind of art of love, inasmuch as it assumes relationships between
friends and lovers. In the background, of course, is Plato's *Symposium,* as the
paradigmatic form of the dialogue. It is no accident, Origen implies, that
Plato's question of the nature of love should take place at a kind of dinner
party at the home of Agathon. For dialogue is an art of loving — we partake
of one another, we feast not just on foods but on words, and through this exchange of personalities, of ideas, and of desires, we are drawn into a state of
charity with one another, so that the form of the discussion of the nature of
love cannot be separated from the content thereof. Indeed, the discussion of
the nature of love in the *Symposium* is in a sense the performance of the very
object of the speeches. As Origen himself says,

> Among the Greeks, indeed, many of the sages, desiring to pursue the search
> for truth in regard to the nature of love, produced a great variety of writings
> to show that the power of love is none other than that which leads the soul

---

36. Origen, *Commentary,* Prologue 1, pp. 23-24.

37. Cf. Origen's *Commentary on John,* Book 13.3-192, in Joseph W. Trigg, *Origen* (London:
Routledge, 1998), p. 160: "Once her first five husbands, along with the one left after them whom
she supposed to be her husband, are confuted, the heterodox opinion of those dealing with the
Scripture, not being able initially to see who the Word refuting them is, says that he is a prophet,
as if he were someone divine who had about him some superhuman quality, but not as great as
he actually was. That is why she says, as if somehow looking up and considering herself in a state
of contemplation *(en theoria):* 'I behold that you are a prophet.'"

38. Cf. Carruthers' treatment in *The Craft of Thought,* pp. 77-81.

from earth to the lofty heights of heaven, and that the highest beatitude can only be attained under the stimulus of love's desire. Moreover, the disputations on this subject are represented as taking place at meals, between persons whose banquet, I think, consists of words and not of meats.[39]

Thus the route towards *theoria*, the beatific vision, is in the form of dramatic dialogue. As one must learn the grammar of love's language before approaching the Song, reading the Song itself is the performance of this grammar, the gradual drawing-near of the Bride toward the Bridegroom. Indeed, the itinerary of the reading soul is, as Origen understands it, coextensive with the *exitus* of the Bride from bondage in Egypt. The virgin's journey is narrated in the seven "songs" of the Law and Prophets, culminating in the Song of all songs.[40] It signifies, for Origen, both the journey of the chosen people of God to the Holy Land in the Incarnation, and the route of the individual soul towards the beatific vision. This "flexibility" in Origen's understanding, however, suggests that the two can never be divorced from one another. The itinerary of the whole Church towards beatitude in Christ is not something other than that which the individual soul follows. For Origen this song is the seventh, and therefore greatest, of all the songs of the Hebrew Scriptures, as it marks the climax of an ascent from bondage into the pure light of blessedness. It is both the journey of the people of God towards the New Jerusalem, and of the Bride toward the marriage bed. As Origen has it, the bridal bed is the "body that she shares with the Bridegroom" — the Bride's body which partakes of the body of the Bridegroom. Thus the goal of this narrative is this bridal chamber, the participation of the Body of the Bride in the Body of the Bridegroom; i.e., the eucharistic participation of the Church in the very Body of Christ, by which it is united with him in the body. Lest Origen be charged with the repression of sexual lusts by way of the "escape" into allegory, it is important to note that here, at the teleological consummation of the long journey of the Church/soul to the wedding feast of God, she is more emphatically embodied *now* than at any other point along the way from her Egyptian bondage.[41]

39. *Commentary*, Prologue 2, pp. 23-24.

40. "A man will sing this song, however, only when he has first been freed from bondage to the Egyptians; but after that, when he has traversed all those things that are written in Exodus and in Leviticus, and has come to be admitted to the divine Numbers, then he will sing another, a second song, when he has emerged from the valley of Zared, which means Strange Descent, and has come to the well of which it is written: *And the Lord said to Moses: 'Gather the people together, and I will give them water to drink* from the well.'" *Commentary*, Prologue 2, pp. 47-48.

41. See E. Ann Matter's discussion of various modern critical readings of Origen and the eroticism of the Song of Songs, from Patricia Cox Miller and William Phipps to Mary Daly in *The Voice of My Beloved: The Song of Songs in Western Medieval Christianity* (Philadelphia: Uni-

Origen does not, at least in the texts which survive, as Bernard of Clairvaux does, explicitly link the marriage bed with *theoria*. In his twenty-third sermon on the Song of Songs, Bernard writes:

> By your leave, then, we shall search the Sacred Scriptures for these three things, the garden, the storeroom, the bedroom. The man who thirsts for God eagerly studies and meditates on the inspired word, knowing that there he is certain to find the one for whom he thirsts. Let the garden, then, represent the plain, unadorned, historical sense of Scripture, the storeroom its moral sense, and the bedroom the mystery of contemplation.[42]

Though not mentioned explicitly, Origen is clearly the subtext for Bernard's treatment.[43] Though the three senses of Scripture are, by the twelfth century, a commonplace in biblical exegesis, the reference to the route through the three *scientiae* of Solomon, culminating in inspection or *theoria,* is unmistakably Origenist. Yet this metaphor of the bridal chamber for *theoria* is neither entirely new to Bernard nor lacking in Origen:

> . . . with what stately steps the Bride, as she makes her entrance, attains by way of all these to the nuptial chamber of the Bridegroom, passing *into the place of the wonderful tabernacle, even to the House of God with the voice of joy and praise, the noise of one feasting.* So she comes, as we said, even to the Bridegroom's chamber, that she may hear and speak all these things that are contained in the Song of Songs.[44]

The nuptial chamber, then, represents for Origen the union of the soul with the knowledge of God, the *skopos* of the text. With regard to the *Glossa Ordinaria,* then, the route of the reader of the Song (and here it is clear that one need not take the "reader" to refer *either* to the Church *or* to the individual soul, as the two are ultimately incapable of being abstracted from one another) is "lined" not just with rhetorical markers and cues for the memory,

---

versity of Pennsylvania Press, 1990). Phipps' claim that "Allegory came to the rescue" when it became apparent that the Song might serve as a warrant for carnal indulgence is, for Matter, curiously close to Daly's claim of "escape" from "sadomasochistic obsessions" into what she terms "sado-asceticism." Matter is right, I think, to point out that these critiques miss the way in which "allegory seeks to emphasize, rather than diminish, the erotic tension of the text" (p. 33), not to mention the fact that these readings are remarkable for the lack of attention they pay to particular historical readings of certain scriptural texts and to specific theological treatments of them.

42. Bernard of Clairvaux, *On the Song of Songs,* vol. III, Sermon XXIII.II.3, tr. Killian Walsh, O.C.S.O., Cistercian Fathers Series 7 (Kalamazoo: Cistercian Publications, 1976), p. 28.

43. On Bernard's relationship to Origen, see Matter, *The Voice of My Beloved,* pp. 38-39.

44. Origen, *Commentary,* Prologue 4, p. 50.

but particularly with a series of guides along the way. The peculiar interest of the *Glossa* is in that it suggests to the reader that this itinerary may never be the lonesome journey of the individual seeking after God, but is rather the collective journey of the Church towards beatific vision. Put more appropriately, the journey is a paradox, as far as Origen is concerned: one might describe it as the collective journey of the individual soul towards the nuptial chamber. The reader is guided along this route from "Egyptian captivity" to the freedom of the marriage chamber by a set of "tour describers," or manuductors, who point the reader in the direction of the well-ordered memory. Thus a good reading of the *Glossa* to the Song, for instance, will necessarily involve the association of memorial cues with their ultimate object, namely the Bridegroom, and the performance of these cues will direct and lead the reader to the goal of the text, which is described in the Prologue as *dilectio dei* — a deliberately bodily image of the tasting of the sweetness of the Bridegroom, which is perfectly in keeping with the character of the Song itself.

Thus the *Glossa* narrates the divine drama of the Bride and Bridegroom, and their gradual drawing near to one another, as well as the route of the reader towards the bridal chamber. In other words, the *skopos* of the text is one with the *finis* of the reader, and here it is impossible to dissociate "Scripture" from "tradition" as far as reading is concerned; for the interpretation of the narrative is of one piece with its renarration. The "Bible in the center" tells the story of the Bride and Bridegroom, and the glosses themselves, when read together with the Song, as they must be, simply lead the reader toward the goal of both text and interpretation: union with God. It is assumed that if one reads the text faithfully, it will become a narrative not just "about" the Church, or the soul, but a narrative of the reader herself. In other words, the reader becomes in some sense identical with the narrative of the Song, as she performs this narrative through the activity of the memory.

The *Glossa Ordinaria,* then, forestalls the tendency to reify the continuing interpretive tradition of the Church into a tradition of writings, as opposed to a tradition of saints, where these writings may be abstracted from the person of the author on one hand, but more importantly on the other hand, from the life of the Church in which those authors' lives were situated and given meaning. Reading the *Glossa,* like reading any medieval text, is a performance of the memory. Chirographically, the *Glossa* symbolically re-presents the presence of the Scriptures in the living memory of the Church, their "residence" in the center of on ongoing community of interpreters. Particularly in the case of the Gospels, the *Glossa* is a chirographical image of the liturgical reading of the Gospel during the Mass, where the lector processes to the center of the congregation and orally makes Christ present among his followers, recalling further the presence of Christ among his disciples. As such, the *Glossa* becomes a figure of the body of Christ itself, wherein the Son of God dwells in their midst, and they in him. This re-enactment of the Scriptures is therefore no mere dramatic spectacle, but rather the performance of the Church's memory as one body. As such, the *Glossa* textually re-enacts this presence of the Word of God among his followers, and among their words, in a kind of textual *anamnesis*.

Thus the *Glossa* is a truly medieval (and indeed theological) example of "intertextuality," in the sense that the text of Scripture is not only surrounded by commentary, but even interwoven, as it were, with it. This may be described as a grammar of participation in that the ongoing community of interpreters (i.e., the Church) is both "gathered" by the biblical narratives, and continually performs these in worship, as the form of the mutual indwelling of Christ and his Church.

In the next chapter, I will turn attention to the *Summa Theologiae* of Thomas Aquinas, and show how modern modes of reading have made possible, or at least necessary, the translation of the medieval *quaestio* into the modern paragraph. Such a strategy is evidence of a fundamental transformation of the rhetorical itinerary of Thomas into a modern theological map. In contrast to the modern habit of reading the *Summa* as a kind of encyclopedia of theology, I hope to show the centrality of the metaphor of manuduction in Thomas' theological curriculum, and how his pedagogical project is of a piece with his understanding of *sacra doctrina* as participation in God's self-knowledge.

In the next two chapters, I aim to examine the structure of the *Summa Theologiae* with respect to Thomas' understanding of participation in *sacra doctrina* as the manuduction of the soul toward the beatific vision. In so doing, I will concentrate on the two hinges of the work which connect the three parts together, namely (in Chapter Five) the transition from the end of the first to the beginning of the second part, and (in Chapter Six) the transition from the second to the third. It is at these junctures between the parts that it becomes clear, it seems to me, that Thomas understands his role as a teacher of Catholic doctrine not simply to impart information but to lead the reader towards a certain form of life.

5 The Manuduction of Desire: Will and the Structure of the *Summa Theologiae*

Almost immediately after its author's death in 1274, the *Summa Theologiae* was summarily cut up into separate books. This came about partly owing to pragmatic considerations, given the sheer size of the work, and the unrealistic expectation of producing it in what would have been one enormous and unwieldy manuscript volume. On the other hand, the reception of the *Summa* among Dominicans themselves illustrates the extent to which Thomas' pedagogical project was quickly, and perhaps permanently, rendered impossible to realize.[1]

In the late thirteenth century and following, the *Summa* was almost never read as a whole. Rather, its constitutive parts were divided into separate volumes — one each for the first and third parts, and two for the second. Both within and without the Dominican order, the most popular section was by far the *Secunda Secundae,* his treatment of the virtues. As Leonard Boyle and, following him, Mark Jordan argue, the deficiency in standard treatments of theology which Thomas attempted to remedy (as he states in the prologue) was the separation of moral teaching from theology.[2] In the generations between the founding of the Order of Preachers and the beginning of the writing of the *Summa,* Dominican libraries abounded with moral manuals written by and for members of the order, for use in preaching and hearing confession.[3] In the

---

1. I am indebted here to the work of Mark D. Jordan, particularly "The *Summa's* Reform of Moral Teaching — and Its Failures," in Fergus Kerr, ed., *Contemplating Aquinas: On the Varieties of Interpretation* (London: SCM, 2003), pp. 41-54.

2. Leonard E. Boyle, O.P., *The Setting of the* Summa Theologiae *of Saint Thomas,* The Etienne Gilson Series, 5 (Toronto: Pontifical Institute of Medieval Studies, 1982).

3. Boyle lists some of the better known of these, from the *Summa de casibus* of Raymond of Peñafort (c. 1224) to Hugh of St. Cher's *Speculum ecclesiae* (c. 1236), Willelmus Peraldus' *Summa*

Summa, Aquinas resituated moral teaching within a theological itinerary of the soul's return to God, apart from which it was otherwise unintelligible.

The composition of the *Summa,* as Boyle argues, arose out of Thomas' attempt to construct an entire theological curriculum for *incipientes* at the "*studium personale*"[4] established around him at Santa Sabina in Rome, where he taught from 1265 until 1268.[5] Thus the *Summa* had two original purposes: to function as a pedagogical curriculum, and to contextualize moral teaching as a part of theology, not a discrete "kind" of theology unto itself. As far as we know, Thomas never taught the *Summa* per se, nor did he intend it to be used as a teacher's script. For one reason or another, Dominicans after him rejected the pedagogical project of the *Summa.* Moreover, they tended to extract the moral section, particularly the *Secunda Secundae* of the work, and treat it as a self-contained "moral theology" as opposed to one stage of what Henri de Lubac calls an "itinerary of return"[6] to God. Thus the very goal of the *Summa* — to resituate moral thought within a theology of exit and return — was quickly and perhaps irrevocably subverted by Thomas' own religious Order.

Two well-known textual events in particular point to this. First is Galien de Orto's abridged version of the *Secunda Secundae,* commissioned sometime during the 1280s by the General of the Dominican Order, John of Vercelli.[7] Second is the *Summa Confessorum* of John of Freiburg, written in 1298. As Jordan writes, "[t]his confessors' *Summa* would itself be abridged, simplified, and alphabetized — so that we have pieces of Thomas now twice or three times redacted. More interesting even than these Dominican revisions is their popularity: there are between two and three times as many copies of one alphabetized redaction, the *Summa Pisana,* as there are of the Secunda Secundae of the *Summa.* Thus if Aquinas' intention was to narrate moral

---

vitiorum (c. 1236) and *Summa virtutum* (c. 1236 x 1249-50), Vincent of Beauvais' *Speculum maius* (1244 x 1259), and James of Varazze's *Legenda aurea* (1265 x 1267). See Boyle, *Setting,* p. 2. For Boyle, it is as much to these texts as to the *Sentences* of the Lombard that Aquinas implicitly refers in the Prologue to the *Summa.*

4. Boyle, *Setting,* p. 9.

5. Cf. Jean-Pierre Torrell, O.P., *Saint Thomas Aquinas,* Volume One: *The Person and His Work,* tr. Robert Royal (Washington, D.C.: Catholic University of America Press, 1993), pp. 142-59.

6. Henri de Lubac, *Theology in History,* tr. Anne Englund Nash (San Francisco: Ignatius, 1996), p. 151.

7. See Leonard Boyle, "The *Summa Confessorum* of John of Freiburg and the Popularization of the Moral Teaching of St. Thomas and of Some of His Contemporaries," in *Facing History: A Different Thomas Aquinas* (Louvain-La-Neuve: Fédération Internationale des Instituts d'Etudes Médiévales, 2000), pp. 37-63; Torrell, *Saint Thomas Aquinas 1,* p. 159; Jordan, "Aquinas' Reform of Moral Teaching," p. 7.

teaching in the context of a theological itinerary, his effort was either deliberately ignored or simply misunderstood. In any event, the Dominican appetite seems to have been for more of "*quae a diversis scripta sunt*" which Aquinas attempted to correct. Thus from the very beginning of the *Summa's* history within the Dominican Order, its "curricular ideal"[8] was passed over, and the text became not a single map of theological science (as it would later), but a set of distinct and discrete maps of particular theological *loci.*

Thus the tendency towards the transformation of Thomas' itinerary into something more like an encyclopedic map of theology was already nascent among his readership even in the final years of the thirteenth century — though it was only after the various "parts" of the *Summa* had been already segregated from one another, and thereafter treated as individual "textbooks."

One significant example of the way in which the "curriculum of persuasion" envisioned by Thomas in his *Summa* is rendered something far less dynamic, if not less persuasive, is the way in which the *Summa* is often adapted for modern readers. Nowhere are the presuppositions behind such transformations more evident than in Timothy McDermott's one-volume translation of the *Summa Theologiae.*[9] McDermott's intent is to make accessible to "twentieth-century reading habits" the difficult and "impressive"[10] text of Aquinas and to simplify its often bewildering and labyrinthine itinerary into a straightforward and easy prose. In McDermott's edition, "the format is modern: paragraphed, with paragraphs grouped in titled sections. And sections gathered into chapters." He notes that while the disputational format of the *Summa* is "powerful," it is "difficult for the modern reader," and thus he has "preferred a modern format of paragraphed, continuous text."[11] While such an attempt may have something to commend it, it betrays several presuppositions concerning the relationship between the reader and the "text" which might in the end not simplify Thomas' magnum opus, but indeed, make it even more perplexing.

When one comes to read a particular question of the *Summa*, if one is encouraged — as I dare say most readers are — to skip over the various objections and the *sed contra*, and head directly to the "body" of the text, or to "what Thomas says," one not only loses the context against which Thomas is arguing, but also, and perhaps more seriously, the text is reconfigured such that it does not challenge the very mode of reading with which most of us

8. Jordan, "The *Summa's* Reform of Moral Teaching," p. 47.

9. Timothy S. McDermott, ed., *Summa Theologiae: A Concise Translation* (Westminster, Md.: Christian Classics, 1989).

10. McDermott, "Editor's Note," *Summa*, p. xiii.

11. McDermott, "Editor's Note," p. xiv.

come to the text to begin with. That is to say, simplifying the *Summa* in this way gives one the impression that Thomas would have done much better simply to "get to the point," and not bother the reader with all of these technicalities. This approach betrays our modern predilection for "pure prose," for language which is not only "easy," but follows a direct line from proposition to exposition. Thus the matter of translation is not one of "ease" at all, but at a much deeper level, it is a question of the types of readers that we are.

But why did Thomas Aquinas not write in "pure prose"? McDermott's attempt here with respect to the *Summa* is not unlike Martin Luther's purging the Scriptures of its glossal accretions.[12] The aim in both moves is to free the text from its moorings, to make available the plain sense of the words, and to preclude the possibility of violence against the original. Whereas the removal of the glosses is the reduction of the text to its original, taking away external commentary, this "abridgement" of the *Summa* removes elements of style and argumentation which are integral to the original itself, so that there is a violence of some kind which is altogether inevitable. However, my concern here is not with "faithfulness to the original," which, though important, is not only in the strictest sense impossible in an abridgement which condenses over 1,500,000 words to about one sixth that amount, but has also been dealt with elsewhere.[13] For, by definition, an "abridgement" must omit some sections (in this case about five sixths of the original), most of which are for McDermott "mainly of historical interest."[14] My concern, on the other hand, is less with the accuracy or the fluidity of McDermott's translation or even with the question of whether he is successful in attempting genuinely "to give the feel of Thomas's treatment." Rather, what is prior to all of these concerns is the unspoken assumptions about the relationship between texts and their readers.

It must be said in McDermott's defense that his volume is intended "only

12. See my previous discussion in Chapter Four, "Memory and the *Glossa Ordinaria.*"

13. For example, see Romanus Cessario's review in *Theological Studies* LII (March 1991), pp. 147-49. "I do not think, however, that a reader (or reviewer) can approach this sort of book with an eye towards discovering to what extent it faithfully represents the original. Why? Because M. does not translate the *Summa;* rather, he abridges it. When one chooses an abridgement of a classic, one does not expect to find a faithful rendition of the original. An abridgement gives us some idea about whether or not we might like eventually to pick up the unabridged version, even in translation" (p. 148). Thus, Cessario is unclear as to why McDermott chose to call his work a "concise translation." In any case, it *is* an abridgement, but nevertheless of McDermott's own translation. While I do not disagree with Cessario's assessment, I think a more important question concerns the understanding of readership which makes "abridgements" possible, much less necessary, in the first place, and the assumption of theological neutrality to the way in which texts are organized.

14. McDermott, "Editor's Note," p. xiii.

as a useful translation for first reading."[15] He even refers the interested reader to the Blackfriars sixty-one-volume edition "with its Latin text, notes, appendices and glossaries." Yet, once more, my argument is not directed so much at McDermott or his translation, or even his editing. Rather, I want to suggest that one must raise the question of why such a text is needed in the first instance, and in the second, to what kind of readers his volume is directed. As we have seen, this is a text intended for beginners. But was not Thomas' *Summa*, in its original form, also aimed at theological novices?[16]

One reviewer writes:

> Regardless of the merit of various criticisms of Thomistic methodology, Aquinas did accomplish a brilliant synthesis of medieval learning while transforming the philosophical framework of theology in his day from platonic idealism to aristotelian realism. At the same time he tried to address the most significant of all questions: Is there a God? How can we know? Do we freely choose? What makes an action good or bad? How can there be evil in a world created by a good God? What is law and virtue? What did Christ's suffering mean? Why did God become a man? What did Christ know? What is sin and why do we need grace? These are questions worth studying. What we need is access to the work of Aquinas. The multi-volume set still inhibits. Until now![17]

To be precise, none of these are specifically Thomas' questions. This is not to say that he does not address issues of God's existence, our knowledge of sensibles, the Incarnation, and so on. But the implication in this particular review is that Aquinas can be read as giving answers to the commonplace questions of modern theology. To be sure, Thomas does in some sense give answers to these questions, but only in a very qualified sense. That is, the answers, *qua* answers, are not precisely Thomas' insofar as the questions are not precisely his. As another reviewer comments, when reading McDermott's version, "one is not reading Aquinas, but a version of Aquinas filtered through the sensibility of one person. One misses the push and pull of Aquinas' dialectical mind at work just as one misses the force of the objections

---

15. McDermott, "Editor's Note," p. xiv.

16. John I. Jenkins argues that the *Summa* is in fact not meant for pure novices, but for those who have had some theological training. See his *Knowledge and Faith in Thomas Aquinas* (Cambridge: Cambridge University Press, 1997), pp. 79-90.

17. L. Russ Bush, review of *The Summa Theologiae: A Concise Translation*, ed. Timothy S. McDermott, *Faith and Mission* VIII (Spring 1991), p. 108.

(which may, at times, be ornamental but elsewhere tell us what the argument is all about) with which he begins each article."[18]

The "push and pull" of the *Summa* are precisely part of what is lost in McDermott's version, but the question here is: what happens to the text when these are removed? Or then again, what has already happened to make such a thing not only possible, but indeed, now "readable"? In other words, what is it about other editions that makes their readability problematic?

To reiterate, the problem here lies with the presumed mode of reading which makes such a "translation" thinkable and even "useful." McDermott's attempt to make this text accessible concedes that modern reading habits differ to such a degree from medieval ones that not only do words need to be translated, but so do *genres*. And thus McDermott is precisely right in suggesting that "the format" of his translation "is modern: paragraphed, with paragraphs grouped in titled sections, and sections gathered into chapters."[19] It *is* modern, but *prima facie* this is only a problem of anachronism which may or may not be a problem. The hidden presupposition here is that a medieval text such as this can be adapted to "modern" format without some violence to the original. Perhaps McDermott himself would concede this point, but this is not the only issue. Another, much more subtle one is the kind of reading which this reorganization of knowledge likewise presupposes. In the final analysis, the adaptation of the *Summa* to modern format raises, and perhaps comes down to, questions of epistemology and of ontology.[20]

This last point may seem odd. The words, after all, are still Thomas'. The aim of the translation is, of course, is to "give the feel of Thomas' treatment."[21] One may indeed get the "feel" of Thomas' treatment of these various *loci* of theology, but what is lost is not only the sense of Thomas' dialectical mind, not only the "force of the objections." What has already been lost, long before any of these questions arise, is the type of training required to be a good reader of the *Summa*. That is to say, as I argue elsewhere, good reading of the *Summa* requires a liturgically trained memory. This claim depends upon several prior claims, which I will flesh out.

Reading is an inescapably theological enterprise, insofar as it is an act of human *poiesis*, of participation in divine self-knowledge. Only in the modern period have we come to understand reading as a "receiving" of some-

18. Lawrence S. Cunningham, review of McDermott, *Commonweal* CXVII.2 (26 January 1990), p. 61.

19. McDermott, "Editor's Note," p. xiv.

20. Alasdair MacIntyre has expressed related sentiments in *Three Rival Versions of Moral Enquiry: Encyclopaedia, Genealogy, and Tradition* (London: Duckworth, 1990), pp. 133ff.

21. McDermott, "Editor's Note," p. xiii.

thing, or the reader as a passive recipient of something there, frozen in space but noetically transmitted to the intellect by way of the visual "receptors." This understanding of vision as reception is an inversion of the classical and medieval understanding of sight as something active, an act performed upon an object.[22] Insofar as reading is an exercise of this type of vision, the reader has an active relationship to the page — contrary to our modern predisposi-tions — and becomes like a participant in a conversation or dialogue with the text. From the earliest days of the Church, reading has been understood as a profoundly ethical (and corporeal) endeavor. At least from the time of Origen on, good reading of the Scriptures is realized only in the ascent from the literal sense to the spiritual, in the arrival at the point at which the reader becomes in some sense a part of the text, and at which the text becomes a part of the reader. Thus in order to understand what is problematic about a translation like McDermott's, one must situate this edition within a longer history of reading and of texts which privileges the visual, first of all, over the oral. We could attempt to date when this shift begins, but whatever the precise or imprecise date of the beginning of this shift, it is most emphati-cally fixed with the invention of moveable type in the middle of the fifteenth century.

McDermott's is an attempt to "distill" the text of Aquinas into manage-able units, whole in themselves. But more than a mere reduction of the text to manageability, this "distilling" of the text is quite literally also a "stilling" of the text, the taming of an unwieldy and labyrinthine work. It is, moreover, an attempt to spatialize a text which, from beginning to end, refuses the stillness of the paragraph. In other words, for various reasons, the text of the *Summa* prohibits by its very structure the reduction to localized units which may be read as wholes unto themselves. To be sure, no text can *qua* text resist stillness utterly; there is always an irreducibly spatial character to texts insofar as they are, visually, nothing more than words on a blank page. But I suggest that the

22. For example, see Augustine, *The Trinity*, tr. Edmund Hill, O.P. (Brooklyn: New City, 1991), IX.i.3, p. 273: "We see bodies with our bodily eyes because the rays which shoot out from them touch whatever we observe." The inheritance is of course Platonic, and comes from the *Timaeus*, 45: "They arranged that all fire which had not the property of burning, but gave out a gentle light, should form the body of each day's light. The pure fire within us that is akin to this they caused to flow through the eyes, making the whole eye-ball, and particularly its central part, smooth and close-textured so that it would keep in anything of coarser nature, and filter through only this pure fire. So when there is daylight round the visual stream, it falls on its like and coalesces with it, forming a single uniform body in the line of sight, along which the stream from within strikes the external object." In Plato, *Timaeus and Critias*, tr. Desmond Lee (Lon-don: Penguin, 1965, 1971), p. 62.

character of the *Summa, qua* text, defies this "idolatrous spatialization" inasmuch as it obstinately defies the possibility of the reduction of its flux to independent, chewable units.

This is for several reasons. The first is that, unlike modern theologies, at least from Melanchthon and Cano onward, the *Summa* does not treat successively the various *topoi* peculiar to theological discourse. For this reason Bush's review of McDermott's version is at once both perplexing and unsurprising. It is perplexing in the sense that Thomas does not set out to "give answers to" the various commonplace topics of theology, as does the modern tradition of *Loci Communes* (of which Melanchthon's is the earliest and most notable Protestant example, and Cano's the first in Roman Catholicism).[23] This tradition presupposes a circumscribable "domain" to theological speech, which is for all intents and purposes off-limits to other discourses, above all "philosophy." This is the result of the theological abandonment of the "philosophical," the vacation from "philosophical space" of theology. On this account, theology leaves to philosophy its own *loci communes,* which have little to do with the commonplaces of theological speech. What Bush's review reveals — and this is why it is unsurprising — is the extent to which our understanding of theology as concerned with a particular "subject matter" is so pervasive as to make our ability to understand Aquinas as anything but a "systematic" theologian *par excellence* all but impossible.

---

23. See Philipp W. Rosemann, *Understanding Scholastic Thought with Foucault* (New York: St. Martin's, 1999), esp. Study 3, "Scholastic Intellectual Practices," in which he argues that "in thirteenth century Scholasticism we find the first germs of a dissociation of a text from reality — not a breaking of the bond, to be sure, but a loosening of the grip of the text over reality, and indeed over the subject." Rosemann points to the *Tabula* of Robert Grosseteste, completed circa 1230, in which he arranges 217 topics under nine *distinctiones,* such as *de Deo, de Verbo, de creaturis,* etc. Grosseteste, progenitor of the "light-metaphysics" later made famous in Roger Bacon, insisted upon the instrumental usefulness of mathematics as a descriptive apparatus, as well as the "use of observation and experiment controlled by logical methods of analysis and verification." (See David Knowles, *The Evolution of Medieval Thought,* 1st ed. [London: Longmans, 1962], p. 283.) His "mathematical" arrangement of material, in many ways, prefigures later developments in Agricolan and Ramist place-logics. Rosemann's use of Grosseteste's *Tabula* is illustrative of the tension already developing in the thirteenth century with regard to the science of texts. The prevalent modern tendency to read every Scholastic text as a "map" is, as I argue later on, problematized by several examples. I hope to show that the *Summa Theologiae* of Aquinas, in its compositional architecture, is more akin to live oral disputations and liturgical paradigms of memory and performance than to a table or catalog of theological sentences. This is simply to suggest that the tension described by Rosemann is not *resolved* by the publication of Grosseteste's *Tabula,* given that the *Summa,* a generation later, attempts to resist the spatializing tendency of such theological maps. In fact, one might illustrate this tension by the opposition of two types: the *Tabula* on the one hand, and the *Summa* on the other.

The second implication of the stilling of the text is that, if anything, the overarching *sense* (or McDermott's "feel") of the entire *Prima Pars* is one of *motion*. While the subject matter of the first forty-three questions may be "God as He is in Himself,"[24] the dominant motif of this section (and the ones that follow) is of *procession*. Indeed, the forty-third question of the *Prima Pars* concerns the "mission of the divine Persons."[25] The remainder of the first part of the *Summa* then deals with the going-out of God from himself to creatures. Curiously, the itinerary here is from abstract discussion of the existence of God in the second question, to the altogether mundane questions at the end of the *Prima Pars* dealing with whether semen is produced from surplus food.[26] From the exalted and much-discussed heights of the first and second questions of the first part, by the end of that part we have proceeded to altogether more terrestrial affairs.[27]

Here it might be worth rehearsing the well-known prologue to the *Prima Pars*, found immediately before the second question:

> So, because, as we have shown, the fundamental aim of holy teaching is to make God known, not only as he is in himself, but as the beginning and end of all things and of reasoning creatures especially, we now intend to set forth this divine teaching by treating, first, of God, secondly, of the journey to God of reasoning creatures, thirdly, of Christ, who, as man, is our road to God.
>
> The treatment will fall into three parts: first, his nature, secondly, the distinction of persons in God, thirdly, the coming forth from him of creatures.

By the end of the first part, we have concluded that section dealing with "the coming forth from him of creatures," in Questions 118 and 119, on human reproduction with respect to the soul and the body.[28] However it is the question

---

24. *ST* Ia.i, Proemium.

25. *ST* Ia.xliii, Proemium. "Mission" here translates of course *missio*, "sending."

26. *ST* Ia.cxix.2.

27. If there were any reasons to doubt that Thomas was serious in the first question about *sacra doctrina* treating "all things . . . under the aspect of God," those doubts should by now have been put firmly to rest.

28. This latter question, it should be noted, ends on a Christological note: "However, Christ is said to have been in Adam with respect to bodily substance but not with respect to the seminal cause. For the matter of his body supplied by the Virgin Mother was derived from Adam, but the active power was not derived from Adam because his body was not formed by the power of the male semen but by the operation of the Holy Spirit. For such a birth was fitting for him who is God, blessed above all things, forever. Amen." *ST* IaIIae.cxix.2, ad 4, Blackfriars.

that precedes these final two which, I think, provides the most illuminating clue as to the aim and structure of the *Summa* as an itinerary of the soul's return to God. This is Question 117 of the *Prima Pars*, three questions from the end of the first part of the *Summa,* in which Thomas discusses human activity. In fact these final three questions form a unit, according to Thomas, who says in the *proemium* to Question 117, "We next must consider what pertains to the activity of man, a composite being of spirit and body. First, we discuss human activity (117); second, we discuss propagation of man from man (118-119)."[29] But it is in Question 117 that the principal rhetorical function of Thomas as "teacher of Catholic truth" *(catholicae veritatis doctor)* becomes audible.

The first article of that question asks *utrum unus homo posit docere alium, causando in ipso scientiam* ("whether a man can teach another man, causing him to know"). Interestingly, the first objection, drawing on Matthew 23:8 and Jerome's interlinear gloss thereon, argues that "[T]o be a teacher then properly belongs to God"; thus humans most certainly cannot teach one another. The second objection argues that knowledge is an active quality like heat, which, when in proximity to another object, produces an effect in it which is like itself. The third objection suggests that illumination is required, and the fourth argues that "[a] teacher does nothing to his pupil save to put certain signs before him which signify something either by words or gestures." In each of the responses to the objections, Thomas grants the legitimacy of each argument. He seems here to resist the exaltation of the role of the teacher in such a way that would make God *not* the true cause of knowledge, but at the same time insists all the more firmly on the claim that God alone teaches, but through teachers.

> Now the teacher leads the learner on from the already known to the unknown in two ways: first, by putting before him certain means which his mind can use in acquiring knowledge, for example, as when he puts before him less certain universal propositions on which the learner can form a judgment from previous knowledge, or as when he puts to him concrete examples, either likenesses or opposites or something of the kind, from which the learner's mind is led on to knowledge of the truth of what was previously unknown *(ex quibus intellectus addiscentis manuducitur in cognitionem veritatis ignotae).*[30]

29. *ST* IaIIae.cxvii, Proemium, Blackfriars.
30. *ST* IaIIae.cxvii.1, *resp.,* Blackfriars. For further discussion of this, see below, Chapter Six.

One reason why this passage is so curious is due to where it appears in the *Summa*. There is also quite a clear sense in which the text here refers to itself. The point is that this is not just a question about the nature of knowledge or education; it is about the readers themselves, and about the author of the *Summa Theologiae*. The implied question that Thomas must have anticipated from his reader must have been something like, "How can this text teach us? Or, more importantly, how can another person teach me?" If the end of all knowledge is beatific vision, then it becomes a very important question as to the ability of one's instructors adequately and rightly to lead one to the proper *telos* as a human being. Thus the question here is entirely apposite, coming as it does at the end of the *Prima Pars*. It refers us all the way back to the prologue to the entire work, which set out the task of the doctor of catholic truth. Now, at the conclusion of the first segment, having addressed God as the origin of all that is, including all knowledge, it is necessary to ask about the agency of God in theological education, such as that in which the reader of the *Summa* is now participating.

However, what makes significant the placement of Thomas' discussion of the teacher at the end of the *Prima Pars* is the context by which it is framed. I have already suggested that that context is the hinge between the first two parts. But in terms of the *ductus* of Thomas' argument, it is significant because it falls in the middle of a discussion of the ability of will and intellect to move one another.

Thomas' favorite term for the way in which participants in *sacra doctrina* are led to knowledge, and hence to the beatific vision is *manuductio*, "leading by the hand." He uses the term in the fifth article of the very first question of the *Summa*, in which he describes the nature of *sacra doctrina* as subaltern not to other human sciences but to *scientia divina*, the knowledge God has of himself. Holy teaching therefore makes use of other sciences, all of which are "subsidiary and ancillary," because "our understanding is wanting, which is the more readily guided into the world above reason, set forth in holy teaching, through the world of natural reason from which the other sciences take their course."[31] Thus at the very outset of the *Summa*, manuduction is already linked to participation in divine self-knowledge. The *Summa* itself is, as we shall see, a kind of itinerary of the soul, by which we as readers are led by the hand toward the vision of God face-to-face.

The term *manuduco* and its cognates make a number of appearances throughout the works of Aquinas, particularly the *Summa Theologiae* and the *De Veritate*. He uses the term at least twenty times in the *Summa*, but what is

31. *ST* Ia.1.v, *ad* 2, Blackfriars.

more interesting is *when* he uses it. I have already hinted at the significance of Thomas' discussion of the teachability of human beings at the end of the *Prima Pars*, and we have seen that in that discussion (Question 117, Article 1), he mentions the "leading by the hand" of the mind of the learner from the known to the unknown. So already we have an instance of the reference to manuduction at one of the "hinges" of the *Summa's* three finished parts. In fact, over half of these uses of the notion come at or near the end of each of these three sections.

Similarly, at the end of the *Secunda Secundae*, Thomas uses the term six times within one question, namely Question 180. Five of these instances appear in Article Four, wherein Thomas commends the religious life to his readers. As I have argued elsewhere, the self-conscious use of *manuductio* here at the end of the *Secunda Secundae* suggests that Thomas not only wants his readers to be convinced of the merits of religious life, but that he wants to lead them by his own hand into the religious life itself.

In the meantime, however, another curious appearance of the term is in the final article of the final question of the *Prima Secundae*, in Question 114, Article 10. In fact it is quite nearly the final word of the whole part:

> All things happen equally to the good and the wicked, as regards the substance of temporal good or evil; but not as regards the end, since the good and not the wicked are led to beatitude by them [*quia boni per huiusmodi manuducuntur ad beatitudinem, non autem mali*].[32]

It makes sense that Thomas ends this way, speaking about the good being led by the hand to beatitude, since his discussion of virtue and vice is what will occupy the whole of the *Secunda Secundae*.

Before turning to the beginning of the *Prima Secundae*, it is worth considering how this particular passage from the end of the first to the beginning of the second part is itself framed by an argument about will. In Article 4 of Question 82 of the *Prima Pars*, Thomas asks whether the will moves the intellect. In the previous article, Thomas argued that the intellect is higher than the will, since its object is more simple and abstract.[33] In the first objection, Thomas cites St. Augustine's *De Genesi ad Litteram*, wherein the latter writes that "the agent is nobler than the patient" (with confirmation from Aristotle's *De Anima* III.5). From this it would seem that the will does not move the intellect, since the former would be analogous to the patient and not the agent, on account of its lesser nobility. However, Thomas distinguishes two kinds of motion:

32. *ST* IaIIae.cxiv.10, *ad* 4.
33. *ST* Ia.lxxxii.3, *resp.*

First, as an end: for instance, when we say that the end moves the agent. In this way the intellect moves the will, because the good understood is the object of the will, and moves it as an end. Secondly, a thing is said to move as an agent, as what alters moves what is altered, and what impels moves what is impelled. In this way the will moves the intellect, and all the powers of the soul, as Anselm says . . .[34]

Similarly, both the intellect and will can be considered in two ways, as "apprehensive of universal being and truth, and as a thing and a particular power having a determinate act."[35] Thus there is a reciprocal relationship between the two, since the will can move the intellect and the intellect can move the will, depending upon the object of the movement. "From this we can easily say why these powers include one another in their acts, because the intellect understands that the will wills, and the will wills the intellect to understand. In the same way good is contained in truth, inasmuch as it is an understood truth, and truth in good, inasmuch as it is a desired good."[36] Nonetheless, Thomas concludes this article with the claim that "every movement of the will must be preceded by apprehension, whereas every apprehension is not preceded by an act of the will; but the principle of counseling and understanding is an intellectual principle higher than our intellect, namely, God."[37]

Sacra doctrina, of course, is a kind of scientia which is derivative of this higher intellectual principle, scientia divina. The intellect, insofar as it knows or understands anything, participates in the knowledge God has of Himself, and therefore understanding and will are mutually implicated in one another in an ongoing itinerary of the soul towards the consummation of that motion. The Summa, then, conducts the reader toward this goal by the manuduction of desire and understanding.

We have already seen how Thomas uses this metaphor of manuductio for that activity in which the teacher participates, particularly in Question 117 of the Prima Pars. This discussion is set up by the argument twelve or so questions earlier, wherein Thomas asks whether God can move the created intellect and will immediately. The analogy he uses is that of the teacher, as in the sed contra to Article 3: "a teacher moves the mind of a learner. According to the Psalm, God teaches man knowledge."[38] God "moves man's mind" accord-

---

34. ST Ia.lxxxii.4, resp.
35. ST Ia.lxxxii.4, resp.
36. ST Ia.lxxxii.4, ad 1.
37. ST Ia.lxxxii.4, ad 3.
38. ST Ia.cv.3, sed contra.

ing to Thomas because "the intelligible exemplars of all things exist first in God and then pass on to other minds so that these have actual knowledge."[39] The mind, then, is moved by its object, which is God.

So it is also with the will. The will is moved by its object, which is the universal good. According to Aquinas, God is the sole cause of the power of willing, since willing means a responsiveness to God who is the universal good. Coercion arises when the will is directed in a way "contrary to its own leaning"; thus God "gives the will its natural leaning."[40] This is important because it highlights the claim that God's being the sole cause of the movement of the intellect and the will does not mitigate against the freedom of these to move themselves, because whatever natural desire there is in the soul is always already graced with derivation.

Turning now to the beginning of the *Secunda Secundae:* recall that the *Prima Pars* closed with a kind of descent, corresponding to the ontological procession of all things from God, down to the very corporeal production of one human being from another. That movement ended with the Amen at the end of Question 119.

Having descended thus far, Thomas turns in the Prologue to discuss the last end of human beings. The implication here is that one can understand the origin of man only by knowing his end, a claim which is made explicit here:

> Man is made in God's image, and since this implies, so Damascene tells us, that he is intelligent and free to judge and master of himself, so then, now that we have agreed that God is the exemplar cause of things and that they issue from his power through his will, we go on to look at this image, that is to say, at man as the source of actions which are his own and fall under his responsibility and control.
>
> The first matter to come up is the destiny of human life, and next how it may be reached or missed: remember, all our plans get their meaning from their final purpose. Happiness is set down as being this; accordingly we shall start with human teleology in general, and then relate it to happiness.[41]

Notice the self-conscious rhetorical reference here: "now that we have agreed," etc. This would seem to imply, quite obviously, that the purpose of the *Prima Pars* was to convince us of this claim, namely that "God is the ex-

39. *ST* Ia.cv.3, *resp.*
40. *ST* Ia.cv.4, *ad* 1.
41. *ST* IaIIae, Prologue, Blackfriars.

emplar cause of things and that they issue from his power through his will." If that is so, then we would be justified in thinking that the aim of the coming part is, in reflection upon the *imago dei* and its final destiny, to participate in the divine initiation of movement of the will from potency to act — as a movement always "from," "towards," and "into" God — through the transformation of desire in proportion to the human being's "responsibility and control." In other words, seen from the perspective of this transition, the goal of the second part is more clearly not simply to *describe* the will's movement, but actually to move the will itself.

On the other side of the prologue, Thomas returns in Question 9 of the *Prima Secundae* to the question we have already been considering, although this time the order is altered. Whereas in Question 82 of the *Prima Pars* he had asked whether the intellect is moved by the will, here he asks whether the will is moved by the intellect. This would on the face of it seem to be redundant. We had, after all, "agreed that God is the exemplar cause of things and that they issue from his power through his will," and that God is the sole cause of the movement of the intellect and the will. Why then do we return to the question?

To begin with, the stress of the discussion in the latter article is on the movement from potentiality to actuality, while in the former he did not retrace this familiar terrain.

> None other than God can be the cause of man's willing. Two reasons make this clear. First, because the will is a power of the rational soul, which is caused by God alone by creation, as we have shown in the *Prima Pars*. Second, because of the will's bearing on universal good, none other than God, who is the universal good, can cause it to act. Everything else is good by participation and a sort of particular good.[42]

The stress on the movement from potency to act, on the movement of the will to the object of the will, the universal good, is essential to understanding the remainder of the *Secunda Pars*, in which Thomas discusses the virtues and vices. But more importantly, it is not simply that Thomas aims to convince his readers of the veracity of his claims; rather, it seems to me, he intends to aid in their translation from potentially good to actually good. In this sense we can see the *Summa's* structure as an itinerary of the soul towards union with God, in which the role of the author or teacher is not simply relegated to that of the encyclopaedist. The teacher's vocation is to move the soul, by a

42. *ST* IaIIae.ix.6, *resp.*

participation in the movement of the intellect and will whose agent is God alone. This makes the task of the teacher of sacred doctrine both more demanding and less central: it is God alone who is the agent of understanding and good desire. Furthermore, it is precisely because the teacher's role is derivative and not primary that gives it its nobility. It is because the teacher is not the true agent of knowledge that renders that intellect its integrity, since it is a participation in divine self-knowledge.

In spite of the fact that much criticism of the *Summa* ignores it, Thomas as an author seems to be quite aware of his own audience. For example, in Article 3 of the sixth question of the *Prima Secundae*, on whether there can be voluntariness without act, Thomas argues that will can be expressed both directly in action and indirectly in inaction. In the reply to the second objection, he says,

> 'Non-willing' has a double meaning. First, when taken as a single term, *non velle*, the infinitive of *non volo* or *nolo*, not to wish or to be unwilling. So that if I say, 'I am unwilling to read', I can be taken to mean, 'I am willing not to read', so that willing not to read and not willing to read are equivalent: in this sense 'not-to-will' causes involuntariness. Second, when taken as a sentence, and then no act of will is posited: in this sense 'to will not' does not cause involuntariness.[43]

This is a rare instance of Thomas' use of the word *legere*, "to read," in a context other than the citation of an authority, for example, by saying, "as we read in Augustine." Further, it is a curiously witty remark. It is as if Thomas anticipates the sense among his readership that he is trying their patience, that reading the *Summa* is demanding work. Perhaps he "hears" the claim "I am unwilling to read" being murmured under the breath of his readers at this point!

Reading requires patience, and it does so because the reader, in tracing the return of the soul to God, is in the process of a difficult transformation. There is a subtle sense here of the will being bent into shape, of desire being reordered to its proper object. The passage of the learner from the known to the unknown depends upon the gracious agency of God, who, as divine charity, moves all things to himself, including human minds. At the same time, it seems that, from this reading of the structure of the *Summa*, Thomas the teacher of catholic truth intends not simply the impartation of information, but the bending of the will towards that to which it ought to be directed. To read *sacra doctrina* well, then, is to be caught up in the "procession" which serves as the ordering principle of the *Summa*, a movement of the divine per-

---

43. *ST* IaIIae.vi.3, *ad* 2, Blackfriars.

sons from and to each other, which is a motion without beginning and with-out end. To know, then, is to participate in this divine motion in such a way that the will itself is moved — not simply by the author of the text, but by the divine author of knowledge itself.

"Learning," writes Otto Bird, "supposes a certain motion or process on the part of the student, and teaching can at most help to bring that motion about; it cannot actually constitute the motion."[44] Here it might be clearer how the un-derstanding of the page itself is inseparable from its pedagogical purpose, and from the end to which it is ordered. Thus *sacra doctrina* uses human reasoning in order "to make manifest some implications of its message"[45] or "to make clear other things that are put forward in this doctrine";[46] *ad manifestandum aliqua quae traduntur in hac doctrina. Traduntur,* of course, is suggestive of its root, *trado,* from which *traditio.* The implication here is that that which is passed on, or what we call "tradition," is no fixed and intractable code of teach-ing, but is always in need of clarification, of manifestation. "Reason" *(ratio humana)* therefore is not an intellectual faculty over and against *sacra doctrina*; rather it is the *activity* of seeking clarification through the dialectical narrative of *auctoritates.* It submits to what is already given and received by the Church, and as such is not therefore the arbiter of truth, but the discursive activity of the continuing community of interpretive voices, directed towards a clearer mani-festation of the truth. Though each article may be said to conclude with a kind of *manifestatio* in the authorial response, it does not, as Jesse Gellrich rightly states, "validate articles of faith, but replicates in its style the divine ordo."[47]

44. Otto Bird, "How to Read an Article of the 'Summa,'" *The New Scholasticism* XXVII (April 1953), p. 149.

45. *ST* Ia.i.8, *ad* 2, Blackfriars.

46. *ST* Ia.i.8, *ad* 2, Fathers of the English Dominican Province.

47. Jesse M. Gellrich, *The Idea of the Book in the Middle Ages: Language Theory, Mythology, and Fiction* (Ithaca: Cornell University Press, 1985), p. 67. See also p. 66: "The *manifestatio* of which summae are capable, first of all, is the *summa* itself, not only the 'highest' reaches of spec-ulation, but the 'totality' or complete itemization of all aspects of an issue; such treatises must be composed of adequate *articuli,* constituent 'parts' or 'members,' and subdivided into finer el-ements; the pattern of ordo of the whole is preserved by proper comparisons, *similitudines,* and sufficient contrasts, *distinctiones;* the inclusion of precise diction, harmonious sentences, and rhyme will foster mnemonic devices for rapid memorization; finally the last item in an argu-ment must affirm the *concordantia* of the whole, the principle that no contradictions remain as all opening objections are conclusively refuted." While Gellrich is basically right about the structure of the article, and particularly its mnemonic cues, his overall reading of the *Summa* of Thomas is seriously flawed. First of all, the characterization of the *Summa* as the *manifestatio* of the "highest" reaches of speculation is not only anachronistic, but also betrays a curious com-monplace of a codified twentieth-century "Thomism," namely that the *Summa* is essentially a totalizing synthesis of all of theology — a theology which is, finally, an entirely speculative sci-

In the next chapter, I will spell out the sense in which Thomas understands the teaching of *sacra doctrina* as participating in the ongoing *traditio* of the teaching of Christ. As we shall see, "tradition" is not a source alongside Scripture, but the activity of apprenticeship in holy teaching. Any attempt to find a correlate of the modern notion of tradition in the *Summa Theologiae* will therefore be shown to be misguided. To that end, I hope to re-emphasize the oft-neglected rhetorical character of this text, in which Thomas unites the persuasive function of rhetoric to the *telos* of the whole human life.

---

ence, in the modern sense — i.e., it has nothing to do with "reality." It also contradicts what Thomas himself says about the speculative character of *sacra doctrina* — it is not purely speculative, but only more speculative than practical, insofar as it concerns actions only as they relate to their end (*ST* I.i.5, *resp.*). Moreover, Gellrich suggests that Thomas (along with Bonaventure and the Lombard, whom he also cites — neither of whom, incidentally, ever wrote a *summa*) "submitted" to the form of the article out of sheer convention. His suggestion that this *manifestatio* is a "highly formalized principle of the projection of schemata and the spatialization of thought that begins long before Aquinas, Gregory, and Augustine" (p. 68) implies a severance of the order of the arrangement of the text from its pedagogical goal. It divorces, in other words, the formal from the ontological. In brief, he makes a map out of what is essentially a narrative itinerary. But as I have shown, the rhetorical goal of the *Summa* is identical with the ontological goal of creation, and as the textual order "replicates" the cosmological, it does so in a theological taxonomy of participation and not of mere representation. Furthermore, Gellrich's narrative of "spatialization," owing much to Derrida, assumes a kind of univocity to the character of "*the* book" which is ultimately ahistorical.

Finally, Gellrich's Derridean assumptions about the "idea of the book" impute a host of modern assumptions about "totality" to texts which do not share them. The implication here, with specific regard to the *Summa Theologiae*, is that the author aims at a conclusive refutation of all objections, and removes all contradictions. This is an act of closure, by which the monologue of Aquinas overwhelms and silences all other voices. A fundamental violence is therefore implied in the totalizing drive of medieval theological "syntheses," which, Gellrich argues, attempt a "complete itemization of all aspects of an issue." From what I have shown, completeness and closure are precisely *not* the goals of the *Summa*. Compared with the Quodlibetal question, the *Summa* is far less "complete" in terms of its range of objections. With its more abbreviated and, I submit, rhetorically sophisticated style, it does not aim at conclusive refutation, but attempts the very *manuductio* ("leading by the hand") toward union with God which it narrates. Gellrich is unable, finally, to reconcile his account of *manuductio* with his spatialization thesis, because he is too ahistorical in his attempt to give a theological account of this space and how it is performed.

As a curious postscript, consider the fourth article of the first question of the *Summa*, which deals with whether *sacra doctrina* is a speculative or practical science. In place of specific responses to the objections, Thomas has, *Et per hoc patet responsio ad objecta* (*ST* I.i.4, *resp.*), which the Blackfriars edition translates "This leaves the way open for the answer to the difficulties" (pp. 16-17), and which the English Dominican edition translates "This is a sufficient answer to the objections" (p. 3). Either way, this is explicitly not a word of closure, but of the presumption of the possibility of further comment and qualification. Nowhere does Thomas seek a *conclusive* answer to all "difficulties," but only a *sufficient* one to some of them.

6 Reading as *Manuductio* as *Traditio* as *Reditus*

In his books *Whose Justice? Which Rationality?* and *Three Rival Versions of Moral Enquiry*, Alasdair MacIntyre presents Thomas Aquinas as a figure who "understood philosophical activity as that of a craft and indeed of the chief of crafts."[1] MacIntyre's reading of the *Summa Theologiae* in particular portrays Thomas' pedagogical project as ordered towards the "possession and transmission of [a] kind of ability to recognize in the past what is and is not a guide to the future."[2] Moral philosophy, then, is a kind of apprenticeship in the knowledge of particular goods which depends upon friendship in order to learn well what is *the* good.[3] This friendship is both synchronic and diachronic, insofar as it involves a "leading by the hand" by friends both present and past. In this chapter I hope to extend MacIntyre's account of moral philosophy as craft to Aquinas' more specific treatment of *sacra doctrina*, which the latter treats as a kind of apprenticeship in the self-knowledge of God, in connection with the logic of participation in the Trinity.

In *Three Rival Versions*, MacIntyre describes "the Augustinian conception of moral enquiry" as a pedagogy of reading, and asks,

> What then does progress in reading and understanding texts, including the text of nature, consist in? It consists at one level in activities characterizable by an external observer as an identification of discrepancies within texts, the formulation of hypotheses for overcoming them and a search for evi-

1. Alasdair MacIntyre, *Three Rival Versions of Moral Enquiry: Encyclopaedia, Genealogy, and Tradition* (London: Duckworth, 1990), p. 127.

2. MacIntyre, *Three Rival Versions*, p. 128.

3. Alasdair MacIntyre, *Whose Justice? Which Rationality?* (Notre Dame: University of Notre Dame Press, 1988), pp. 179ff.

dence to confirm or disconfirm such hypotheses, the integration of newly discovered or rediscovered texts into the body of knowledge, and the construction of ever more adequate ways to classify and systematize what has been learned. In these activities dialectical argument is employed both to investigate the underlying ontology of the scheme of knowledge and to elucidate the problematic issues arising in the course of enquiry. But all of these contribute to and are constituted as progress only insofar as the mind of the enquirer engaged in such activity moves from an initial stage, in which it does not know either itself or other finite beings or God as exhibiting the degree and kind of perfection which belongs to each of these, towards such apprehensions as it is capable of, of the perfection of each; and in achieving this progress it also perfects itself.[4]

According to MacIntyre, Aquinas inherited this craft under Albert the Great's tutelage at the Dominican *studium generale* in Cologne during the years 1248-52.[5] According to this scheme, he writes, "when I first believe in order that I may go on to understand, I do not evaluate evidence, but put my trust in certain persons as authorized to represent the apostolic testimony, something which I may come to do in many different kinds of ways, none of which will be at that preliminary stage good-reason-providing, because I cannot as yet know how in this area to evaluate reasons as good or otherwise."[6] Despite the material revisions to this concept of enquiry that Thomas was to contribute, he retains the Augustinian understanding of theology as a craft of reading well. Thus for Aquinas, training in *sacra doctrina* requires first of all the virtue of humility, through which the reader is disabused of the temptation to autonomy. But in addition to humility, Thomas' understanding of pedagogy will be shown to require, as well as to cultivate, the virtue of prudence, as this is understood as the ordering of thoughts and actions to their proper end, the Wisdom who is the second person of the Trinity.

A recent current in studies of St. Thomas has emphasized his nuanced doctrine of participation in God, which, in response to a long history of the "Aristotelianizing" of Thomas' thought, has reasserted the Platonic elements in his work.[7] In one of these works, Anna Williams has argued that

4. MacIntyre, *Three Rival Versions*, p. 95.

5. MacIntyre, *Three Rival Versions,* esp. ch. V, pp. 82-105.

6. MacIntyre, *Three Rival Versions*, p. 92.

7. Chief among these are (in no particular order): Leo J. Elders, *The Metaphysics of Being of St. Thomas in a Historical Perspective,* Studien und Texte zur Geistesgeschichte des Mittelalters 34 (Leiden: Brill, 1993); Rudi A. te Velde, *Participation and Substantiality in Thomas Aquinas,* Studien und Texte zur Geistesgeschichte des Mittelalters 46 (Leiden: Brill, 1995); Oliva

the *Summa* is "both an exhortation to contemplation and an act of contemplation."[8] For Thomas, she argues, "theology is a form of reflection deriving from a kind of active participation in God's self-knowledge, which is no less than God's own self. . . . Theology is thus construed not so much as a human task, but as a divine self-giving, the means by which we are drawn into God's own existence."[9] To be sure, theology *is* a human task, an ongoing pedagogy of the prudential ordering of our knowledge and will towards their proper end, a task which, though it is indeed an act of divine self-giving, is not separable from the perichoretic operations of intellect and will, of memory and understanding, and the love which unites these — a love which is not only given but is also learned. Learned, that is, as a response to something already given — and in this way the rather mundane training in the use of authorities in theological disputations and writings must be considered as part of this gift of love, whereby the mechanics of education, and particularly of reading, are understood as the instruments of divine self-gift, mediated through the wisdom of the Fathers and the saints, and performed in memorial composition. In other words, the notion that "things participate in God to the extent that God communicates himself in a different manner to each of them and attunes the being he gives, to each particular subject"[10] is the principle, as it were, which undergirds the need to order our memory, and our desire, by an act of on-going *anamnesis*, to remember the cause by which we are created and the end to which we are ordained. Therefore contemplation, "the intellect's absorption into God,"[11] as an act of reading the world rightly, has as its end the beatitude of the perpetual enjoyment of God.

In the third question of the *Prima Secundae*, as to whether happiness is something uncreated, Thomas writes,

---

Blanchette, *The Perfection of the Universe According to Aquinas: A Teleological Cosmology* (University Park, Pa.: Penn State University Press, 1992); A. N. Williams, *The Ground of Union: Deification in Aquinas and Palamas* (Oxford: Oxford University Press, 1999); A. N. Williams, "Mystical Theology Redux: The Pattern of Aquinas' *Summa Theologiae*," *Modern Theology* XIII.1 (January 1997), pp. 53-74; and John Milbank and Catherine Pickstock, *Truth in Aquinas* (London: Routledge, 2001). See also Mark D. Jordan, *The Alleged Aristotelianism of Thomas Aquinas*, The Etienne Gilson Series 15 (Toronto: Pontifical Institute of Mediaeval Studies, 1992); Wayne J. Hankey, *God in Himself: Aquinas' Doctrine of God as Expounded in the* Summa Theologiae (Oxford: Oxford University Press, 1987).

8. Williams, "Mystical Theology Redux," p. 56.
9. Williams, "Mystical Theology Redux," pp. 58-59.
10. Elders, *The Metaphysics of Being*, p. 228.
11. Williams, "Mystical Theology Redux," p. 62.

I answer that, as stated above (Q.1, A.8; Q.2, A.7), our end is twofold. First, there is the thing itself which we desire to attain: thus for the miser, the end is money. Secondly, there is the attainment or possession, the use or enjoyment of the thing desired; thus we may say that the end of the miser is the possession of money; and the end of the intemperate man is to enjoy something pleasurable. In the first sense, then, man's last end is the uncreated good, namely, God, Who alone by His infinite goodness can perfectly satisfy man's will. But in the second way, man's last end is something created, existing in him, and this is nothing else than the attainment or enjoyment of the last end. Now the last end is called happiness. If, therefore, we consider man's happiness in its cause or object, then it is something uncreated; but if we consider it as to the very essence of happiness, then it is something created.[12]

This passage recalls the rhetorical distinctions between *skopos* and *ductus,* between the goal of a text and the manner through which one arrives there. For Thomas, our end as human beings, our *skopos,* as it were, is God, the uncreated good, who himself is beatitude by his essence.[13] Humans therefore participate in this uncreated beatitude by participation in happiness, which is created. Thus the created participation in God's beatitude in this life is the result of human operations, as Thomas says in the very next question:

In so far as man's happiness is something created, existing in him, we must needs say that it is an operation. For happiness is man's supreme perfection. Now each thing is perfect in so far as it is actual; since potentiality without act is imperfect. Consequently happiness must consist in man's last act.[14]

He goes on further to state that with final perfection, the operation of beatitude is not continuous because the human operation of happiness is perfectly joined to happiness itself in God. Beatitude is now made essentially one in the Trinity. However, in the present life, "in so far as we fall short of the unity of that operation, so do we fall short of perfect happiness." And here Thomas explicitly links beatitude with the activity of contemplation as the *ductus* which leads us unto beatitude. Though the beatitude of God in which we participate through contemplation in the present life is an imperfect one,

Nevertheless it *is* a participation of happiness: and so much the greater, as the operation can be more continuous and more one. Consequently the ac-

---

12. *ST* IaIIae.iii.1, *resp.*
13. *ST* IaIIae.iii.1, *ad* 1.
14. *ST* IaIIae.iii.2, *resp.*

tive life, which is busy with many things, has less of happiness than the contemplative life, which is busied with one thing, i.e., the contemplation of
truth. And if at any time man is not actually engaged in this operation, yet
since he can always easily turn to it, and since he ordains the very cessation,
by sleeping or occupying himself otherwise, to the aforesaid occupation, the
latter seems, as it were, continuous.[15]

The image of contemplation which Thomas supplies is reminiscent of the
monastic art of memory which emphasized clarity and order in the construction of artificial memory palaces, the chief enemy of which is crowding or
randomness, or *curiositas,* or the busyness with many things which he mentions here.[16] The one whose memory is well-trained and well-ordered to the
contemplation of the truth will not be distracted by the "mental fornication"
of a mind wandering about in disorder, with no route to follow, but rather has
the power to cease at will to perform other tasks, "since he ordains the very
cessation." In any case, the groundwork is now laid for what will be the goal of
the rest of the *Summa,* leading the reader to beatitude, no matter how par-
tially participated this might be.

As he writes in article eight of the same question, "Final and perfect happiness can consist in nothing else than the vision of the Divine Essence."[17] As
the final cause of creation, it is therefore linked with the goal of the theological itinerary. As knowledge of God may be called true only inasmuch as it
participates in divine self-knowledge, the end of knowledge, the end of contemplation, is the very essence which effects such knowledge and makes it
possible. That is to say, the beatitude towards which we are drawn by virtue of
our creation is the same beatitude towards which our intellect strives by its
necessity for perfection; and the route towards this beatitude is effected by the
grace of divine creation. Or to put it more succinctly, "We run to God along
the road of God," as Hugh of St. Victor says.[18]

In other words, the reality of the eschatological consummation of our
knowledge in God's own knowledge is mirrored in the activity of the mind
engaged in imaginative dialogue with the interpretive fellowship I mentioned
earlier, such that participation in the triune life of God cannot be seen as a

15. *ST* IaIIae.iii.3, *ad* 4, emphasis mine.
16. See Mary Carruthers, *The Craft of Thought* (Cambridge: Cambridge University Press,
1998), pp. 82ff.
17. *ST* IaIIae.iii.8, *resp.*
18. Hugh of St. Victor, *In Praise of Charity,* ch. IV, in A Religious of C.S.M.V., tr., *The Divine
Love: The Two Treatises* De Laude Caritatis *and* De Amore Sponsi ad Sponsam (Oxford: A. R.
Mowbray & Co., 1956), p. 15.

kind of an *a priori* metaphysical first principle. Rather, the extent to which our lives participate in the life of the Trinity is inseparable from the "form of life" which makes Christians the kind of people they are, by training in the virtues of faith, hope, and charity, learned through the sacramental habituation of desire, or the liturgical ordering of memory, understanding, and will. Therefore Oliva Blanchette is quite right explicitly to relate the cosmological perfection of the universe with the perfection of the human being, as the latter is "the key and the center" of the former.[19]

Turning back to the first question of the *Summa,* we read in article six that *sacra doctrina* is "wisdom above all human wisdom," i.e., the very wisdom of God himself. Here Thomas identifies divine wisdom with divine knowledge, and indeed *sacra doctrina* is "especially called wisdom," because it participates in the perfectly ordered knowledge of God, in whom origin and end are one. The function of *sacra doctrina* therefore is to order our knowledge of God according to the divine pattern, wherein we must come to understand that our origin and our end are one and the same God. Thomas writes,

> This doctrine is wisdom above all human wisdom; not merely in any one order, but absolutely. For since it is the part of a wise man to arrange and to judge, and since lesser matters should be judged in the light of some higher principle, he is said to be wise in any one order who considers the highest principle in that order: thus in the order of building he who plans the form of the house is called wise and architect, in opposition to the inferior laborers who trim the wood and make ready the stones: *As a wise architect I have laid the foundation* (1 Cor. iii. 10).[20]

A medieval reader of this passage might have recognized immediately the mnemotechnical resonances of the artificial memory as a building which one must imaginatively construct in the mind. Thomas' invocation of 1 Corinthians 3:10 is also entirely appropriate, for this passage in effect became the foundation for an entire tradition of monastic memory-construction, so much so that it "gave license to a virtual industry of exegetical architectural metaphors," and during the Middle Ages "became the authority for a fully developed mnemonic technique, using the *planus* (and sometimes the *elevatio*) of a building laid out in one's mind as the structure for allegorical and moral meditation, the 'superstructures' *(superaedificationes)* of *sacra pagina.*"[21] And

19. Blanchette, *The Perfection of the Universe,* p. 7.
20. *ST* Ia.I.vi. *resp.*
21. Mary Carruthers, *The Craft of Thought: Meditation, Rhetoric, and the Making of Images, 400-1200* (Cambridge: Cambridge University Press, 1998), p. 17. It might also be argued that this

lest there be any suspicion that any correlation between Thomas' Pauline citation here and the medieval art of memory is purely accidental, it might be
dispelled by the fact that the Dominican order was "chiefly responsible for the
dissemination of the architectural mnemonic,"[22] and was the "single most active proponent and popularizer of memory as an art, and especially of the
principles of Tully."[23] Frances Yates speaks of a "well-head of enthusiasm for
artificial memory which is spreading throughout the Dominican Order" in
the thirteenth and fourteenth centuries.[24] Much of this is of course attribut-
able to Thomas Aquinas and Albert the Great; however, it reflects a long tradition of Dominican training in the art of memory which persisted up
through the fifteenth-century Italian Renaissance, during which it indeed
thrived, and into and beyond the Reformation period. Thomas Aquinas was
so identified with the art of memory that he became a kind of commonplace
authority on it (perhaps even its "patron saint") in sixteenth-century memory manuals, and his authority had not waned by the time of the publication
of Gregor von Feinaigle's *The New Art of Memory* in 1813.[25]

In any case, Thomas suggests that *sacra doctrina* resembles a house, which
is the product of wisely ordered composition. God has laid the foundation,
and it is the task of the theologian to invent upon this groundwork, to build
in proper order, the teaching of God's own knowledge. *Sacra doctrina* is,
therefore, not a set body of teaching *per se,* but the wisdom of God which is
the appropriate ordering of human knowledge to its proper end. Prudence is
the virtue required of the one who would be wise, and it is no accident that already in the very first question of the *Summa* we are given a hint as to what it

---

text became a foundation for an entire tradition of architecture as well, which understood the
structure of the cathedral (and the parish church) to function as "furnishing the routes of
prayer" (p. 261), and, particularly in the Gothic period, conceived churches as "meditation ma-
chines." See esp. ch. 5, "The Place of the Tabernacle."

22. Mary Carruthers, *The Book of Memory: A Study of Memory in Medieval Culture* (Cambridge: Cambridge University Press, 1990), p. 101.

23. Carruthers, *The Book of Memory,* p. 154.

24. Frances Yates, *The Art of Memory* (London: Routledge & Kegan Paul, 1966; Pimlico,
1992), p. 97.

25. Gregor von Feinaigle, *The New Art of Memory* (London: Sherwood, Neely, and Jones,
1813). See Frances Yates, *The Art of Memory,* pp. 93-94. "Thus a side of Thomas Aquinas who was
venerated in the ages of Memory was still not forgotten even in the early nineteenth century. It
is a side of him which, so far as I know, is never mentioned by modern Thomist philosophers.
And though writers on the art of memory are aware of II,II, 49 as an important text in its history, no very serious inquiry has been undertaken into the nature of the influence of the
Thomist rules for memory" (p. 94). Evidently the situation has not changed much since Yates
wrote this in 1966.

will behoove us to practice in this science. Though Thomas will not treat of the virtue of prudence directly until the *Secunda Secundae,* it is already clear that this is required for good reading, and along with prudence (good ordering) goes memory. It is perhaps more than curious that out of 512 questions in the *Summa,* the one dealing with prudence is the 280th in the series, which, regardless of whether one includes the *Supplementum,* falls roughly in the very middle of the work. Prudence, says Thomas, "consists in a right estimate about matters of action."[26] It is, as Josef Pieper writes, the "cause, root, mother, measure, precept, guide, and prototype of all ethical virtues; it acts in all of them, perfecting them to their true nature; all participate in it, and by virtue of this participation they are virtues."[27] It is therefore the first of the cardinal virtues, and for this reason it is mentioned at the very beginning of the *Summa.* For without that virtue which knows how to order things, signs, words, ideas, actions, and so forth to their proper referent, there can be no virtues at all. Moreover, there can be no good reading in the absence of the prudential ordering of associations. As I have already suggested, this requires the student to be both humble and patient, for the study of *sacra doctrina* requires that one's own knowledge be situated within an ontologically prior fellowship, which is to a large degree determinative of any theological statement which one might contribute to this ongoing discourse.

Prudence, then, is the virtue required if one is to become wise and to be led to union with Wisdom itself. As Aquinas writes,

> in the order of human life, the prudent man directs his acts to a fitting end: *Wisdom is prudence to a man* (*Prov.* x. 23). Therefore he who considers absolutely the highest cause of the whole universe, namely God, is most of all called wise. Hence wisdom is said to be the knowledge of divine things, as Augustine says (*De Trin.* xii. 14).[28]

The direction of acts to a fitting end (among which is included the consideration of the highest cause; i.e., contemplation) is therefore not divorceable

---

26. *ST* IIaIIae.xlix.4, *resp.*

27. Josef Pieper, *The Four Cardinal Virtues: Prudence, Justice, Fortitude, Temperance* (New York: Harcourt, Brace & World, 1965), p. 8. See Aristotle's discussion of the relationship of *phronesis* to the other virtues in *Ethics* VI.xiii, where he argues, modifying Socrates, that the other virtues are not forms of prudence, but rather imply it (p. 224): "So whereas Socrates thought that the virtues are principles (because he said that they are all forms of knowledge), we say that they imply a principle. Thus we see from these arguments that it is not possible to be good in the true sense of the word without prudence, or to be prudent without moral goodness." Aristotle, *Ethics,* tr. J. A. K. Thomson (London: Penguin, 1955), pp. 223-25.

28. *ST* Ia.i.7, *resp.*

from the activity of the memory, which is a constitutive component of prudence. Thomas' reference to Augustine's *De Trinitate* XII.14 is most curious, as that section of the book describes Augustine's account of sin as when the soul, "loving its own power, slides away from the whole which is common to all into the part which is its own private property."[29] The sin of the soul is the result of the wandering memory, which, by greed, assumes its own authority for the assignation of references for the things held in the memory.

> And so [the soul] finds delight in bodily shapes and movements, and because it has not got them with it inside, it wraps itself in their images which it has fixed in the memory. In this way it defiles itself foully with a fanciful sort of fornication by referring all its business to one or other of the following ends: curiosity *(curiositas)*, searching for bodily and temporal experience through the senses; swollen conceit, affecting to be above other souls which are given over to their senses; or carnal pleasure, plunging itself in this muddy whirlpool.[30]

This brings us back to the matter of *curiositas,* or that "mental fornication" which is the chief enemy of a well-ordered memory. This citation of Augustine, however, is perhaps sufficient to establish Thomas' inheritance of the Augustinian connection between a well-ordered memory and virtue; for as Aquinas links prudence with a good memory, Augustine here explicitly links sin (particularly as greed) with a bad one, using the very rhetorical categories of *curiositas* and "business" which invoke the Ciceronian tradition of memory arts. For Augustine, as for Aquinas, humanity is most itself when it is properly ordered to God as its own source and end, when it is engaged in that "return journey"[31] to God, for which, for Aquinas, the tour guide is prudence.

If wisdom is knowledge of divine things, as Aquinas hears Augustine say, then our knowledge of God must in some sense always *become* divine self-knowledge, as we are turned toward God through the practice of the cardinal and the theological virtues. In this sense, participation in divine knowledge is not an epistemic *a priori*, as I said before, which we can simply take for granted on account of our createdness. Rather, this participation is embodied in the social reality of the pedagogy of the church, where we learn that we are *made* partakers in the divine nature by God's self-gift, a reality which is never finally secured, but always somewhat precarious. Training in the virtues is

---

29. Augustine, *The Trinity* XII.14, p. 330.
30. Augustine, *The Trinity* XII.14, p. 330.
31. Augustine, *The Trinity* XII.14, p. 330.

therefore the "form" of our participation, the *ductus* of the proper orientation of our desire towards God. "For man's true honor is God's image and likeness in him, but it can only be preserved when facing him from whom its impression is received."[32]

As MacIntyre has suggested, theology is a kind of craft ordered towards the possession and transmission of skills, habits, and virtues, not to mention languages, necessary for any knowledge of God. As such, a "craft in good order has to be embodied in a tradition in good order. And to be adequately initiated into a craft is to be adequately initiated into a tradition."[33] This, however, points to the question of the relationship between "tradition" and the text which is said to inaugurate or constitute it, namely the Scriptures. If, then, training in *sacra doctrina* is a kind of apprenticeship of manuduction, how does the concept of tradition emerge in the *Summa Theologiae*? Does Aquinas have an account of it? And more importantly, what is the relationship between his notion of *traditio* and his theology of participation, both metaphysical and social?

Before turning to the *Summa*, it is significant to note that the concept of "tradition" is, at least in the modern period, most closely associated with the modern conception of *authority*, understood here as a static and codified deposit of irrefutable and incontrovertible probative truths. As George Tavard and Yves M. J. Congar have argued, the distinction between Scripture and the Church as two distinct authorities for theology begins with Henry of Ghent, who, in his *Commentary on the Sentences* (1276-92), asked the "regrettable" question: "Must we believe the *auctoritates* (= the *dicta*, the texts) of Sacred Scripture rather than those of the Church, or vice versa?"[34] Henry's answer to this question is not, according to Tavard, surprising. He simply "restates the classical principle, universally sponsored before him, that there is no ultimate discrepancy between the Church and Scripture."[35] Thus already in the generation immediately following Thomas Aquinas, the questions which will come to crisis in the sixteenth century are already incubating, and are beginning to be formulated in a way which, despite the attempts at an "orthodox" response to them from the likes of Henry of Ghent, initiates the point of no return for the question of the relation of Scripture and Tradition as two distinct "containers" of truth. Posing the question this way leaves one with one of two al-

---

32. Augustine, *The Trinity* XII.14, p. 331.

33. MacIntyre, *Three Rival Versions*, p. 128.

34. Yves M. J. Congar, O.P., *Tradition and Traditions: An Historical and Theological Essay* (London: Burns & Oates, 1966), p. 99. See also George Tavard, *Holy Writ or Holy Church: The Crisis of the Protestant Reformation* (New York: Harper & Bros., 1959), pp. 22ff.

35. Tavard, *Holy Writ or Holy Church*, p. 23.

ternatives: "To see the Church as subservient to Scripture is one way of doing this. There would be another: to view Scripture as thoroughly depending on the authority of the Church."[36]

By contrast, Heiko Oberman suggests that the notion of Scripture and Tradition as two distinct "sources" goes back at least to Basil the Great, who, in the treatise *On the Holy Spirit*, introduces "for the first time explicitly the idea that the Christian owes equal respect and obedience to written and to unwritten ecclesiastical traditions, whether contained in canonical writings or in a secret oral tradition handed down by the Apostles through their successors."[37] The specific context concerns the use of the word "with" as opposed to "in" in phrases such as "Glory to the Father *with* the Son, *together with* the Holy Spirit."[38] It bears noticing, however, that the distinction Basil makes is *not* between "Scripture" and "Tradition," but between *written* and *unwritten* teaching.[39] It is implied that Basil includes, under the heading "written teaching," not simply the canonical texts, but also the commentaries of the Fathers before him. The question therefore seems to be more about *writing* than about "sources." Basil's emphasis on the legitimacy of grammatical usage which has no *written* precedent, but only the precedent of historical usage, suggests that his criticism is directed towards those who demand something be validated by a written text before it can be used or spoken in worship. Thus for Basil, the unwritten traditions of the Church point towards the notion that theological usage, and indeed exegesis, is not entirely enclosed within the written text (a notion which, as I have argued, is a much later innovation). Rather, for Basil as for Augustine after him, the written traditions provide, in a sense, the cues for rhetorical invention, for imaginative performance of the written texts, which, though "containing" all things necessary for salvation, are not totalizing.[40]

36. Tavard, *Holy Writ or Holy Church*, p. 29.

37. Heiko A. Oberman, *The Harvest of Medieval Theology: Gabriel Biel and Late Medieval Nominalism*, 3rd ed. (Grand Rapids: Baker, 2000), p. 369.

38. St. Basil the Great, *On the Holy Spirit*, tr. David Anderson (Crestwood, N.Y.: St. Vladimir's, 1997), p. 17.

39. The text in question is found in *On the Holy Spirit* 66: "Concerning the teachings of the Church, whether publicly proclaimed *(kerygma)* or reserved to members of the household of faith *(dogmata)*, we have received some from written sources, while others have been given to us secretly, through apostolic tradition. Both sources have equal force in true religion" (p. 98).

40. This is a different position from that of the Fourth Session of the Council of Trent, where the "written books" are explicitly identified with the canonical books. "Scripture" therefore is defined according to the rules of Protestantism, whereby the Word of God is identical with the physical text of Scripture, thus rendering the prior notion of the coinherence of "Scripture" and "Tradition" unintelligible.

Therefore, it does not seem to be acceptable to make St. Basil, as the late medieval nominalists do, the legitimate Patristic progenitor of the "two-source" notion of authority. Inasmuch as Basil did become the accepted authority on this point, his fate seems to have rested on an unhappy translation of his τὰ μὲν . . . τὰ δέ ("on the one hand . . . on the other") into the Latin *partim . . . partim,* which was to become the conventional post-Tridentine formula.[41] The ambiguity of the Greek, then, does not allow us to attribute to Basil a fourth-century "theory" of Scripture and Tradition, nor to make of him a proto-Tridentine theologian. It is only later that the notion of Tradition as "the written and unwritten part of the apostolic message as approved by the Church" comes to be formulated in such a way as to begin the process of the reification of the two into separate "containers" or "sources." Although printing cannot be said to *cause* this reification, it certainly facilitates it, by actually contributing to the understanding of, first of all, the Bible as a physical "thing," and secondly, by hastening the rise of the "scriptural economy."

Oberman thus locates the "decisive late-medieval demarcation line" between the two different understandings of Tradition current in the fourteenth century. One of those lines, which he names "Tradition I," refers to the sufficiency of Scripture as the final authority in theological matters, but understands Tradition as the "mode of reception of the *fides* or *veritas* contained in Holy Scripture."[42] "Tradition II," by contrast, essentially refers to the "two-source" theory of written and unwritten apostolic traditions, and is regarded as the prototype of the Tridentine definition.[43] As Oberman, Congar, and Tavard have all shown, the chief proponents of the second description are Henry of Ghent, Gerard of Bologna, and the nominalists Pierre d'Ailly, Jean Gerson, William of Ockham, and Gabriel Biel.[44]

Therefore Oberman seems to be quite right in claiming that "late medieval nominalism can be regarded as the forerunner of the Tridentine formulation of the relation of Scripture and Tradition," but wrong to continue, "and is therefore in agreement with beliefs basic and characteristic for what has come to be known as Roman Catholicism." He concludes, "When catholicity is understood in this sense, we are altogether willing to defend the thesis that late medieval nominalism should be viewed as a basically catholic move-

---

41. Congar, *Tradition and Traditions,* p. 48.

42. Oberman, *The Harvest of Medieval Theology,* p. 372.

43. While the first of these two definitions of Tradition in the late medieval period does not seem to be entirely satisfactory, the second does more or less adequately illustrate the position that was to win out in the sixteenth century.

44. See Oberman, *The Harvest of Medieval Theology,* pp. 373-412; Tavard, *Holy Writ or Holy Church,* pp. 22-43; Congar, *Tradition and Traditions,* pp. 94-101.

ment."[45] This seems to me to be a tautology. It amounts to saying that if Catholicism can be understood as basically nominalist, then the nominalists are therefore quite catholic. This assessment entirely ignores the question of whether the Tridentine understanding of Tradition can rightly be regarded as "catholic," at least in a sense which is not bound to a radical separation between text and interpretation, between form and content, and finally, between rhetoric and ethics.

What Henry of Ghent established was the question of Tradition as a *problem*. While there were certainly those who thought of Tradition in terms of a source independent of Scripture, Henry's contribution was to set up Scripture and Tradition (or the Church) as two "sources" whose relationship requires resolution. While Basil had sought to recognize the legitimacy of unwritten "traditions," he suggested that these unwritten forms are more or less interpretative performances of the written texts.

Like Basil, Thomas Aquinas' use of the notion of Tradition has largely to do with the use of gestures and words in the liturgy, which are not necessarily found in Scripture. Of the mere eleven instances of the word *traditio* in the *Summa Theologiae,* nine of these are found in the *Tertia Pars,* and even there their use is quite varied. Two of these uses have nothing whatsoever to do with the modern concept of "tradition," in particular in Question 83, in which Thomas uses *traditio* to refer to Judas' betrayal of Jesus;[46] and also in a reference to Dionysius in Question 66, which mentions the "*conferring* of our most sacred and Godlike regeneration."[47] The other uses, though sparse, do illuminate what Thomas understands by "tradition."[48]

First of all, in the *Summa Theologiae, traditio* never refers to a codified deposit of teaching, as it would in later generations. Moreover, not only is *traditio* not explicitly opposed to *scriptura,* but in fact the latter performs the former. I say "performs" because for Aquinas it would be misleading to say that Scripture "contains" Tradition in the sense that Tradition is a kind of *item. Traditio,* rather, is a function of Scripture itself. As an objection to the question of whether the image of Christ should be adored *(latria),* he says, "But Scripture does not lay down anything concerning the adoration of images."[49] This trans-

45. Oberman, *The Harvest of Medieval Theology,* p. 428.

46. *ST* IIIa.lxxxiii.5, *ad* 3.

47. *ST* IIIa.lxvi.1, *ad* 1.

48. For an account of the variety of uses of *traditio* in Thomas Aquinas, with a focus on the Biblical commentaries, see Walter H. Principe, "'Tradition' in Thomas Aquinas' Scriptural Commentaries," in Kenneth Hagen, ed., *The Quadrilog: Tradition and the Future of Ecumenism. Essays in Honor of George H. Tavard* (Collegeville, Minn.: The Liturgical Press, 1994), pp. 43-60.

49. *ST* IIIa.xxv.3, *obj.* 4: *Sed nulla traditio in scriptura invenitur de ~~adorationis~~ imaginibus.*

adorandis

lation does not convey the sense of *traditio* in Thomas' words which, to take them literally, could read, "But there is nothing to be found in the tradition in Scripture concerning the adoration of images." "The tradition in Scripture": that is to say, that which is "handed down" in the sacred texts. What later came to be called "Tradition," then, in a certain fashion merely participates in the same function of Scripture, which is to pass on *sacra doctrina*. It is for this reason that Thomas identifies, in the first question, *sacra scriptura* with *sacra doctrina*.[50]

Therefore, *any* talk of the "place of tradition" in Thomas Aquinas (as in other contemporary writers such as Bonaventure) is destined to be misleading, for we are now virtually incapable of imagining either "scripture" or "tradition" in any other way than by analogy to books, independent repositories of "revealed" or "unrevealed" data.[51] Moreover, any discussion of "scripture" and "tradition" not only in Thomas, but especially in him, is bound to frame the question in Henry of Ghent's "regrettable" sense — i.e., in terms of an opposition between competing authorities. The caution must be, therefore, against employing the concept of Tradition as a kind of Agricolan *locus* or *topos*.

Thus we modern Ramists look in vain in the index or table of contents to the *Summa Theologiae* for the question on "Tradition." There is none. Far from being a *topos* in the Agricolan sense, it is not even a *topos* in the sense of one in a catena of sites ordered toward a rhetorical end, namely beatific vision, which, as I have shown, is Thomas' sense of the "topic." Nowhere does he treat the "concept" of Tradition because it is not for him a concept. It is rather an activity. Though there is no such thing as the "theory" (much less the "doctrine") of "Tradition" in Aquinas, there is the frequent *use* of *traditiones*, particularly in the scriptural commentaries. It is clear, then, that "Thomas nowhere presents a formal analysis of the theme of tradition."[52]

On the other hand, what *does* he mean by *traditio*, and in what sense can it be called a "source"? As I suggested earlier, Tradition is not a *locus* but an activity. Thus Walter Principe writes, "The active, dynamic force of Thomas Aquinas' use of the noun *traditio* can be grasped only by examining it in conjunction with the verb *tradere* from which it derives."[53] Though it may have other meanings, the overarching sense in which Aquinas uses *tradere* is in the sense of "handing over." Thus *tradere* is often employed in relation to

50. *ST* Ia.ii, *ad* 2.

51. G. Geenan, O.P. "The Place of Tradition in the Theology of St. Thomas," *The Thomist* XV (1952), pp. 110-35.

52. Walter H. Principe, "'Tradition' in Thomas Aquinas' Scriptural Commentaries," p. 51.

53. Principe, "'Tradition' in Thomas Aquinas' Scriptural Commentaries," p. 44.

doctrina, as well as to liturgical practices and customs, whether verbal or non-verbal. Hence in the reply to the objection above, he writes,

> The Apostles, led by the inward instinct of the Holy Ghost, handed down to the churches certain instructions which they did not put into writing, but which have been ordained, in accordance with the observance of the Church as practiced by the faithful as time went on. Wherefore the Apostle says (2 Thess. ii.15): *Stand fast; and hold the traditions which you have learned, whether by word* — that is by word of mouth — *or by our epistle* — that is by word put into writing. Among these traditions is the worship of Christ's image. Wherefore it is said that Blessed Luke painted the image of Christ, which is in Rome.[54]

The emphasis here, as in Question 83 on the rite of the Eucharist, is upon the active aspect of "handing on." In the latter we read, "As is stated in the last chapter of John (*verse* 25), our Lord said and did many things which are not written down by the evangelists; and among them is the uplifting of His eyes to heaven at the supper; nevertheless the Roman church had it by tradition from the apostles."[55] *Traditio* performs the same function as Scripture, that of handing down, passing on, teaching and practice. Yet the Scriptures themselves do not, as Aquinas points out, claim irrevocable closure for themselves. Indeed, the task of *tradere* is transmuted to the Apostles, and, by extension, to the doctors of the faith. As John implies, the continuing task of "writing" the Gospels falls upon the Apostles and their heirs, and writing does not necessarily guarantee the veracity of unwritten traditions.

Unlike later authors, Thomas does not, however, identify the Tradition (understood in the sense of transmitting teaching, whether verbal or nonverbal) of doctrine explicitly with the Magisterium.[56] The stress on writing seems to be important, insofar as Thomas' account does not privilege the textual character of an *auctoritas* over an unwritten custom. It is in this context that he writes,

> The custom of the Church has very great authority and ought to be jealously observed in all things, since the very doctrine of catholic doctors derives its authority from the Church. Hence we ought to abide by the author-

54. *ST* IIIa.xxv.4, *ad* 4.
55. *ST* IIIa.lxxxiii.4, *ad* 2.
56. For a treatment of Thomas' view of the teaching office of the Pontiff, see Francis A. Sullivan, S.J., *Magisterium: Teaching Authority in the Catholic Church* (New York: Paulist, 1983), pp. 71-75.

ity of the church rather than by that or an Augustine or a Jerome or any doctor whatever.[57]

The custom in question is the baptism of Jewish children against their parents' will. However, this does not seem to suggest that the "custom" of the Church has inviolable supremacy over the "authority" of a catholic doctor. The latter, to be sure, receives its doctrine from the Church, but in terms of a question of practice such as this, the unwritten custom of the Church is opposed not to the "authority" *per se* of catholic doctrine as found in the Fathers, but to the assumption that a written *auctoritas* has greater weight than an unwritten one on the sheer virtue of its being written. Thus Thomas here uses the concept of *auctoritas* (which in the thirteenth century suggests primarily a written text) against itself, as if to say, authority does not derive its essence from being written but from its handed-down character. Therefore it is not the case that Augustine and Jerome are not authorities to be trusted, but their written doctrine must be qualified, not by what we call "Tradition," but by the ongoing, interpretative teaching of the Church as we receive it. The locus of the Church's authority is not therefore entirely identical with the Magisterium, for even this derives its force by virtue of its being "handed over" by Christ to Peter.

The Magisterium, then, is not one "source" over and against the authority of Church doctors; on the contrary, both derive their prestige from the same act of *traditio* or handing-over: on the one hand the *traditio* of the teaching of Jesus to Peter, and on the other, the subsequent *traditio* of this *doctrina* to the apostles and their followers. Both acts of handing-over are, however, a single event, and whenever the Church teaches, whether it be the Magisterium or the doctor of the Church, it participates in the same single activity.

We can see that this is the case from Thomas' own use of the term *tradere* to refer to the exercise of theology. He describes, in the prologue to the *Summa,* that his aim in this work is *ea quae ad Christianam religionem pertinent, eo modo tradere, secundum quod congruit ad eruditionem incipientium* ("to hand down that which pertains to the Christian religion in a manner which befits the training of beginners"). He therefore refers the task of the transmission of Catholic teaching not to the bishops alone, but to himself, and, by extension, to other doctors.[58] In the prologue to the second question of the *Prima Pars,* he explains,

---

57. *ST* IIaIIae.x.12, *resp.*
58. See Per Erik Persson, *Sacra Doctrina: Reason and Revelation in Aquinas,* tr. Ross Mackenzie (Philadelphia: Fortress, 1970), p. 47.

Because the chief aim of sacred doctrine is to teach the knowledge of God, not only as He is in Himself, but also as He is the beginning of things and their last end, and especially of rational creatures, as is clear from what has already been said, therefore, in our endeavor to expound this science, we shall treat: (1) Of God; (2) Of the rational creature's advance towards God; (3) Of Christ, Who as man, is our way to God.[59]

Principalis intentio huius sacrae doctrinae Dei cognitionem tradere. The principle intent of Sacred Doctrine is to "hand over" the knowledge of God. Thus *traditio* is a theological performance, insofar as it describes the function of the theologian in transmitting teaching to his hearers. Here Alasdair MacIntyre's suggestion that theology is a kind of craft is most apposite. One might even say that for Aquinas, theology is, in the deepest sense, not only a craft but a *trade*.[60] From the very beginning of the *Summa Theologiae*, Thomas suggests to his readers that theology, the knowledge of God, is not the function of some kind of innate intuition of Being-Itself, but rather apprenticeship in the love of God at the feet of masters who must lead the student by the hand *(manuductio)* along the itinerary which he outlines in this prologue.[61] The whole enterprise of *sacra doctrina* involves a motion, from God back to Him-

59. *ST* Ia.ii, *prol.*

60. "Trade" (e.g., fishing, husbandry, etc.) seems to suggest less of a sense of mere utility to theology than "craft," which seems to suggest making something useful for some other purpose (e.g., woodworking, hide tanning, etc.), whereas *sacra doctrina* is not studied for the sake of some other science, but for its own sake. On the other hand, "trade," as the *Oxford English Dictionary* notes, comes not from the Latin *tradere*, but from the Middle English *trade*, whence "track." It too must be distinguished as a form of life as opposed to the trafficking in commodities, as, for example, "day traders." Nevertheless, the use of "trade" preserves at least the homophonous connection with *tradere*. Finally, the language of both "craft" and "trade" risks the reading of theology as one of the *artes serviles*, as opposed to that art alone which is done for its own sake, and to which all other sciences are subaltern (see Josef Pieper, *Leisure, the Basis of Culture*, tr. Gerald Malsbary (South Bend, Ind.: St. Augustine's, 1998). In this respect, "craft" does retain the explicit connection to the "seven crafts" of the medieval liberal arts curriculum (see *Oxford English Dictionary*, s.v. *craft*). In any case, both words suggest the connection between *sacra doctrina* and the training in skills and virtues necessary for such knowledge.

61. See also *ST* Ia.i.8, *ad* 2: "This doctrine is especially based upon arguments from authority, inasmuch as its principles are obtained by revelation: thus we ought to believe on the authority of those to whom the revelation has been made [the apostles]. Nor does this take away from the dignity of this doctrine, for although the argument from authority based on human reason is the weakest, yet the argument from authority based on divine revelation is the strongest. But sacred doctrine makes use even of human reason, not, indeed, to prove faith (for thereby the merit of faith would come to an end), but to make clear other things that are put forward in this doctrine [*ad manifestandum aliqua quae traduntur in hac doctrina*]."

self, through rational creatures, to and through Christ.[62] This motion corresponds to the same event of *traditio* which I just described: the movement of the reader towards God, the *skopos* of the *Summa,* is analogous to the movement of the continual handing on of the *doctrina* of the Church. Thus like the Church, and like the believer, the reader is never the beneficiary of an impetuous impartation of knowledge and wisdom; rather, the Church is inexorably joined to temporality as is the reader of the *Summa,* who, from the very outset of the text, learns that the process of training in the knowledge of God is a long and arduous one, requiring first of all the humility of a servant. As I showed in reference to the reading of the Song of Songs in the *Glossa Ordinaria,* the destiny of the individual reader may never be abstracted from the eternal goal of the Church, union with God. The historical, continuous *traditio* of the Church likewise implies the motion of the pilgrim city of God towards its own source and end, and as students of *sacra doctrina,* our future is of a piece with it. Students and teachers participate in the *traditio* of the Church, not as mere noetic dispensers and receptacles of information, but as its performers.

Hence what one might call the "coup" in Thomas' prologue, at least as far as modern ears are concerned. The declaration that *principalis intentio huius sacrae doctrinae Dei cognitionem tradere* places the role of the *doctores* at both a higher level and at a higher risk. The task of teaching sacred doctrine *is* a function of the bishop, but it is also the onus of the Dominican regent-master. Thus Thomas situates himself as an organ of tradition. But in doing so he also brings with him the chorus of voices and languages that constitute the *Summa.* Therefore "tradition" is, even for the regent-master, participation in the ongoing community of interpretation that is the Church, and therefore Aquinas simultaneously exalts and relativizes the position of the theologian.

Thus the *catholicae veritatis doctor* quite plainly points to Thomas himself, who understands it to be of the essence of his magisterial vocation to lead beginners out of ignorance *(e-rudire),* to reorder the disordered mind of the student towards its proper object: *ad eum pertinet etiam incipientes erudire.*[63] But the "doctor of Catholic truth" also points to the reader himself, as the fu-

---

62. See Rowan Williams, "What Does Love Know? St. Thomas on the Trinity," *New Blackfriars* LXXXII.964 (June 2001), p. 272: "Our relations to the other are continuous with and reflective of an eternal act; so much is implicit in the doctrine that we are made in the divine image, and in the connected recognition that all finite intelligent action is *activated* by the fact that God is eternally engaged in something like understanding. But this eternal engagement is never a possessing, because it is the act (the knowledge) of love; what is understood prompts and grounds something other than 'simple' intellection. That something other is not just an attitude of consent or approbation, but a movement to which desire is analogous."

63. *ST* Ia, *prol.*

ture teacher of theology. As Victor White explains, "the *doctor* or teacher is the reader for whom the book is designed and intended, the *incipientes* are among those whom he has to teach; for in fact there is nobody whom the teacher of Catholic truth can exclude from his teaching."[64] However, the *incipientes* themselves are to be understood, according to John Jenkins, as future "Masters of the Sacred Page."[65] This is simply to re-emphasize the pedagogical purpose of the *Summa*, which, as I have argued, is not merely to instill good disputational skills (though it includes that), but more profoundly, to lead the beginner into truth, towards God himself.

In this alone, says Thomas, resides the only hope of human well-being, *salus*. It is necessary for the rough-minded *(rudis)*, as it were, to know their true end *(finis)*, before they embark on the long apprenticeship of *sacra doctrina*. "But the end must first be known by men who are to direct their thoughts and actions to the end. Hence it was necessary for the salvation of man that certain truths which exceed human reason should be made known by divine revelation."[66] In the first question, Thomas shows the reader that the goal of the text, the *skopos*, is *salus*.[67] Moreover, the motion and direction

---

64. Victor White, O.P., *Holy Teaching: The Idea of Theology according to St. Thomas Aquinas* (London: Blackfriars, 1958), p. 12.

65. John I. Jenkins, C.S.C., *Knowledge and Faith in Thomas Aquinas* (Cambridge: Cambridge University Press, 1997), pp. 85-95. Jenkins' case, it seems to me, is overstated. Though he makes a strong argument that the *Summa* is intended for "a student pursuing a degree in theology, for an aspiring *Magister in sacra pagina*, or for someone at a comparable level" (p. 87), I do not think it follows that Thomas intended it to serve as a "final, comprehensive course for theology students" (p. 89). To state it flatly, Thomas makes no pretensions to finality or comprehensiveness. Jenkins' argument qualifies, in an important way, the stress on *incipientes*, while at the same time perpetuating a misplaced *topos* of twentieth-century Thomism, namely the reification of the *Summa Theologiae* into an encyclopedic "summary textbook" of the whole of the "scientific" study of theology — a notion which owes more to Rudolf Agricola and Peter Ramus than to Thomas himself.

Similarly, in light of the work of Leonard Boyle, who has argued that the *Summa* was composed to remedy specific deficiencies in Dominican moral teaching, it seems incorrect to conclude, as G. R. Evans does, that "It was the existence of a growing public and the need to find a means of organizing teaching on a large scale which provided the stimulus to which Aquinas responded in trying to provide a comprehensive textbook, a *Summa Theologica* [sic], for use by students of theology as an academic discipline." G. R. Evans, *Old Arts and New Theology: The Beginnings of Theology as an Academic Discipline* (Oxford: OUP 1980), p. 13. See also Leonard E. Boyle, O.P., *The Setting of the Summa Theologiae of Saint Thomas*, The Etienne Gilson Series 5 (Toronto: Pontifical Institute of Mediaeval Studies, 1982).

66. *ST* Ia.i.i, *resp.*: "But the end must first be known by men who are to direct their thoughts and actions to the end. Hence it was necessary for the salvation of man that certain truths which exceed human reason should be made known by divine revelation."

67. See White, *Holy Teaching*, p. 10: "'*Salus*' is not just 'salvation' in the sense of pie-in-the-sky:

of the work is implied, *ad humanam salutem; unde necessarium fuit homini ad salutem* — the *traditio* of holy teaching leads one to *salus,* which is, finally, the Triune God.

Thus we have seen how the character of the *Summa,* from the *exitus-reditus* scheme of the whole to the particular apparatus of the *quaestio* itself, is defined by a certain *motion. Sacra doctrina,* as *traditio,* is always first a movement of the soul into God, and as such, is an aspect of the human creature's participation in God himself. The peculiar type of *scientia* which is holy teaching is therefore always "borrowing" its principles from God.[68] Hence the role of the doctor is more aptly described as a "leading into" than as an "imparting of" knowledge. *Traditio* is a "handing over," not just of something known, but of the soul itself. In this sense, the *catholicae veritatis doctor* "hands over" his student to the teaching of the Church, to be led into wisdom, towards participation in the divine self-knowledge.

The beginner in theology, as I have said, benevolently "poaches" from her master — but not only from the master alone but from all the authorities to whom she is trained to listen. Theology has the character of being something "on loan" in perpetuity, as it were, in the sense that God alone is the teacher of catholic truth, and "the rest of us are its *doctores* only as the instruments for the imparting of a *veritas* which he alone strictly knows."[69] The assumption which Thomas makes throughout the *Summa* is that one is led into *salus* by relinquishing the wrongly-ordered desire for autonomy and placing oneself into the hands of masters, whose skills one acquires by participating in them by imitation. This teaching, which is "passed on" from the teacher to the student, inculcates in the latter a set of habits, skills, and virtues, which are likewise learned by *mimesis* of those to whom one must entrust oneself as higher authorities. Thus to practice the trade of theology is to deal in "copies," to teach and to learn a craft which one inherits by participation. In this sense,

---

it must be given its full significance of 'health', 'weal', 'well-being', 'total integration', here as well as hereafter. For similarly we must interpret *finis* not merely as the terminus of a yet uncompleted journey, but give it with St. Thomas the amplitude of *telos,* rounding-off, fulfillment or completion: an eternal life which not only awaits us hereafter but is already dwelling in us." One must resist the temptation to understand *salus* in a purely individual sense. For Thomas, the force of *salus* concerns everything which pertains to Holy Teaching. In that sense, one is compelled to understand *salus* as an entirely political activity. See Nicholas Lash, "Beyond the End of History?" in *The Beginning and the End of 'Religion'* (Cambridge: Cambridge University Press, 1996), pp. 252-64; John Milbank, *Theology and Social Theory: Beyond Secular Reason* (Oxford: Basil Blackwell, 1990).

68. *ST* Ia.i.6, *ad* 5: "Sacred doctrine derives its principles not from any human knowledge, but from the divine knowledge, through which, as through the highest wisdom, all our knowledge is set in order."

69. White, *Holy Teaching,* p. 8.

there is not one kind of participation that is "metaphysical" and another that is "social," much less "individual." One's participation in the trade of *sacra doctrina* is participation in knowledge, and as such it is necessarily kinetic. To master this craft is to become more of a "copy": the development of the skills of holy teaching is coextensive with the conforming of the human mind to the divine, and is therefore a continual *traditio* of the soul into God. For this reason, it is quite right to say that "the placing of imitation ahead of auton-omy suggests that, for Aquinas, borrowing is the highest authenticity which can be attained. One must copy in order to be, and one continues only as a copy, never in one's own right."[70]

How then, in terms of rhetoric, does Thomas hand over the apprentice to the mystical union? As Mark Jordan claims, "The *Summa Theologiae* is a structure for ordering the multiplicity of languages around topics and for ordering topics pedagogically to the illumination and attainment of the hu-man end."[71] The ordering of *sacra doctrina* according to its subject matter, God as he is the beginning and end of all things, is not simply a clever ar-rangement of divine *loci* according to how these are arranged in God himself (such a notion makes no sense whatsoever), but according to the origin and destination of all creation. That is to say, the *ordo* of the *Summa,* in mimick-ing the cosmological order itself, in its final return to God, traces the itiner-ary of the knowledge of God as it proceeds toward him. This is, again, an itinerary that must be performed, and it traces spaces which can only but be inhabited and traveled through. Inasmuch as the *ordo disciplinae* corre-sponds to the order of the subject matter of *sacra doctrina,* it can scarcely be over-emphasized that this *ordo* implies, indeed demands, the overarching as-pect of motion, and hence of temporality.[72] Therefore the *ordo disciplinae,*

70. John Milbank and Catherine Pickstock, *Truth in Aquinas* (London: Routledge, 2001), p. 10.

71. Mark D. Jordan, "The Competition of Authoritative Languages and Aquinas's Theologi-cal Rhetoric," *Medieval Philosophy and Theology* IV (1994), p. 87. For our purposes, it might be better to say "voices" instead of "languages," at least in terms of *auctoritates.* Jordan uses the term "languages" in a Wittgensteinian sense, and he intends it to cover three connected sets of linguistic features of the *Summa:* 1) the *modus loquendi,* or what he calls "technical terminolo-gies"; 2) the *auctoritates;* and 3) "the natural language *(lingua)* in which a *modus loquendi* is con-structed" (p. 72). In this context he cites a passage from the *Philosophical Investigations* which proves entirely fitting: "Our language can be seen as an ancient city; a maze of little streets and squares, of old and new houses, and of houses with additions from various periods; and this surrounded by a multitude of new boroughs with straight regular streets and uniform houses." Ludwig Wittgenstein, *Philosophical Investigations,* tr. G. E. M. Anscombe, 2nd ed. (Oxford: Basil Blackwell, 1958), p. 8.

72. See Brian Coffey, "The Notion of Order according to St. Thomas Aquinas," *The Modern Schoolman* XXVII.1 (November 1949), pp. 1-18.

the hierarchical arrangement of languages and voices, is consummated in an eschatological arrival.

However, theology is not a "site" at which one finally arrives; rather it represents the posture of an ever-incipient Church slowly and painfully approaching its goal of union, in an attempt to produce an acceptable response to the command to "follow me."[73] It is a pedagogy in which one is trained to "step back from the idolatry of some familiar tongue, the mother tongue"[74] and to be enlisted as a participant in a continuing community of interpretation, and "to lend one's lived time to the retelling of the text's narrative — which is to say, the reenactment of its teaching. The rhetorically minded reader sees that to read theology well is to be invited in as a protagonist in a curriculum that is a narrative, in a school of comprehensive persuasion."[75]

Thus the vision of apprenticeship in theological teaching which Thomas outlines in the *Summa Theologiae* is at once a grammatical one, by a training in how to read *signa* and *littera,* and a rhetorical one, by a leading out of ignorance as a function of persuasion. This persuasion has its end not in simple delight, but in a real charitable union with the "subject matter" of *sacra doctrina.* The rhetorical character of this persuasion is most eminently illustrated in the metaphor of manuduction, which Thomas uses to describe the act of "handing on" of this doctrine. *Traditio,* teaching, as we shall see, is a *manuductio,* a "leading by the hand."

All beings participate in God insofar as they *are* at all. Yet the need for *sacra doctrina,* as Thomas says, lies in the fact that human beings do not know the end toward which they are ordered. "Participation" may be an index of the creature's existing at all, but this does not imply that human beings partake of God's being merely as cause. Knowledge, participation in God's knowledge of himself, is not on this account an innate intuition which exhaustively perceives all that there is to be known; rather, as rational creatures humans do participate in God's knowledge, like our participation in being, *in via.* To participate in being is therefore to participate in knowledge, for the two are identical in God, but it is an event which is not yet finished. Only by returning to the causal

---

73. See Michel de Certeau, "The Weakness of Believing. From the Body to Writing, a Christian Transit," tr. Saskia Brown, in Graham Ward, ed., *The Certeau Reader* (Oxford: Basil Blackwell, 2000), pp. 214-43. See especially p. 217: "In the past, classical theology legitimately armed itself with references to 'authorities' which had 'truth' value (canonical texts, definitions of a doctrinal authority, 'Fathers' of the church, etc.); that is how theology explained its dependence on ecclesial society, which was, in the last instance, the only body capable of conferring authorization."

74. Jordan, "The Competition of Authoritative Languages," p. 90.

75. Jordan, "The Competition of Authoritative Languages," p. 89.

origin of our being, and thus of our knowledge, are human creatures made complete. God alone, therefore, knows things perfectly because he knows to what ends they are ordered, he alone knows their perfection; i.e., he knows himself perfectly.[76] The function of *sacra doctrina*, as Thomas understands it, is manifestly to participate in this knowledge, to know the true perfections of creatures, sensible and insensible, and most of all the *telos* of human life. To know something truly is to "catch it on its way back to God,"[77] and therefore to know ourselves truly, we must understand ourselves as ordered by God to himself, as our origin and end.

Thus the scope of the *Summa* as a rhetorical composition, and as a "curriculum of persuasion" corresponds to this return, to the leading of the reader back to the God in whom we already exist. As such, it must be stressed that this is not a result of rational exertion, but is ever understood as gift, as the gracious handing over of the rational creature back to its true source and end. This act of learning is simultaneously the process of sanctification, or of deification, of becoming more conformed to the mind of God. As Thomas says,

> For God is in all things by His essence, power, and presence, according to His one common mode, as the cause existing in the effects which participate in His goodness. Above and beyond this common mode, however, there is one special mode belonging to the rational nature wherein God is said to be present as the known is in the knower, and the beloved in the lover. And since the rational creature by its operation of knowledge and love attains to God Himself, according to this special mode God is said not only to exist in the rational creature, but also to dwell therein as in His own temple. So no other effect can be put down as the reason why the divine person is in the rational creature in a new mode except by sanctifying grace. Hence the divine person is sent, and proceeds temporally only according to sanctifying grace.[78]

Thus Aquinas likens the "mission" of the Holy Spirit to the procession of rational creatures towards the knowledge and love of God. The Spirit can then be spoken of as "proceeding" temporally by analogy to the drawing of humans into the divine life. Thus this motion of the *e-rudire* of the *incipientes* is a leading of the intellect into a greater degree of participation in the Trinity, which is, Thomas stresses, always a work of God himself, who is the true agent of our knowledge. To make this claim, then, has two consequences, one

---

76. See Milbank and Pickstock, *Truth in Aquinas*, p. 13.
77. Milbank and Pickstock, *Truth in Aquinas*, p. 12.
78. *ST* Ia.xliii.3, *resp.*

of which I have already mentioned. The first is that all our knowledge, and all our growth in knowledge, is for Aquinas simultaneously a growth in *being,* insofar as to know truly is to participate to some degree in the knowledge which God knows, and to enjoy the objects of our knowledge as ordered to their proper end in God. The second is the fact that the "teacher of catholic truth" likewise participates in the Spirit's mission to the Church, by handing over the soul of the student, and also by participating in the divine leading-toward-himself. In so doing, the *traditio* of sacred doctrine may correspond to the manuduction of the soul into God. Thus the doctor shares in the function of the Spirit, and in a way represents the "form" of the latter's work, as the *cura animarum.*

This brings us to a closer examination of the metaphor of *manuductio,* or "leading by the hand." The two terms, *manuductio* and *tradere,* are brought together in the fifth article of the first question of the *Summa,* where Thomas explains that *sacra doctrina* makes use of lesser sciences which do not borrow their principles, as it were, directly from God by revelation:

> That it thus uses them is not due to its own defect or insufficiency, but to the defect of our intelligence, which is more easily led by what is known through natural reason (from which proceed the other sciences), to that which is above reason, such as are the teachings of this science [*sacra doctrina*].[79]

Facilius manuducitur in ea quae sunt supra rationem, quae in hac scientia traduntur. The intellect, then, is "led by the hand," not simply to sacred doctrine, but to the *object* of sacred doctrine. That is to say, philosophy does not lead one to holy teaching as an irrevocable conclusion; rather, it leads one towards its object, a task which only *sacra doctrina* can complete.[80] Thus that which is "above reason," which is that with which *sacra doctrina* deals, is the

---

79. *ST* Ia.i.5 *ad* 2.

80. *ST* Ia.xii.12, *resp.*: "Our natural knowledge begins from sense. Hence our natural knowledge can go as far as it can be led by sensible things [*unde tantum se nostra naturalis cognitio extendere potest, inquantam manuduci potest per sensibilia*]. But our mind cannot be led by sense so far as to see the essence of God; because the sensible effects of God do not equal the power of God as their cause. Hence from the knowledge of sensible things the whole power of God cannot be known; nor therefore can His essence be seen. But because they are His effects and depend on their cause, we can be led from them so far as to know whether He exists, and to know of Him what must necessarily belong to Him, as the first cause of all things." Thus natural knowledge and *sacra doctrina* both, in some sense, perform the function of *manuductor*: the former can lead only so far, and the latter alone can truly lead one to beatitude. In this sense, the Dantean passage from Virgil to Beatrice as the *manuductor* of the itinerary to Paradise is an entirely Thomistic trope.

goal of the *manuductio*, not (formally, at least) *sacra doctrina* itself. As he states in the commentary on Hebrews, "For the Lord wanted to lead us by the hand to intelligible and spiritual things."[81] In other words, even philosophy aims at some kind of beatitude, though the mind cannot be led to this beatitude except by participating in beatitude itself, which is apprenticeship in holy teaching.[82] Thomas therefore makes an explicit link between the manuduction of the intellect into God and the "handing over" of theological teaching. To be an apprentice in theology is to be led by the hands of one's masters, not unlike children, to whom Thomas likens the *incipientes* in the prologue to the *Summa*.

That which holy teaching passes on leads one to beatitude, and the act of passing on this teaching is, for Aquinas, participation in the work of God in leading the intellect to himself.[83] Therefore to be the object of the discursive *traditio* of the Church's teaching is at the same time to be led by the hand, which in turn is to participate in a procession of the Spirit to creatures, which again is coextensive with the return of the pilgrim city of God to its origin and end. These are all phases, as it were, of the same event. The *traditio* is the *manuductio* is the *reditus*.

This is seen in Thomas' rejection of the Platonic doctrine of recollection, whereby the soul recovers what it knew from the beginning, by being disposed to receive intelligible forms, or, as he puts it, the soul "is roused by [the teacher] to remember what he knows." His reason for rejecting this lies in his

---

81. Thomas Aquinas, *In Hebr.* VIII.5: *Dominus enim voluit nos ad intelligibilia et spiritualia manuduci.* Quoted in Henri de Lubac, *Medieval Exegesis,* vol. II, tr. E. M. Macierowski (Grand Rapids: Eerdmans, 2000), p. 185.

82. It seems to me that John Milbank is therefore quite right to describe "faith" and "reason" as "successive phases of a single extension," because both seek not the same "conclusions," but the same object. For Aquinas the object of philosophy is, as for Aristotle, happiness, but it is through *sacra doctrina* that one is truly led to beatitude by participating in it. In this sense, the "Meno problematic" makes sense in reference to theology: one learns to know and love God by participation in him, and by being led by the hand into the knowledge and love of him. See "Truth and Vision" in Milbank and Pickstock, *Truth in Aquinas,* pp. 18-59.

83. If the teacher can be said really to teach something new to the student that was not known before, then it must be said that the former participates in the illumination of the mind, which is the work of sanctifying grace, as we have seen. For this reason Thomas rejects the notion of recollection in the *Meno,* where learning is described as a recovery of the things known in a previous mode of existence. For Aquinas this is ultimately a denigration of human knowledge, not an exaltation of it. For to claim that nothing new at all can be known is tantamount to claiming that the human intellect lacks the power to lead and to be led into beatitude, which for Aquinas is to claim that there is some kind of knowledge which is outside of God. Likewise, though Thomas does inherit some degree of Platonic recollection, his account is teleologically ordered to the participation in that to which all memory ultimately refers, the Trinity.

insistence that the "passive intellect of the human soul is in pure potentiality to intelligible (species)."[84] The human creature naturally desires beatitude, though it does not know how to name it; this is the function of the "light of the active intellect," which must, in a sense, be "activated" by the teacher. For Aquinas, then, Platonic recollection demands an external act of disposition of matter to receptivity. This is altogether insufficient to account for the interior principle of the created intellect as participated *scientia*. The human creature more real-ly participates in the divine for Aquinas than for Plato, since to learn anything is to be reduced from potentiality to act — that is, to be "caused" by another to know. In this sense, the teacher does not act as a mere disposing agent, but as participating in the divine causality of knowledge. And though the teacher acts as the exterior principle, or as he says, "only brings exterior help," he nonetheless participates in the principal cause of knowledge, God himself. The exterior help of the teacher is therefore not the "principal agent," for this is the "interior light of the intellect"; however, as the physician strengthens nature, and employs food and medicine, of which nature makes use for the intended end,[85] so the teacher truly "moves" the learner toward the object of *sacra doctrina*. In so doing, the *traditio* of holy teaching is seen in its double sense: it is both a handing over of the Church's doctrine, but at the same time a handing over of the learner back to God. Moreover, the restoration to *salus* represents the handing over of the student back to himself. The principle of knowledge lies in the interior light of the intellect, which must now be actualized, and this happens by ordering it to its proper end. In this way, then, the activity of the intellect is not a super-added *scientia*, but the inchoate motion of the soul back to its origin. For this reason, Thomas says, "The Master does not cause the intellectual light in the disciple, nor does he cause the intelligible species directly: but he moves the disciple by teaching, so that the latter, by the power of his intellect, forms intelligible concepts, the signs of which are proposed to him from without."[86]

God is the cause of knowledge of him. However, this is not Platonic recollection redux. On the contrary, Thomas rejects the latter because, for one thing, it is unreasonable to suppose that the union of the soul with the body is the condition that must be overcome in order for the intellect to become receptive to knowledge. As he states, "It is unreasonable that the natural operation of a thing be totally hindered by that which belongs to it naturally."[87] That

84. *ST* Ia.cxvii.1, *resp.*
85. *ST* Ia.cxvii.1, *resp.*
86. *ST* Ia.cxvii.1, *ad* 3.
87. *ST* Ia.lxxxiv.3, *resp.*

is, the body belongs naturally to the soul, and it is not a hindrance to knowledge to be embodied. Rather, for Aquinas, who now overcomes the alleged dualism of soul and body, it is indeed through sensible things that the mind is led back to God. It is through "the signs that are proposed to him from without" that the disciple may form the concepts which "move" him.

The second reason why Thomas' account surpasses simple recollection is that his account is altogether more inscribed in a *body*, in the sense in which I just mentioned, and also in the sense of being responsible to a political community which is historically prior to one's own knowing. In a sense, Aquinas agrees with the assertion that all knowledge is remembering; yet it is not a solipsistic recovery of that which the individual once knew. Instead, all knowledge is, for Aquinas, discipleship in the interior light of faith which leads one from the known to the unknown — an apprenticeship of the embodied intellect in the trade of sacred doctrine. Thus one really *can* learn something one did not know before; but part of what makes such knowledge true is that someone *did* know it before, and knew it to be true, precisely because they had received it. And their reception of this teaching required not the solipsistic disposition towards receptivity; it required a real movement into being, into the transcendental cause of our being, which we find at the same time to be our eschatological destiny. Yet this we can only be taught. Consequently the role of the teacher has a great deal more risk than for the "Platonists." To lead a student back to himself, and back to God, is fraught with a great deal more risk of failure than is the task of making one receptive to what is already there. In other words, in the account of recollection that Aquinas rejects, there is nothing to be learned which threatens one with the specter of unfamiliarity; yet for Aquinas, the training in holy teaching requires a certain amount of suffering knowledge that exposes us to who we truly are. The itinerary of the soul into the unknown and the unloved is fraught with danger, and for this reason one needs to be led by the hand. Moreover, inscribed within the ecclesial community of interpretation, the activity of *sacra doctrina* is a performance of memory, not of mere independent recollection of known data, but of a different kind of receptivity — one which assumes the knowledge one learns is not one's own, and is not property. Instead it is obtained through the posture of prayer, of humbly listening to those who "know better." For this reason Thomas says, "Wherefore anyone who teaches, leads the disciple from things known by the latter, to the knowledge of things previously unknown to him; according to what the Philosopher says (*Poster.* i.1): *All teaching and all learning proceed from previous knowledge.*"[88]

88. *ST* Ia.cxvii.1, *resp.*

This, then, is the role of the master, who "leads [*ducit*] the disciple from things known to knowledge of the unknown"[89] in one of two ways: 1) "by proposing . . . certain helps or means of instruction," such as "less universal propositions" or sensible examples (either similitudes or oppositions); 2) by "strengthening the intellect of the learner," which, he is quick to point out, is not "by some active power as of a higher nature," but by a certain "order of principles to conclusions." In this way, "the intellect of the learner is led [*manuducitur*] to the knowledge of truth previously unknown."[90] Thus the function of demonstration is causing knowledge in a hearer which did not exist before.

Though the *ordo* mentioned here does not explicitly refer to the *ordo disciplinae* of the *Summa*, it might as well, for as I have argued, the rhetorical structure of the text operates as a kind of pedagogical itinerary of the manuduction of the soul to the beatific vision, the tools of which are the "demonstrative" apparatus of the *quaestiones*, taken together in a series which proceeds from God as the cause and origin of creatures to God as their final end. However, it is imperative to insist that Aquinas does not separate "mind formation" from the teleological formation of the whole person, and neither does he separate the "academic" study of *sacra doctrina* from contemplation.

To be a master or an apprentice in *sacra doctrina* is not simply to traffic in demonstrations; it is finally and most fittingly, to live the contemplative life.[91] It is in contemplation that Thomas situates the locus of the activity of the interior light of the intellect, in its movement towards beatitude. Thus the structure of the *Summa* must not be abstracted from its pedagogical purpose of instilling in its readers the skills necessary for the contemplation of the truth which is God. Thomas' aim, if we are to take him at his word, is to lead his students by the hand toward the beatific vision, by means of the practice of contemplation. At the same time, by beatific vision he understands the perpetual, unbroken contemplation of God as he is in himself (Augustine's timeless "reading"), which is only possible in eternity. Contemplation, in this eschatological sense, is synonymous with union, because to be joined to God in eternity is to participate fully in his knowledge of himself, to "see face to face." Thus contemplation is the "end of the whole human life."[92] Having said

89. *ST* Ia.cxvii.1, *resp.*: *"Ducit autem magister discipulum ex praecognitis in cognitionem ignotorum dupliciter."*

90. *ST* Ia.cxvii.1, *resp.*: *"Ex quibus intellectus addiscentis manuducitur in cognitionem veritatis ignotae."*

91. See A. N. Williams, "Mystical Theology Redux: The Pattern of Aquinas' *Summa Theologiae*," *Modern Theology* XIII.1 (January 1997), pp. 53-74.

92. *ST* IIaIIae.clxxx.4, *resp.*

this, it should be evident that it is not the case that he simply wants to convince his readers of the inscrutable validity of his arguments and the irrefutable necessity of his conclusions; rather, he intends to persuade and to move them towards a *skopos*, a particular *kind of life*. And the *Summa*, as a structure designed to lead one into contemplation, is the *ductus* by means of which he attempts to conduct us thereunto.

The contemplative life, then, represents for Aquinas the school of persuasion unto beatitude. Does this mean that all that precedes the 180th Question of the *Secunda Secundae* has not been contemplation, but of another order? In this question, he addresses the question of the contemplative life as such, not "contemplation" *per se*. Whereas I have argued that the whole pedagogical architecture is a kind of *ductus* which leads one to the wisdom which is beatitude, through the prudential ordering of knowledge to its proper ends, it seems to follow that *sacra doctrina* is a training in and towards contemplation, as this is understood as "the simple act of gazing on truth." One has therefore to be trained to gaze in this way — it is not an innate skill. Thus while contemplation may be the result of an education, it also denotes the basic posture of *sacra doctrina*. It is through the appetitive power that the intellect is moved to practice the act of contemplation. And therefore he confirms here what he had said in the third question, namely, that "We draw near to God by no corporeal steps, since God is everywhere, but by the affections of the soul, and by the actions of that same soul do we withdraw from Him."[93]

In fact, when contemplation is understood as the goal of the student of sacred doctrine (even if this is taken to mean the momentary, ecstatic "experience" of union), becoming proficient in this art, as it were, requires a prior movement of the intellect from the consideration of sensible objects, in which all knowledge begins, to the perfection of contemplation in beatific union, in a series of manuductions. Knowledge of sensible objects leads to knowledge of intelligible objects, which leads to judgment, and so on.[94] One must be guided by the hand to the life of contemplation; but the contemplative life itself is understood as the *manuductio par excellence* of the mind to God.[95] As he states, commenting on Romans 1:20, "the contemplation of the divine effects also belongs to the contemplative life, inasmuch as man is guided thereby to the knowledge of God."[96]

93. *ST* Ia.iii.1, *ad* 5.
94. *ST* IIaIIae.clxxx.4, *ad* 3.
95. One must be careful, then, to distinguish between contemplation as the *finis* of human life, and contemplation as the *manuduction* of the intellect towards this end. Nevertheless, they are both "phases within a single extension" (see above, n. 82), and participate in one another.
96. *ST* IIaIIae.clxxx.4, *resp.*

Hence the operation of the intellect is described as movement toward the intellect's perfection.[97] This claim, at the end of the second part, brings us back to the very beginning of the *Prima Pars,* where it was shown that human knowledge possesses an inchoate desire for beatitude, which, we are now shown, is perfected in the movement of the intellect in contemplation. There, in the second question, he says, "For man naturally desires happiness, and what is naturally desired by man must be naturally known to him." God, he says, is man's beatitude. Thus Question Two of the first part already anticipates the reply given much later on, at the end of the second part: "Now contemplation of the truth befits a man according to his nature as a rational animal: the result being that *all men naturally desire to know,* so that consequently they delight in the knowledge of truth."[98]

This brings us to the following conclusions: 1) for Aquinas contemplation is both the *finis* of the whole of human life, and the practice by which one comes to participate more fully in God's self-knowledge; 2) the structure of the *Summa* may be described as "contemplative" in posture, insofar as this is understood as constituted by a series of manuductions from sensibles to the contemplation of God himself; and 3) the interest in persuasion is not merely "academic" but involves the real "movement" of the learner towards the object of *sacra doctrina,* which is finally perpetual contemplation in union with the Trinity.

The manuduction of theology, the rhetorical means by which Thomas convinces and moves his reader to a particular kind of life, comes to a climax at the end of the *Secunda Secundae,* wherein he argues that the religious life is, more than the active, best suited to the contemplation of God. Therefore as a school of persuasion, the life of the religious is eminently ordered towards this end. It is the pedagogical site of the production of the virtues necessary for such a life, and therefore the "privileged regime of moral formation, the state in which one is most likely to be taught how to attain to God."[99] This is so because the religious community is a kind of fellowship of *manuductores* and *incipientes,* masters under whose apprenticeship one may best be personally "led by the hand" unto beatitude. To put it more crudely, the religious life, then, is the "trade school" of *sacra doctrina par excellence.*

Therefore, as Mark Jordan has argued, "Thomas is not describing reli-

97. *ST* IIaIIae.clxxx.6, *resp.*
98. *ST* IIaIIae.clxxx.7, *resp.*
99. Mark D. Jordan, "Thomas Aquinas on Bernard and the Life of Contemplation," in John R. Sommerfeldt, ed., *Bernardus Magister: In Celebration of the Nonacentenary of the Birth of Saint Bernard of Clairvaux: 1090-1990,* Cistercian Studies 135 (Kalamazoo: Cistercian Publications, 1992), p. 458.

gious life as an education; he is proposing the religious life as a response to the reader's desire for contemplative beatitude."[100] Here one finds, at last, the *skopos* of the second part. The goal is not the transmission of information about "contemplation" or the virtues; rather it is the persuasion of the reader to enter the school of charity wherein one may best be led back to the origin and end of all that is. In the penultimate article of the *Secunda Secundae,* Thomas asks "Whether one should induce another to enter religion." He might as well have asked, "Whether *I* should induce *you* to enter religion," for by now it is clear to the reader that Thomas has every intention to recommend the religious life to the reader, and that the itinerary which he has been following leads him here. In fact, the objections to this article anticipate an attitude perhaps not entirely uncommon in undergraduates, who more than once might have been heard to retort a modernized version of the sentiment that "no one should induce another to do what is to his prejudice."[101] Perhaps, if Thomas' students were already Dominicans, this argument would have been already redundant. Nevertheless, it suggests that the pedagogy of persuasion in which Aquinas is involved is also aimed at those *incipientes* who have not entered a religious order, and to those Dominicans who are to persuade others to join them. The result is that the *manuductio* of Thomas' argument has led the reader, hopefully, to the novitiate, and that the Dominican regent-master has, in the course of the *traditio* of holy teaching, participated in the *traditio* of the learner to another set of *magistri,* another set of manuductors, who will continue the training in contemplation.

The metaphor of *ductus* has been shown to be critical in Aquinas' rhetorical-theological curriculum. As I have argued, the *ductus* of the text as a whole, from the treatment of God in the *Prima Pars,* to the treatment of rational creatures in the second part, to the Christ in the third, is one aspect of this. Another is the principle of manuduction, which is the process of "handing over" sacred doctrine, and of being "led by the hand" towards its object. Essential to this notion is the assertion that there is no knowledge which is learned alone or simply "recovered," and that one must be inscribed as an apprentice within an ongoing fellowship, or guild, consisting of those who are more skilled and more virtuous than oneself.

The final metaphor, that of *inductio,* we encounter here, with its explicit relation to persuasion. The question concerning entrance into religious life is framed in terms of a "leading into," which at the same time recalls the necessarily political quality of *manuduction,* but also points to the *ductus* as the

---

100. Jordan, "Thomas Aquinas on Bernard," p. 458.
101. *ST* IIaIIae.clxxxix.9, *obj.* 3.

rhetorical scheme by means of which one is convinced of something or moved to some different kind of *habitus*. Thus the *inductio* into the religious life in which Thomas understands himself to be participating is bound up with the overall rhetorical project of the *Summa*. To persuade, to move, is to lead one into a new form of life, in which one may come to know what and whom one previously did not.

To that end, then, the *Tertia Pars*, whose place in the larger scheme of the text has been the subject of much anxiety among scholars for years, seems to fit quite logically. In fact, the claim made by some (including Chenu)[102] that the Christological part of the *Summa* appears only as a kind of appendix, emerges as altogether misguided. If what I have been arguing is true, and if Jordan is right about Thomas' urgent insistence upon the religious life, and moreover, if contemplation is the goal of human life, and if this contemplation is of God as he is in himself, then it follows that the "Christological part" altogether more emphatically grounds the *esse* of God in Jesus Christ. For to begin to consider God "face to face" is to begin to consider the Incarnation. The building up to this part more decisively situates *sacra doctrina* as an apprenticeship whose basic mode is one of participation in God's self-knowledge. As a result, this will come to a fuller realization in the Eucharist, where the "metaphysical" and "social" aspects of participation are completely integrated.

The religious life, then, offers the preeminent site for the cultivation of a well-ordered memory, chiefly because of its constitution as a fellowship of masters and apprentices in the school of charity. Moreover, the implication of Thomas' recommendation of the religious life is that it is only through participation in the daily liturgy that the training in *sacra doctrina* may be perfected. That is to say, for Thomas Aquinas, the monastery or the priory is the school of persuasion par excellence, because it is the school of the well-ordered memory. As he will show in the *Tertia Pars*, the prudential ordering of knowledge towards wisdom is a skill which is learned and mastered liturgically. To that end, then, in the next chapter I will argue that Aquinas' discussion of the rite of the Eucharist provides a picture of what it might mean to be in possession of a "liturgically trained memory." The liturgy, it will be argued, is the grammar of participation from which all other similar grammars are derived, and to which, one might even say, they are subaltern.

---

102. Marie-Dominique Chenu, O.P., *Toward Understanding St. Thomas* (Chicago: Hugh Regnery, 1964), p. 310.

7 Liturgically Trained Memory

As I argued in the last chapter, Thomas recommends the religious life because it is preeminently the school of charity. As I hope to argue in this chapter, because it represents the ideal form of the pedagogy of love, it is also the school of memory. Through the participation in the liturgical life of the religious community, one is trained how to love rightly. But this can only happen through the proper ordering of the memory and the understanding, which are united together in the will. Thus in Question 83 of the *Tertia Pars,* Thomas' reading of the rite of the Eucharist, he illustrates how the ritual performance of and participation in the liturgy of the Mass train the soul to remember well, in such a way as to guide one toward the beatific vision. As such, it can be argued that, for Aquinas, the liturgy is the only proper art of memory.

From the liturgical ordering of memorial associations to their proper referent, the Trinity, therefore, all other arts of memory are subordinate and derivative. That is to say, the art of memory which the *Summa* itself inculcates as a pedagogical form derives its structure from the antiphonal character of liturgy itself. Thus the famous *sic et non* character of the *Summa* will be seen to be dependent not upon the postulation of a properly "scholastic method," but upon the daily training in memory in which the religious life consists.

The modern reader of Aquinas, particularly in view of the textual presentation of the *Summa Theologiae* in modernity, such as McDermott's version, is in constant need of the reminder that the pedagogical culture in which Thomas studied and taught cannot be abstracted from the "form of life" which makes such inquiry intelligible. Thomas is, after all, a Dominican religious. This point can hardly be overemphasized, given the modern amnesic obsession with separating his "philosophical" material from his "theology." Moreover, it is imperative that one recall that the *Summa* consists not of discrete "topics" or "commonplaces," but rather constitutes a coherent didactic itinerary of the soul. Just as one could not hope to get from London to Aberdeen only by being instructed as to the middle leg of the journey, the pedagogical project of the *Summa* is subverted by turning its "parts" into separate "books." This is already the case in the generation immediately following Aquinas' death, when the *Summa* was promptly divided into separate containers, each consisting of its own discrete theology, whether of God, of morality, or of Christ.

Of all the parts of the *Summa,* the third is by far the least prominent in terms of extant manuscripts. For every one manuscript of the *Tertia Pars,* nearly three exist of the *Secunda Pars,* which is of course the most popular part in the Middle Ages.[1] In the modern period, the third part remains the least discussed and most often ignored portion of the work. This is perhaps due not least to the influence of Chenu, for whom it "would seem to play the role of no more than a part added to the whole as an afterthought."[2] The work of Michel Corbin, for example, has sought to correct this perception by arguing that the third part is in fact the consummation of the whole project.[3] In any case, it is crucial for understanding how, in Thomas' account, rhetoric is consummated in the liturgy.

Thomas treats the Mass as a kind of rhetoric designed to teach, to move, and to persuade. Yet, as I argued in the case of Augustine's account of the conversion of Victorinus in the *Confessions,* the liturgy of the Mass turns out to be the only rhetoric properly so called, since it teaches truly, moves one's affections to God himself, and persuades or leads one into participation in the triune life of God. As such, this participation is at once metaphysical and social, since to participate in the Trinity is at the same time to participate in the ecclesial reality of the Body of Christ, in a sense "effected" by the Eucharist. Thus the rite of the Mass is *the* grammar of participation, from which all others are derived.

Aquinas' treatment of the eucharistic rite in Question 83 is not typically regarded as being of great theological importance. This is partly understandable, given the "provincial" character of much of his discussion of different li-

1. According to my best calculations from H. F. Dondaine, *Codices Manuscripti Operum Thomae de Aquino.* Recensuerunt H. F. Dondaine et H. V. Shooner, cooperantibus sociis Commissionis Leoninae (Rome: Leonine Commission, 1967-). So far, these manuscripts have been cataloged alphabetically only as far as Paris.

2. Marie-Dominique Chenu, O.P., *Toward Understanding St. Thomas,* tr. Albert M. Landry, O.P., and Dominic Hughes, O.P. (Chicago: Hugh Regnery, 1964), p. 310.

3. Michel Corbin, *Le Chemin de la Théologie chez Thomas d'Aquin* (Paris: Beauchesne, 1974), pp. 801-2.

turgical practices and customs. Nonetheless, as the translator of this question, Thomas Gilby, writes in the footnote to this question in the Blackfriars edition,

> The first art. [*sic*] is the only one of directly theological interest; arts. 2-6 are concerned with canonical and rubrical prescriptions and the liturgical words and actions observed in the main, despite a variety of local uses, by the Western Church at the time and for nearly seven centuries afterwards. . . . The discussions, which are characteristic of their period and evince more devotion to the liturgy as a present fact than informed appreciation of its historical development, may be read with profit, and not merely by a medievalist in an archaeological spirit.[4]

Again we are back to McDermott, and to those parts of the *Summa* which are "mainly of historical interest."[5] Evidently articles two to six of this question comprise one of those parts, as they are omitted from McDermott's edition. I suspect the decision to excise them is related to the suspicion that they are not of "directly theological interest," but such a claim would depend upon the assumption that "canonical and rubrical prescriptions" and "liturgical words and actions" are not theological matters. On the other hand, this neglect may arise from the fact that the "sources" invoked in these five articles are not straightforwardly theological or philosophical texts, but rather local traditions, canonical decrees and liturgical customs. Nonetheless, as I showed in chapter five, this suspicion is unfounded.

It is doubtful that Thomas would have considered liturgical words to be of no, or at least scant, theological concern. It is perhaps more symptomatic of modern suspicions of "rhetoric" that McDermott and others disregard the grammatical structure of the liturgical rites as not addressing "real" questions of theology, concerned as these latter are with topics such as "God" and "Christ" and "transubstantiation." However, does not this subtle deafness to the words used in the liturgy betray a strategy of representation, whereby the form is more or less irrelevant to the content of a given subject? In what follows, it should become clear that the words and actions involved in eucharistic performance are conceived by Aquinas to be of paramount theological importance, and indeed, he spends a good deal of time analyzing these words and gestures precisely because he takes them to "mean" something.

Though our modern commentators do not go so far as to call such words

4. *ST* IIIa.lxxxiii.1, n. "a," Blackfriars, vol. 59, p. 132.

5. Timothy S. McDermott, ed., *Summa Theologiae: A Concise Translation* (Westminster, Md.: Christian Classics, 1989), "Editor's Note," p. xiv. See Chapter Five, "Reading Immemorially."

and gestures "ridiculous," Aquinas does seem to anticipate the presumption that these actions are not theologically significant in the response to the fifth objection in Article 5 of Question 83, where he says, "The actions performed by the priest in a mass are not ridiculous gestures, since they are done so as to represent something else."[6] His example here is the priest's outstretching arms, which recall the "outstretching of Christ's arms upon the cross."[7] Thus the function of this gesture is to remind the communicant of Christ's sacrifice — presumably not a theologically uninteresting matter. The gesture is important because it not only teaches us about Christ's death as an offering for us, but it also aims at persuading us to participate in that sacrifice. Hence in this particular liturgical example, the memory is bound together with understanding and will — the recollection of the crucifixion does not simply remind or recollect, it orients one toward the future, and it draws the soul into participation in the political community of the Body of Christ. By imaging this body, the priest re-performs the divine initiative of making the church one body through Christ's sacrifice. In other words, the memory is trained to remember rightly. A man standing in front of an altar with his arms spread wide, points not to anything whatsoever, but to a particular act which is remembered in the historical memory of the church, particularly in the context of the liturgical story. Thus reference to the body of Christ on the cross requires the trope, learned in liturgical practice, that these outstretched arms point not to themselves but to another body, which we are to become.

Therefore, far from denigrating rhetoric to the level of frivolous bombast, Aquinas gives rhetoric its proper place, though reorienting it as an architectonic of desire. By construing the rite of the Mass in terms formerly reserved for the rhetorical arts, he transforms rhetoric into the truly teaching, the truly moving, and the truly persuasive art by arguing that speech is made perfect by becoming praise, and by the liturgical borrowing of language inherited from an ontologically prior community of readers and interpreters. That this community is transformed from a mere collective readership into a universal fellowship of worship represents the final perfection, as it were, of rhetoric, as it is transformed into liturgy.

Hence Aquinas continues what was begun in Augustine's *De Doctrina Christiana,* namely the fusion of rhetorical *inventio* with grammatical *enarratio,* by treating the eucharistic rite as the complex performance of texts, both written and remembered, both visual and auditory. That is to say, "finding something to say" becomes a function of the reading of a "text" (the lit-

6. *ST* IIIa.lxxxiii.5, *ad* 5.
7. *ST* IIIa.lxxxiii.5, *ad* 5.

urgy of the Mass) and also the function of oratorical delivery. In other words, invention becomes the responsibility not simply of the orator, but of the believer in the act of devotion. Invention thus becomes a category of desire, as much as commentary and interpretation become the function of spoken and enacted performance. In this way, *inventio* in some sense becomes a grammatical operation (i.e., of "reading"), just as *enarratio* becomes a rhetorical activity, as the liturgy is understood as a kind of dramatic commentary on the Scriptures.

The role of the believer, then, is cast in terms of invention, of the imaginative renarration of the learned story, by learning to associate particular gestures and words with particular narrative tropes and theological truths. It is not simply the case that the believer is flatly told what to believe — in fact, in Question 83 the "instruction of the faithful" is the function not of the sermon but of the reading of the lectionary[8] — but is rather given the cues for invention, which is not simply "making things up" but is defined within patterns of *mimesis*. Thus he writes that "the priest also bears Christ's image in whose person and by whose power he pronounces the words of consecration, as we have shown. And so in a measure the priest and the victim are the same."[9]

Thomas begins this question by claiming that this rite is "an image representing Christ's sacrifice,"[10] and is therefore discursive in character. Thus the concept of motion, as in his notion of *traditio*, is crucial. For this reason, according to Aquinas, the eucharistic rite is called a "Mass" *(missa)* because it is an act of motion. As he writes in Article 4:

> Or else by the angel we are to understand Christ Himself, Who is the *Angel of great counsel* (Isa. ix.6: *Septuag.* Version), Who unites His mystical body with God the Father and the Church triumphant.
>
> And from this the mass derives its name *(missa)*; because the priest sends *(mittit)* his prayers up to God through the angel, as the people do through the priest. Or else because Christ is the victim sent *(missa)* to us: accordingly the deacon on festival days *dismisses* the people at the end of the mass, by saying, *Ite, missa est*, that is, the victim has been sent *(missa est)* to God through the angel, so that it may be accepted by God.[11]

Thus the motion in the Mass is a twofold ascent of prayers to God and descent of Christ the Paschal victim to the people. As a motion towards God, it

---

8. *ST* IIIa.lxxxiii.4, *resp.*
9. *ST* IIIa.lxxxiii.1, *ad* 3.
10. *ST* IIIa.lxxxiii.1, *ad* 2.
11. *ST* IIIa.lxxxiii.4, *ad* 9.

is also God's motion toward us. Thus to participate in the liturgy of the Eucharist is to partake of this motion of *missio,* as it were to become swept into an already extending economy of motion to and from and, indeed, within God the Trinity. This economy is thus one of complete reciprocal return without remainder, because what is first a gift to us is returned to God as a sacrifice of praise through the identity of the Giver with the gift. Our gift to God is acceptable only because it is a return to God of Himself.

As a kind of motion, the rite fulfils the rhetorical function of *movere,* in terms of moving the affections; but it does so in a way that renders the hearer truly moved, because she is participating in the divine motion of ascent and descent. Thus the goal of *movere* is identical with the source of such persuasion. The soul is moved because it is God who moves it by donation; it is truly moved because the soul is returned to God through Christ and therefore made acceptable.

This brings us back to Victorinus and the borrowing of language. For Aquinas, the Eucharist is different from all other sacraments for two reasons. First, in the Eucharist, the consecration of the material elements involved is more than a simple blessing and the production of a spiritual power. As he states, "the consecration of the matter consists in the miraculous change of substance, which can only be done by God; hence the minister in performing this sacrament has *no other act save the pronouncing of words.*"[12] The second way in which the Eucharist differs from other sacraments lies in the grammatical identity of the speaker. Whereas in other sacraments the blessing is effected (grammatically) by the agency of the priest ("I baptize you," "I confirm you," etc.), in the Eucharist the identity of Christ is, as it were, borrowed by the priest. Hence "the form of this sacrament is pronounced *as if Christ were speaking in person,* so that it is given to be understood that the minister does nothing in perfecting this sacrament, except to pronounce the words of Christ."[13]

The Eucharist, then, paradoxically exceeds the other sacraments for precisely this reason, that the *mimesis* of priestly performance is completed in the loaning of the identity of Christ to the utterance involved. Aquinas speaks of this in terms of a "character," which is "a kind of seal, whereby something is marked, as being ordained to some particular end."[14] The whole rite of the Christian religion, he says, operates on a fundamental derivation of character, derived from the priesthood of Christ.[15] Human priests are mimetic images

---

12. *ST* IIIa.lxxiv.1, *resp.* Italics mine.
13. *ST* IIIa.lxxiv.1, *resp.* Italics mine.
14. *ST* IIIa.lxiii.3, *resp.*
15. *ST* IIIa.lxiii.3, *resp.*

of this one authorial character[16] — not as simple pictorial representations, but as "nothing else than certain participations of Christ's Priesthood, flowing from Christ Himself."[17] The office of the priest, then, is derivative of the identity of Christ by virtue of a real participation. The same could be said of the faithful themselves, who "receive" the character of Christ as gift, which distinguishes their peculiar form of life as ordained to a certain end.[18] Paradoxically, perhaps, the end to which they are ordained is identical with the "character" of the donation; Christ is the identity lent to the priest and people, and Christ is the end towards which they are ordained.

Therefore, the priest does nothing in terms of consecration except "the pronouncing of words." And these words are not his own, but Christ's. The agent of the transubstantiation of the elements of bread and wine is likewise the speaker of the words of consecration, though these words are given voice by the priest. In a sense, then, the words of the priest are only made worthy by themselves being transubstantiated, by being transformed from the mere recitation of a textual narrative into the performative utterance *in persona Christi*. "For since these words are uttered in the person of Christ, it is from His command that they receive their instrumental power from Him."[19] Thus while the voice (i.e., the accidents) of the priest remains, the words themselves are not his, but belong to the borrowed character which he inhabits. Though he speaks them with his own voice, their power is derivative because "these words have no power except from Christ pronouncing them."[20]

The words of consecration then constitute a kind of *enarratio*. The words of Jesus, remembered from his last meal with his disciples, are re-narrated by the priest, who recites them as learned text. Yet, the function of grammatical *enarratio* is here joined with the aims of rhetorical *inventio*, whereby the dramatic reenactment of a scene is designed to inspire, in the "reader" in the pew, a movement of the affections. For this reason, it is appropriate that the Last Supper of Christ and his disciples becomes for us the first instance of unity. Moreover, the function of memory is at the center of its performance. The Eucharist is given at the last so that it will be remembered first. Yet again, it is

16. *ST* IIIa.lxiii.3, *ad* 2: A character "is a sign conferring on a man a likeness to some principal person in whom is vested the authority over that to which he is assigned."

17. *ST* IIIa.lxiii.3, *resp.*

18. *ST* IIIa.lxiii.3, *ad* 2: "And in this way those who are deputed to the Christian worship, of which Christ is the author, receive a character by which they are likened to Christ. Consequently, properly speaking, this is Christ's character."

19. *ST* IIIa.lxxviii.4, *resp.* Here Aquinas explicitly links the borrowed character of Christ's identity to the "greater worth" of the Eucharist above other sacraments.

20. *ST* IIIa.lxxviii.1, *ad* 1.

not a question of mere recall or memorial, but of the guiding of the affections towards charity. Thus "last words, chiefly such as are spoken by departing friends, are committed most deeply to memory; since then especially affection for friends is more enkindled, and the things which affect us most are impressed the deepest in the soul."[21]

Repeatedly, Aquinas insists that the liturgy orders our desire; and it is desire itself that is the condition of faithful reception. Desire for the Body and Blood of Christ is therefore proper desire, and as such, is even sufficient to procure the grace which enables one to lead the Christian life.[22]

In Question 83 of the *Tertia Pars*, Aquinas conceives of the liturgy of the Mass in terms of classical rhetorical schemes. I suggest that Thomas' account of the Eucharistic rite is a transformation of the classical art of memory, as articulated chiefly by the author of the *Ad Herennium*. The description in the latter consists of three principal parts: first, the account of the theory of mnemonic *loci* or backgrounds; second, the theory of images and similitudes; and third, the theory of words. Concomitantly, I will treat Thomas' radical subordination of these categories to liturgy as he reorients them to God, through his own account, in somewhat different order, of: first, the relation of memory to time; second, the role of theological places in the liturgy *(loci);* and third, the account of words and gestures. In all, I hope to show that Aquinas' account of the liturgy of the Mass draws on classical tropes regarding the arts of memory and rhetoric, only to reorient them to theology, and to consummate them in worship. In other words, Thomas reads the liturgy of the Mass as an art of memory, indeed, the art of memory proper.

The *Rhetorica ad Herennium* was composed by an anonymous Roman author at some time between 86 and 82 B.C.[23] Its significance in the history of the artificial memory is tremendous. According to Frances Yates, it draws on Greek sources, none of which have survived. Thus, it is "really the main source, and indeed the only complete source, for the classical art of memory both in

21. *ST* IIIa.lxxiii.5, *resp.*

22. *ST* IIIa.lxxix.1, *ad* 1. See also John Milbank and Catherine Pickstock, *Truth in Aquinas* (London: Routledge, 2001), Chapter Four, "Truth and Touch" for an account of the relation of desire to presence and absence in the Eucharist.

23. For a brief account of the life of the *Ad Herennium,* see Martin Camargo, "Rhetoric" in David L. Wagner, ed., *The Seven Liberal Arts in the Middle Ages* (Bloomington, Ind.: Indiana University Press, 1983), pp. 105-7; James J. Murphy, *Rhetoric in the Middle Ages: A History of the Rhetorical Theory from Saint Augustine to the Renaissance,* Medieval and Renaissance Texts and Studies 227 (Tempe: Arizona Center for Medieval and Renaissance Studies, 1974, 2001), pp. 18ff.

the Greek and in the Latin world."[24] The other classical sources, Cicero's *De Oratore* and Quintilian's *Institutio oratoria,* were both well known, but only through incomplete copies. Owing to the medieval attribution of *Ad Herennium* to Cicero, the work garnered a prominent reputation, and hence came to be known during this period as "the Second Rhetoric of Tullius."[25] As for the medieval reception of the "Second Rhetoric," the medieval *ars memoriae* tradition rested "entirely on the memory section of *Ad Herennium* studied without the assistance of the other two sources for the classical art."[26]

We can be certain that Aquinas was well acquainted with the *Ad Herennium,* since he quotes it in article forty-nine of the *Secunda Secundae,* in recognition of the fact that "memory not only arises from nature, but is also aided by art and diligence."[27] As Yates has shown, the picture of Thomas Aquinas as "patron saint" of the medieval art of memory is one that has long since slipped from modern view, despite his veneration as a master in this respect in his era.[28] Nevertheless, the influence of *Ad Herennium* on medieval arts of memory, even on Aquinas' own account, seems to be so profound as scarcely to require citation. Thus in Question 83, the resonances of *Ad Herennium* will be seen to be implicit, though perhaps obvious to a medieval reader, and considerably revised by Aquinas.

As the author of *Ad Herennium* writes in the third book, the natural memory must be strengthened by an artificial memory, which is trained and practiced through discipline. The first objective in the development of this skill is the establishment of certain imaginary backgrounds, into which one may set at precise intervals the things one wishes to remember.

> By backgrounds *(locos)* I mean such scenes as are naturally or artificially set off on a small scale, complete and conspicuous, so that we can grasp and embrace them easily by the natural memory — for example, a house, an intercolumnar space, a recess, an arch, or the like. An image is, as it were, a figure, mark, or portrait of the object we wish to remember; for example, if we wish to recall a horse, a lion, or an eagle, we must place its image in a definite background.[29]

24. Frances Yates, *The Art of Memory* (London: Routledge & Kegan Paul, 1966; Pimlico, 1992), p. 21.

25. Yates, *The Art of Memory,* p. 68.

26. Yates, *The Art of Memory,* p. 68.

27. *ST* IIaIIae 49.1 *ad* 2.

28. Yates, *The Art of Memory,* pp. 93-94.

29. [Cicero], *Ad Herennium,* tr. Harry Caplan (Cambridge, Mass.: Harvard University Press, 1954), III.xvi.29, p. 209.

One can have a multiplicity of backgrounds, though these should be set in a series, like a house with a series of rooms all linked together by a logical order of passage.[30] These backgrounds should be "of moderate size and medium extent," "neither too bright nor too dim, so that the shadows may not obscure the images nor the luster make them glitter." Moreover, the intervals between each background should be "of moderate extent, approximately thirty feet."[31] The greatest danger in one of these *loci* is that of crowding, that the spaces become too close together so that the images placed therein become confused and cluttered.

The imagined backgrounds therefore are inhabited areas, or de Certeau's "practiced spaces," which must be navigated. Unlike a map of things to be recalled, they are domains which must be walked through. The only way to recall anything is to trace out an itinerary through these backgrounds in the mind, until one finally arrives at that which one sought in the first place. Moreover, these mnemonic places must be "read" properly — thus the pseudo-Cicero's analogy with the palimpsest: "For the backgrounds are very much like wax tablets or papyrus, the images like the letters, the arrangement and disposition of the images like script, and the delivery [of the speech] is like the reading." Thus the memorial recollection is discursive in character, and mimics the oration itself. Indeed, delivery is described here in terms of reading itself, much like grammatical *enarratio*.

Second, the author addresses the theory of images to be stored in these *loci*. These are of two types: likenesses of things *(similitudines rerum),* and likenesses of words *(similitudines verborum).*[32] One invents an image to point to an action, word, or principle to be remembered. When several images are brought together to compose a single mnemonic scene, it may look something like this:

> Often we encompass the record of an entire matter by one notation, a single image. For example, the prosecutor has said that the defendant killed a man by poison, has charged that the motive for the crime was an inheritance, and declared that there are many witnesses and accessories to this act. If in order to facilitate our defence we wish to remember this first point, we shall in our first background form an image of the whole matter. We shall picture

---

30. *Ad Herennium* III.xvii.30, p. 211: "So with respect to the backgrounds. If these have been arranged in order, the result will be that, reminded by the images, we can repeat orally what we have committed to the backgrounds, proceeding in either direction from any background we please."

31. *Ad Herennium* III.xix.31-32, p. 213.

32. *Ad Herennium* III.xx.33, p. 215.

the man in question as lying ill in bed, if we know his person. If we do not know him, we shall yet take some one to be our invalid, but not a man of the lowest class, so that he may come to mind at once. And we shall place the defendant at the bedside, holding in his right hand a cup, and in his left tablets, and on the fourth finger a ram's testicles. In this way we can record the man who was poisoned, the inheritance, and the witnesses.[33]

Thus out of a series of associations — the cup for poison, the tablets for the inheritance, and the ram's scrotum (out of which purses were made) for the witnesses and accomplices who might have been bribed[34] — a single scene is constructed, which is designed to recall the allegations of the prosecution.

Memory by way of the likenesses of words (*similitudines verborum*) proves more difficult, but is useful for recalling particular verses or citations. Here one substitutes images for words, still comprising a rhetorical scene. As an example, pseudo-Cicero cites the phrase *Iam domum itionem reges Atridae parant* ("And now their home-coming the kings, the sons of Atreus, are making ready").

> If we wish to remember this verse, in our first background we should put Domitius, raising hands to heaven while he is lashed by the Marcii Reges — that will represent "*Iam domum itionem reges*" ("And now their home-coming the kings"); in the second background, Aesopus and Cimber, being dressed as for the roles of Agamemnon and Menelaüs in *Iphigenia* — that will represent "*Atridae parant*" ("the sons of Atreus are making ready"). By this method all the words will be represented.[35]

Those images that stick in the mind and remain there the longest are not the ordinary and banal ones, but the extravagant and the exceptional. Thus an eclipse is more easily remembered than a sunrise or sunset, because of the rarity of its occurrence.[36] But most important is the constant repetition of the words and images to be recalled. Thus the author implores his reader "again and again to run over rapidly in the mind all the original backgrounds in order to refresh the images."[37]

For pseudo-Cicero, as for Cicero himself, the purpose of the artificial memory is the efficient recollection of words, phrases, events, actions, and

---

33. *Ad Herennium* III.xx.33, p. 215.
34. See *Ad Herennium* III.xx.33, p. 215, note *b*.
35. *Ad Herennium* III.xxi.34, p. 217.
36. *Ad Herennium* III.xxii.35, p. 219.
37. *Ad Herennium* III.xxii.37, p. 221.

principles for the delivery of a speech in the public realm, especially the jurid-
ical. A good memory is nevertheless the fruit of endless labor, the training in
associations of images, things, and words to their assigned referents.

Turning then to Aquinas, we shall see how he reorients the art of memory
as liturgy, incorporating Ciceronian elements but transforming them by
making memory not a transferable *mathesis* of recollection for the delivery of
a speech, but the historical and political activity of a community as opposed
to an individual mental discipline. For this reason, he begins his treatment of
the Eucharistic rite with a discussion of *time*.

Whereas classical arts of memory assume the artificial memory to be the
product of individual discipline, the liturgical commemoration of Christ's
Passion assumes time to be determinative of its meaningfulness. The crucifixion therefore orders time itself, and orients all memory towards itself. So
rather than being a simple *mathesis* of recollection for a proscribed use, the liturgical art of memory orders memorial associations according to the calendar, arranged around the particularities of the story of Advent and Passion.

Moreover, memory is not mere recall, but a reenactment. The *imagines* in
the *Ad Herennium* are more or less arbitrary associations according to the
convenientia of the individual. In the liturgy, associations are not arbitrary,
but are instead ordered according to the theological *convenientia* of the figure
and the reality. Figures, for Aquinas, analogically participate in the realities
which they represent, and for this reason, "When the reality comes its figure
ceases."[38] Figures are derived from the realities which they image, and not
vice versa. Thus the Eucharist, as a figure of Christ's Passion, is not celebrated
on Good Friday, because the commemoration as figure gives way to the commemoration as reality. The Passion, therefore, is commemorated once a year,
while the Eucharist is commemorated daily. In other words, the commemoration of Good Friday is a reenactment of the Passion by participation in its
historical eventuality. Thus "at Passion-tide Christ's Passion is recalled inasmuch as it was wrought in Him Who is our Head."[39] Or, as the Blackfriars
edition has it, "his Passion is recalled as enacted in him who is our Lord."[40]
On Good Friday, then, the Passion is "recalled as it was really accomplished."[41] Thus participation in the liturgy of Good Friday is the instance of
participation in the "reality" of Christ's Passion *as reality*, not as figure. The
radical implication here is that by re-narration of the historical event in litur-

---

38. *ST* IIIa.lxxxiii.2, *ad* 2, Blackfriars: *veniente veritate, cessat figura.*
39. *ST* IIIa.lxxxiii.2, *ad* 1.
40. *ST* IIIa.lxxxiii.2, *ad* 1, Blackfriars: *recolitur prout realiter gesta est.*
41. *ST* IIIa.lxxxiii.2, *ad* 2.

gical time, one takes part in the very event that is commemorated. Thus memory is transformed from noetic recall into the performance of participation in the divine.

This is not to suggest that figures have a lesser reality. On the contrary, it is through the figures that "we are made partakers of the fruit of our Lord's Passion."[42] Because the figures used in the Eucharist become identical with the reality which they represent, one cannot distinguish the figure from the reality in terms of an ontological hiatus. It is not as though the daily celebration of the Mass is a lesser participation than the commemoration of Good Friday — indeed, for Aquinas the reason for celebrating daily is not simply so that we may recollect Christ's sacrifice, but so that we may "share in its fruits and hold it in constant memory."[43] To "hold in constant memory," therefore, suggests the continual disciplining of the memory towards its ordering to the Passion, so that to remember it is to share in it, however analogously.

Different times occasion different memories, as is the case with the three masses said on Christmas Day. Each is designed to recall different aspects of the birth of Christ. The first, said at night, points to his eternal birth from the Father; the second, said at dawn, signifies his "spiritual birth in time"; and the third, sung in broad daylight, refers to the bodily birth of Jesus to Joseph and Mary. This latter is for us "a sign that he came to the darkness of our infirmity," in order that our recollection of his bodily birth be joined to the penitent remembrance of our own sin, which in turn aids in the ordering of our affections to true charity.

In all, liturgical time orients memory not only to that past, but to the present and future as well, as the reenactment of the Passion at differing times suggests differences of emphasis on the affection to be inspired. As such, time, for Aquinas, is determinative of how one learns to remember well.

In view of the *Ad Herennium*'s account of mnemonic backgrounds, we can see how these *loci* themselves, as Thomas conceives of them, are likewise more thoroughly conditioned by the ontological relation of time to memory. In the third article of Question 83, he asks whether or not the sacrament ought to be celebrated in a building and with sacred vessels.

Aquinas frames the architectural setting of the church's liturgy in terms of a mnemotechnical *locus*. As a background, it likewise signifies something to be remembered. The building itself, he says, signifies the church, and does not simply "house" it. Thomas seems to be thinking in terms of the Gothic un-

---

42. *ST* IIIa.lxxxiii.1, *resp.*
43. *ST* IIIa.lxxxiii.2, *ad* 1, Blackfriars.

derstanding of ecclesiastical architectural structures as "meditational mechanisms" that "furnish the routes of prayer."[44] Pseudo-Cicero's intercolumnar spaces, arches and recesses all find their articulation as sites of memory production in the medieval Gothic cathedrals and parish churches. Though Aquinas does not give an account of these specific places, it seems clear that his understanding of the church building is as a kind of rhetorical background against which the sacraments are performed. That is to say, the visible is here incorporated within a complex economy of figuration. The building itself is a sign, and is ordered towards an end by consecration. As a *locus,* it too orders affections through the memory. By entering the liturgical space (which is always liturgical because always liturgically practiced space) one is reminded that this particular structure is dedicated to a precise use. The entire orientation of the structure is towards the altar, which itself signifies the holiness of Christ, and the cross on which he is sacrificed.[45] Moreover, it points to the disposition of one who enters such space, by signifying "the holiness required in those who would receive" the Eucharist.[46]

Otherwise arbitrary objects are given meaningfulness by their use. "The church, altar, and other inanimate things are consecrated, not as though they were receptive of grace, but they acquire spiritual force by being adapted to divine worship, in that men gather a certain devotion because of them, and are made open to difline [*sic*] things, and not held back by irreverence."[47] Hence, the rhetorical backgrounds of pseudo-Cicero are no longer morally or theologically neutral *loci* in which to deposit objects, but rather function as actual sites directed to a proper use, for the ordering of the affections towards the altar.

Within these backgrounds, other objects are consecrated for the commemoration of the sacraments. Like the scene described in *Ad Herennium,* all of these objects (altar, chalice, linen, etc.), when put together, form a coherent rhetorical composition, which when "read," constitute their delivery. That is to say, the church building and its concomitant apparatuses of worship come to signify by being performed or dramatized. The activity of the memory is the "reading" of all these signs together with one another, which, in terms of the *Ad Herennium,* is coextensive with the "delivery" of the oratory. However, reading is here not a function of the priest alone, much less of the believer alone, but of the whole church.

44. See Mary Carruthers, *The Craft of Thought: Meditation, Rhetoric, and the Making of Images, 400-1200* (Cambridge: Cambridge University Press, 1998), pp. 257ff.
45. *ST* IIIa.lxxxiii.3, *ad* 1.
46. *ST* IIIa.lxxxiii.3, *ad* 1, Blackfriars.
47. *ST* IIIa.lxxxiii.3, *ad* 3.

In his recent work on *The Hermeneutics of Sacred Architecture,* Lindsay Jones attempts to counteract the "well-worn, though insidious, assumption that architectural configurations have intrinsic, stable significances — that buildings have inherent meanings that can be objectified and recovered."[48] Alternatively, he argues that sacred buildings must be read not as having univocal meanings according to original authorial intent, but rather as sites productive of a multiplicity of fluid interpretations, based upon the dynamic ritual interactions between buildings and their "readers," or what he calls "ritual-architectural events."[49]

While Jones is somewhat successful in overturning the modern treatment of buildings as "books" which "contain" meaning, by recovering the sense in which these spaces are practiced (an analogue to the relationship between the itinerary and the map), he is less specific about the character of the interplay of signs as these are performed in particular liturgical rites. Moreover, despite the fact that his is an attempt to rehabilitate the pre-modern understanding of religious buildings as "texts" to be read through the practicing of space, he fails to link this with the medieval arts of rhetoric and grammar, with which the architecture of the Gothic cathedral is so closely linked. A better course, it seems to me, would be to link the function of specific architectural sites to the notion of rhetorical backgrounds for the *inventio* of the readers. Thus rather than simply construe them as "texts" which are productive of a variety of meanings for modern visitors, through the experience of the "eventfulness" of architecture, they function, according to Aquinas at least, in terms of the Ciceronian *loci* of the memory, as a composite which, when linked together in a catena of sites made intelligible by itinerant performance, not only induce *inventio* and *enarratio,* but order desire.

By contrast with Jones' thesis, Emile Mâle has famously described medieval iconography as a kind of script, a calculus and a symbolic code, composed and read according to established grammatical, mathematical and semiotical rules which are not precisely "laid out," but which are learned by practice and habituated by liturgical performance.[50] The art and architecture

48. Lindsay Jones, *The Hermeneutics of Sacred Architecture: Experience, Interpretation, Comparison.* Volume One: *Monumental Occasions: Reflections on the Eventfulness of Religious Architecture* (Cambridge, Massachusetts: Harvard University Press, 2000), p. 3.

49. Jones, *The Hermeneutics of Sacred Architecture,* p. xxviii.

50. Emile Mâle, *The Gothic Image: Religious Art in France of the Thirteenth Century,* tr. Dora Nussey (New York: Harper and Row, 1972), pp. 1-22. See especially his illuminating discussion of Gulielmus Durandus' commentary on the liturgy of Holy Saturday, pp. 16ff. While Mâle's book is now considered somewhat dated, his emphasis on the rhetorical and memorial functions of architecture seem a helpful corrective to Jones' abstraction of these from their *use.* Mâle seems

of the medieval cathedral together constitute a kind of visual grammar or vo-cabulary which is learned through the "enactment" of this space.[51] These buildings were understood to be "meditational mechanisms, structures that not only housed and abetted, but *enabled* the *opus Dei*."[52] That is to say, the iconographic is both grammatical and programmatical. It is a language that must be learned and practiced, by liturgical performance: it must be deci-phered, and it must be read and performed. For the intelligibility of such rhe-torical cues is dependent upon certain actions and operations on the part of the reader — not the actions of a modern tourist who, for a small fee, is led around a medieval cathedral by a tour guide, who points out the objects of interest and what they quaintly "mean" or once "meant" — but rather, the operations of the daily office and the rite of the Eucharist. In other words, one learns that the aureole surrounding the Blessed Virgin signifies her sanctity not simply by being *told* this, but by hearing stories about her in the lections, by the celebration of a feast in her honor, by genuflecting during the Creed at the mention of the Virgin Birth, and so on.

In other words, modern visitors to a Gothic cathedral are taught to read poorly such a text by being told (by an umbrella-toting tour guide) what the images and order of the place might have "meant" to "medieval people." In contrast, to read such a space rightly, then, is to participate in its use, to "prac-tice" this space in worship. That is to say, we read a cathedral well not when we simply collect information about what it signified to someone in less "en-lightened" times (and no longer does to us), but when we are led to the desire of God.

Such a practice of reading, set against the rhetorical backgrounds of the church structure, is necessarily processional. The movement of the liturgy corresponds, then, to the movement of the ecclesiastical body towards the Trinity. Like the ambulatory recollection of the mind, the liturgy is a peripa-tetic passage through the great halls and storehouses of the church's memory,

---

to me *not* to be arguing that "architectural configurations have intrinsic, stable significances — that buildings have inherent meanings that can be objectified and recovered" (Jones, p. 3), but rather analyzing the functions of buildings in the context of liturgical performance. For a more recent treatment, see Eamon Duffy, *The Stripping of the Altars: Traditional Religion in England, 1400-1580* (New Haven: Yale University Press, 1992).

51. One could even speak of various "dialects" of this language, from the austere *sensus literalis* of Cistercian architecture, to the more allegorical, "Dionysian" *modus loquendi* of Abbot Suger. See Carruthers, *The Craft of Thought*, pp. 257-61. She writes (p. 257), "It is significant . . . that both Bernard of Clairvaux and Hugh of St. Victor, using Suger of St.-Denis as his surrogate, thought to realize their *meditational* reforms in terms of building reforms."

52. Carruthers, *The Craft of Thought*, p. 258.

along whose way are placed the *imagines* which recall the story of the church as the tale of God's love for his people.

The liturgy of the Mass, in particular, has the character of a journey. This is seen in the structure of the Mass itself, but is characteristic of every office. A prime analogy is the practice of the stations of the Cross. Here, one traces a route in memory, but also in person, recalling the way of Jesus to his death. In this case, the actual route in Jerusalem becomes figured in the architectural circuit indoors. The placing of the fourteen tableaux at regular intervals marks, as in *Ad Herennium,* the series of *imagines* linked in order.[53] Yet here, as in all liturgical rites, the activity of remembrance is linked to the motion of the soul in its return to the origin and end of its being. Thus internal to liturgy itself is processional motion, which is the movement of the *manuductio* of desire towards God.

Thus what Lindsay Jones also misses is the sense in which medieval Gothic ecclesiastical structures are rhetorical structures, constructed around a certain theological rhetoric that aims at the teaching, moving, and persuading of the soul unto its sole source of rest. This is the case in, for example, the contrasting rhetorical-architectural visions of Bernard of Clairvaux and Suger of St.-Denis. The former favored a radical economy of space and light, while the latter preferred a more labyrinthine and low-lit style. Nevertheless, both styles assumed a theological rhetoric, and both schools constructed edifices around the assumption that the processional motion within these structures relied on the uses of stone, light, and negative space to teach, delight, and move.[54]

53. The resemblance of the Stations of the Cross to the architectural memory described in pseudo-Cicero and Quintilian is not, I think, mere coincidence. A curious investigator might want to attempt to discover if any medieval Gothic architects ever followed pseudo-Cicero to the letter, by placing either stations of the Cross (which seems to be a late Gothic practice) or other kinds of station exactly thirty feet apart.

54. Cf. Erwin Panofsky, ed. *Abbot Suger: On the Abbey Church of St.-Denis and Its Art Treasures,* 2nd ed. (Princeton: Princeton University Press, 1979). Bernard's emphasis on austerity of style is illustrated in his polemic against what he perceived as excesses among the Cluniacs, *Apologia ad Willelmum Abbatem Sancti Theodorici.* See "Cistercians and Cluniacs: St. Bernard's Apologia to Abbot William," tr. Michael Casey, in *The Works of Bernard Clairvaux,* Volume One: *Treatises I,* Cistercian Fathers Series 1 (Spencer, Mass.: Cistercian Publications, 1970), pp. 33-69. Bernard's argument against lavish decoration is not anti-aesthetic but rather is determined by his understanding of reading (p. 66): "What excuse can there be for these ridiculous monstrosities in the cloisters where the monks do their reading, extraordinary things at once beautiful and ugly? Here we find filthy monkeys and fierce lions, fearful centaurs, harpies, and striped tigers, soldiers at war, and hunters blowing their horns. . . . All round there is such an amazing variety of shapes that one could easily prefer to take one's reading from the walls instead of from a book. One could spend the whole day gazing fascinated at these things, one by one, instead of

Thus such buildings can be seen as the mnemotechnical backgrounds for a kind of memory-art. Mary Carruthers cites the example of the Carolingian monastery of Centula-Saint-Riquier, whose eleven altars and set of four stations provided the set of stopping points for remembrance in stational liturgies.[55] As Carol Heitz describes these,

> Images, *imagines* — stations for prayer — marked out the liturgical itinerary. . . . The first of these, that of the Nativity, was placed on the porch, above the entry door in the crypt of the Savior. . . . The three other *imagines* were found in the nave and transepts, more or less aligned. In the center, behind the altar of the Holy Cross, was the image of the Passion of Christ. To the north, doubtless at the end of the aisle, the Resurrection; to the south, in the same position, the Ascension.[56]

Thus within a church building itself, the various images and structures become sites along a route of worship, with its goal the remembrance of heaven — not simply as in a past sense, but as the *telos* of creation.

However, the *loci* of the church's memory are (though preeminently the structures which are consecrated for divine worship) not exclusively the buildings which signify the church. Early and medieval Christian stational liturgies suggest that the city itself was seen as such a *locus*, and that the processional character of liturgy was not limited to the services within the church walls. As John Baldovin argues, the city itself was seen to be holy, and its constitutive sites were incorporated into the worship of the church. Like rhetorical cues for the memory, or the *similitudines rerum*, "[m]onuments, public places, thoroughfares, the center, the edge, and important outlying spots are the vocabulary"[57] of this urban grammar. The suggestion is that in order to be read properly, the city itself must, as it were, be performed liturgically. In so doing, the city becomes more itself than ever before, as it too is made into a rhetorical background for the placing of *imagines* designed to recall the love of God, and by providing the routes of our return to him.

---

meditating on the law of God. Good Lord, even if the foolishness of it all occasion no shame, at least one might balk at the expense."

55. Carruthers, *The Craft of Thought*, pp. 266-69. See especially Figure C, a drawing of the routes of the stational liturgy at Centula-Saint-Riquier.

56. Carol Heitz, "Architecture et liturgie processionelle à l'époque préromane." *Revue de l'Art* (Paris, CNRS) XXIV (1974), pp. 30-47; quoted and translated in Carruthers, *The Craft of Thought*, p. 268.

57. John F. Baldovin, S.J., *The Urban Character of Christian Worship: The Origins, Development, and Meaning of Stational Liturgy*, Orientalia Christiana Analecta 228 (Rome: Pont. Institutum Studiorum Orientalium, 1987), p. 267.

To return to Question 83, then, we have seen how Thomas understands the apparatuses of Christian worship to be like the *imagines* in the memory, which one understands how to read only by making the journey through the liturgy. Thus the *locus* (i.e., the background) for these similitudes is chiefly a church building, inasmuch as it is consecrated to a specific use, but can be any space whatsoever, since "the whole world might serve as the house for Christ's Passion."[58] Having treated the function of the backgrounds in the first part of article three, then, in the responses to objections three through eight he turns from the consideration of the *loci* to the consideration of the *imagines*, or the *similitudines rerum* themselves.

In these latter responses, he treats, respectively, the dedication of a church, the materials used for the altar, the chalice, and the corporal. Each of these instruments "signifies" something to be recalled. In the case of the altar, it is to be made of stone, since Christ is the rock, because he was buried in a stone tomb, and also because stone is universally available. Moreover, its material composition is not of gold or bronze (as argued in the fifth objection) in order that the affections may not be inordinately directed.[59] Each of these similitudes points to something to be remembered, not simply for the recollection of information but, as I have said, for the good association of learned images and words with their true referents in the liturgical story, and therefore with proper *intentio* towards those objects.

Likewise the chalice is to be made of a suitable metal that befits the reverence for that which it contains, and also for the practical considerations of its strength and durability. The corporal, too, is to be made of linen, as it was in linen that the body of Jesus was wrapped and buried. Again, it is also "befitting to denote purity of conscience," and because of "the manifold labour with which it is prepared," it points to the Passion itself.[60] The thrust of Thomas' account, then, is that these various "canonical accessories"[61] function as the mnemotechnical *similitudines rerum* of Ciceronian memory-arts, yet they differ in that they exist in an economy of memory that is aimed not at utilitarian recollection for delivery of a speech, but at the ordering of desire. Thus unlike the memory-arts, liturgy, as Thomas describes it, takes the activity of remembrance to be coextensive with the journey towards God, not anterior to it. The "delivery" in pagan memory-arts thus becomes in Aquinas the practice of worship, the bodily participation in the sacramental mysteries.

---

58. *ST* III.lxxxiii.3, *ad* 1, Blackfriars.
59. *ST* III.lxxxiii.3, *ad* 5, Blackfriars.
60. *ST* III.lxxxiii.3, *ad* 7, Blackfriars.
61. *ST* III.lxxxiii.3, *ad* 8, Blackfriars.

The form of this participation is the itinerant recollection of the soul as it liturgically perambulates the church with all its canonical and non-canonical accessories (chalice, paten, corporal, altar, as well as niches, statuaries, stations of the cross). We will see this more emphatically as we turn to Article Four of Question 83.

First, though in Article Four Thomas treats the grammatical forms of the celebration of the Mass, beginning with the two introductory parts, the preparation and the instruction. The first part is similarly divided into four. Each of these is spoken of in terms of a "commemoration." The first of these is in the Introit, where one is exhorted to the praise of God by a recitation of the forty-ninth Psalm, "The sacrifice of praise shall glorify me, and that is the way by which I will show him the salvation of God."[62] The verbal recollection of this verse places the worshiper in the stature of David, and therefore borrows the identity of the psalmist in order worthily to perform the preparation of praise. There is a kind of transfer of the "I" from its authorial origin to the synchronic utterance of the believer, whereby the latter, from the outset, "prepares" herself by being ridded of the idolatrous desire for autonomy, the desire to make one's words one's own.

The second part of the preparation is the commemoration of present misery *(commemoratio praesentis miseriae)*,[63] followed by the plea for mercy in the Kyrie. The third part is the "memory of heaven," as sung in the Gloria. Again, Aquinas inverts the classical assumptions that memory is only of things past (as opposed to foreknowledge) by asserting (with Augustine) that it recalls future destinies. The third "calling to mind" involved in the singing of the Gloria is, like the three other parts of this section of the Mass, described in terms of "commemoration": *Tertia autem pars commemorat coelestem gloriam ad quam tendimus post praesentem vitam et miseriam.* The fourth and final part is the collect, "which the priest makes for the people that they may be made worthy of such great mysteries."

Thus we have the introduction to the Mass, the preparation of the soul for the worthiness of the sacrament. There are, therefore, four "commemorations" framed on either side by an act of rhetorical "poaching." In the first instance, it is the poaching of the identity of David's praise, and in the second, the priestly vocation in the praying of the collect. The shifting of the "I" continues, from the worshiper to the psalmist to the priest, who now prays on behalf of the people *(pro populo facit),* thus returning the original "sacrifice of praise" in the Introit as a petition *for* the original "I." In all, the speaking sub-

62. *ST* III.lxxxiii.4, *resp.,* Blackfriars.
63. *ST* III.lxxxiii.4, *resp.,* Blackfriars.

ject is made the *object* of a petition for sacramental dignity, by the gradual transferal of a borrowed identity.

The second part of the introduction is the instruction of the faithful (*instructio fidelis*), which consists of the readings of the lectionary texts. This is perhaps the most overtly grammatical and rhetorical section (in the classical sense) of the entire liturgy, since it involves the reading aloud of a written text for the purposes of instruction. The worshiping community, now having been made the object of petition, is taught through the reading of the Prophets and Apostles, the singing of the Gradual and the Alleluia, and the reading of the Gospel. The readings trace a route from prophecy to fulfillment, consummated in the teachings of Christ, in which "the people are fully instructed."[64]

As I argued in Chapter Four, the "Word of God" is present here as *voiced text*. It is written only so as to be read aloud. Moreover, the series of readings constitutes a kind of procession, recapitulating the "motion" of God's drawing near to the world, culminating in the Incarnation, to which the congregation responds by singing the Creed. The readings of the Biblical texts, strung together according to the liturgical calendar, then form a coherent narrative which instructs the community about particular things at particular times — hence the mention of the feasts of Christ, the Virgin Mary and the Apostles, whose commemoration leads us to the confession of faith. In other words, the remembrance of certain individuals recalls ultimately the activity of God towards the church. Therefore the memory of personae in the feasts of the church is in essence anamnesic — it gathers the affections of the collected body and orders them to faith by confession. The creedal confession then marks the end of the preparatory section of the Mass, the *synaxis*, and the beginning of the eucharistic liturgy proper.

The offertory then reflects the joy of the body in praise, now having been gathered into one by the singing of the Creed in the first person. The "I" has now become the congregation itself, not the individual worshiper nor the aggregate of these. Following this, the "People are roused to devotion" in the Preface, and then "devoutly praise Christ's Godhead, saying with the angels, *Holy, Holy, Holy,* and his humanity, saying with the children, *Blessed is he that cometh.*"[65] After this, the priest "quietly recalls" (*secreto commemorat*) "those for whom the sacrifice is offered, namely the universal Church and *those in high places,* and especially those who offer or for whom the mass is offered (i.e., the *Memento*); next the saints, for whom he invokes their pa-

---

64. *ST* III.lxxxiii.4, *resp.,* Blackfriars.
65. *ST* III.lxxxiii.4, *resp.,* Blackfriars.

tronage from above, when he says *Communicating with and honouring the memory,* etc."[66]

Again, there is the threefold act of commemoration, of those future, those present, and those past. All three are gathered together in the prayer of the offertory. But what is different here is the implication that commemoration of these (as they are all partakers of the eternal life of God in some sense, and are therefore neither literally past nor future) takes place through communication with them. The honoring of their memory is at the same time participation in the sacrament of the Eucharist with them. Thus, as I suggested at the very outset of this chapter, one "remembers" most truly by eating and drinking. Thus for Aquinas, memory *(memoria)* is most properly *memory with (commemoratio)*. In this way, he points to the consummation of pagan memory arts in the political activity of *anamnesis* in the eucharistic liturgy of the church. That is to say, the *commemoratio* of Christian worship is not simply mathetic, but truly productive of a body. In this way, the (borrowed) prayers of commemoration by the priest on behalf of the body are paradoxically productive of that body. By gathering the universal church around the altar in commemoration, memory becomes truly political by re-membering the formerly broken body of Christ into one. Thus "[t]he Eucharist is the sacrament of unity for the entire Church, and therefore in this sacrament especially, more than in the others, reference should be made to all that relates to salvation in the universal church."[67]

The aim of this liturgical rhetoric, then, is to inspire devotion. Thus in the Preface, "the people are roused to devotion" *(primo excitatur populus ad devotionem in praefatione).*[68] Such devotion, he suggests, is a function not of the individual believer, but of the whole church. The Eucharist, then, calls for greater devotion "because it contains the whole Christ."[69] Thomas here refers not to the Host itself — since he never talks in a crude locational sense about the elements "containing" Christ — but to the Church, the "mystical body, which is signified by this sacrament."[70] Thus "the devotion should be more communal, namely of the entire people, since it is offered for them, not only the recipients of the sacrament, as with the other sacraments."[71]

---

66. See Josef A. Jungmann, S.J., *The Mass of the Roman Rite: Its Origins and Development,* 2 vols., tr. Francis Brunner (Allen, Texas: Christian Classics, 1986, 1949), II.159-79, for a treatment of these prayers.

67. *ST* III.lxxxiii.4, *ad* 3, Blackfriars.

68. *ST* III.lxxxiii.4, *resp.,* Blackfriars.

69. *ST* III.lxxxiii.4, *ad* 5, Blackfriars.

70. *ST* III.lxxxiii.4, *ad* 9, Blackfriars.

71. *ST* III.lxxxiii.4, *ad* 9, Blackfriars.

Finally, in the fifth article, Aquinas addresses a series of objections as to the appropriateness of the actions performed in the liturgy of the Eucharist. His response begins with the claim that "the sacraments signify something in a twofold manner, by words and by actions."[72] At this point, Thomas introduces a new element into his transformation of rhetoric. Whereas we saw in pseudo-Cicero the two types of mnemonic cues, *similitudines verborum* and *similitudines rerum*, Aquinas has a third, the likenesses of gestures and actions performed by the priest and by the congregation. I suggest that these constitute a third category of signs which order the memory rightly, what one might call *similitudines factorum* (or *gestorum*). These likenesses, together with the *similitudines rerum* of the Mass, suggest a way of reading the liturgy as a kind of itinerary through the "great hall" of the church's memory towards union with God.

The *similitudines rerum* in this article are the apparatuses of the rite itself: water,[73] incense,[74] cross,[75] host,[76] chalice,[77] and wine.[78] These objects, as he said earlier, "acquire spiritual force by being adapted to divine worship, in that men gather a certain devotion because of them."[79] Thus the use of these *imagines* form the *similitudines factorum*. These are: washing of the hands, censing, making the sign of the cross, the fraction of the host, and the dipping of the host into the wine in the chalice. Each of these actions is designed to recall one or more points: the reverence due to the sacrament in the washing of hands and the censing of the altar, the demonstration of the effects of grace by the analogy of the aesthetics of smell, the various events of Christ's Passion in the sign of the cross, the breaking of his body, its distinction and the distribution of the graces flowing from his Passion, the "bliss of the blessed" in the dipping of the host into the chalice, and finally, the cleansing effects of the blood of Christ owing to the properties of wine itself. In all of these gestures, the congregation is instructed and led to devotion.

"The truth should correspond to the figure," Aquinas says.[80] As figures, these similitudes correspond to that which they image by way of the logic of participation. All of this is brought together in the central act of *anamnesis* in

72. *ST* III.lxxxiii.5, *resp.*, Blackfriars.
73. *ST* III.lxxxiii.5, *ad* 1, Blackfriars.
74. *ST* III.lxxxiii.5, *ad* 2, Blackfriars.
75. *ST* III.lxxxiii.5, *ad* 3, Blackfriars.
76. *ST* III.lxxxiii.5, *ad* 7, Blackfriars.
77. *ST* III.lxxxiii.5, *ad* 9, Blackfriars.
78. *ST* III.lxxxiii.5, *ad* 10, Blackfriars.
79. *ST* III.lxxxiii.3, *ad* 3, Blackfriars.
80. *ST* III.lxxxiii.5, *ad* 11, Blackfriars.

the Eucharist, where the hall of memories through which the congregation has been moving is gathered together in the one memory of Christ's body. Yet here, as we have seen, is no mere memorial meal, but the instantiation of an ever-to-be-achieved political body by the commemoration, oddly, of itself. The church universal — past, present, and future — therefore, participates in this sacrament by the analogical gathering around the Messiah for the meal which makes them one. "Though we are many, we are one body, because we all share in one bread."

All of these images and gestures involved in the rite may rightly be seen as cues for the memory, but of a memory construed in a radically different way than older memory-arts. I have argued that Thomas construes the liturgy of the Mass in terms of rhetoric, yet he reconceives rhetoric in a way that suggests his theology of participation in God. The rite of the Eucharist may then be read as an itinerary of persuasion, of knowledge of stories and identities learned through their constant retelling, ordered towards the proper source and object of all such knowledge. The *excitatio* which the eucharistic rite evokes is therefore not a superficial *delectio* in the surfaces of words and gestures, but because the truth corresponds to the figure, and because the figure in some way really participates in its perfection, the words themselves and their uses draw one into real delight, indeed into delight itself. Thus, Aquinas reorients classical rhetoric, through his reading of the rite of the Eucharist, as that art of memory which truly teaches by instructing one as to the proper ends, as Thomas describes the function of *sacra doctrina* in the second question of the *Summa*. It truly moves, because it is the function of a comprehensive *manuduction* of persuasion by a universal and diachronic communion of saints who are commemorated into one body through prayer. And finally, it truly delights, because it leads one into participation in the reality which the figure represents, and because the end of the itinerary is also its origin, God the author and the finisher of the faith. *Finis, dilectio dei.*

Conclusion

Tsar: *What's this?*
Fyodor: *A map of Muscovy, which shows our empire*
  From end to end. Look, father, here is Moscow,
  Here's Novgorod, here's Astrakhan. The sea
  Is here, and here is Perm's primeval forest.
  And there's Siberia.
Tsar: *But, son, what's this*
  That makes a winding pattern here?
Fyodor: *The Volga.*
Tsar: *How fine! These are the honeyed fruits of learning!*
  You can survey at one glance all the empire
  As from the clouds: its frontiers, cities, rivers.

Alexander Pushkin, *Boris Godunov*[1]

Nowhere in the *Summa Theologiae* does Thomas Aquinas give an account of rhetoric, much less of reading. There is no question on the mechanisms of reading — what to read, how to read. In fact Thomas rarely uses the word "read" except when supporting arguments from Scripture or some other authority, as, for example, "as we read in Luke." Among the exceptions, however, there is one that is unique. In the *responsio* to the first article of the eighth question of the *Secunda Secundae*, in a famous etymological moment, Thomas says that "[u]nderstanding implies intimate knowledge,

---

1. Alexander Pushkin, *Boris Godunov*, tr. Philip L. Barbour (Westport, Conn.: Greenwood Press, 1953, 1976), p. 63.

for *intelligere* (to understand) is the same as *intus legere* (to read inwardly)."[2]

What might it mean to "read within"? After all, every kind of knowledge "begins with the outside of things as it were." How is the understanding, so to speak, led inside? For Thomas, the "stronger the light of the understanding, the further it can penetrate into the heart of things."[3] This is for Thomas the nature of understanding — to pierce the veil which separates the mind from the essence of a thing.

The language Thomas uses for this involves a spatial relation — he speaks of substantial reality as "hidden under" accidents, of meaning "lying hidden under" words, of the truth being "hidden under" likenesses and figures. Underlying all of this is the claim that "the intelligible word is 'enclosed within,' while the sensible world is perceived externally."[4]

Does this mean, as Michel Henry notes, that "[l]anguage, as long as there is nothing else but language, can only be lying"? Is language then "the universal evil"?[5] Does Christianity posit an original deceit in the form of the chasm between substance and accident, between form and content, between faith and reason?

So far in this book I have tried to problematize at least one of these *loci*, that of the relationship between the form of written theological pedagogy before modernity and the implicit *telos* of that pedagogy. In so doing, I have suggested that the notion of the deception of language is only as good as the ontology which is "hidden under" it. In offering new ways of reading the *Glossa Ordinaria* and the *Summa Theologiae*, as informed by Augustine's account of rhetoric, I have suggested that there is an ontological character to reading which is not just "behind" the text, but inseparable from it.

Understanding is reading within — within not just the inviolable privacy of the mind, but within the continuing *traditio* of the Church. To read within is to refuse reading without — without community, without reason, without faith. Reading inwardly implies that there is no naked confrontation with the page, that the fundamental metaphor for knowledge is not that of the mapreader who stands above the text and panoptically overlooks a comprehensive tableau of information. Rather knowledge is disclosed in the performance of it. It does not simply arrive as an end, but is always constantly arriving, out of divine generosity.

2. *ST* IIaIIae.viii.1, *resp.*
3. *ST* IIaIIae.viii.1, *resp.*
4. *ST* IIaIIae.viii.1, *resp.*
5. Michel Henry, *I Am the Truth: Toward a Philosophy of Christianity* (Stanford: Stanford University Press, 2003), pp. 8-9.

Throughout this book I have tried to make a connection between reading and being. To come to know is to be led by the hand, and coming to know is at the same time a coming to be. Learning is therefore truly a becoming (and the formula could just as easily be reversed), but it is not a becoming *different*. Christianity does not demand that we repent and become someone different than who we are (Jesus after all commands us to "love one another *as ourselves*"). Rather Christ instructs us to "become what we are," to be not other than what we were, but in a way, more fully what we are.

Because knowledge is participation in divine self-knowledge, there can be nothing "behind" the objects of our knowledge. God simply is the object of our minds. Theology, then, has no particular subject matter.[6] There is no circumscribable domain within which theology speaks with authority. It is not concerned with a specific set of questions. Nor does it simply offer answers to those questions. Instead, because God is the object of holy teaching, theology is about all things as they pertain to God as their source and end. Theology has no outside.

Does this then make of theology a panoptic science? Is theology therefore the map of all maps? Is it not of all disciplines the most hubristic and encyclopedic?

To return to the image with which I began, that of the Ebstorf *mappamundi,* then, any answer to the question "Where am I?" might be better answered not when one is able to "locate" oneself in terms of a particular spatial locus, but rather when one finds oneself already situated within the prior narrative tale of the church. In other words, a "text" like the Ebstorf map might well tell me a great deal more about where I am and where I am going, even though my specific location is nowhere to be found on it. It implies that my being is more truly disclosed to me not by my own self-location and self-description, but through the mediation of a fellowship of others who participate in my coming to know where I am, and hence who I am.

The Ebstorf map is a picture of the world, but it images the world in the form of a Eucharistic host. It is as if the world itself were the Eucharistic bread, stamped with the image of Christ.[7] By reorienting the points of the compass to the extremities of the Logos, the map in a way illustrates the

6. *ST* Ia.i.7, *resp.*

7. Whether the author of the Ebstorf map was in fact conscious of this analogy we of course cannot be certain. However, the practice of stamping of Eucharistic bread with the sign of the cross, or with an image of the body of Christ was established as early as the fourth century. See George Galavaris, *Bread and the Liturgy: The Symbolism of Early Christian and Byzantine Bread Stamps* (Madison: University of Wisconsin Press, 1970).

claim that the Incarnation is the *true law of the physical*.[8] It is not therefore for theology to seek out strategies of "engagement" or "adaptation," but rather to replicate, with style, the divine persuasion that draws all things to itself.

To read within is to read within the *catholica*, "a region whose middle point is everywhere,"[9] and in the world. Yet this world is not simply reducible to phenomenal appearance, but is as it were "veiled" with Christ, who as St. Augustine says is "this New Man spread about over the whole world."[10] For this reason Jerusalem is in some sense the ontological center of the world: it is the Jerusalem already transfigured by the Passion of Christ, yet infinitely dispersed and repeated throughout the world, the Jerusalem which is in some way not yet what it is.

The world is not Christ, yet Christ is "hidden under" the world in such a way that makes the world itself possible. Christ is therefore the possibility of every thought and desire, inasmuch as he is their proper object. The Incarnation of the Word makes all words themselves the site of an incipient grace — a grace which cannot be refused but which everywhere makes itself known. There is no place, no word, no desire that can know itself to be utterly in the absence of the Christ.

For that reason, reading the world theologically sustains the possibility of a genuinely peaceful persuasion, as the object of such is peace itself. To read the world theologically is to read it like a child, because reading in this way is an expression of hope. And hope, says Charles Péguy, is a little girl: "[t]his little girl hope."[11]

As I have tried to show, it is precisely because theology as knowledge understands itself as the performance of the soul's return to God in the company of faith that it must refuse to be encyclopedic. Because God is infinitely knowable, there can be no end to knowledge. Theology refuses the possibility of "survey[ing] at one glance all the empire/As from the clouds" because there is no outside to the cloud to begin with. We see not from a cloud to an-

---

8. Flannery O'Connor, Letter to "A.," 6 September 1955, in Sally Fitzgerald, ed., *The Habit of Being* (New York: Farrar, Straus and Giroux, 1979), p. 100.

9. Hans Urs von Balthasar, *Explorations in Theology*, Vol. IV: *Spirit and Institution*, tr. Edward Oakes, S.J. (San Francisco: Ignatius, 1995), p. 65.

10. St. Augustine, *In Psalm. 85 and 122* (PL XXXVII), pp. 1085, 1630, quoted in Henri de Lubac, *Catholicism: Christ and the Common Destiny of Man*, tr. Lancelot C. Sheppard and Sister Elizabeth Englund, O.C.D. (San Francisco: Ignatius, 1988), p. 46.

11. Charles Péguy, *The Portal of the Mystery of Hope*, tr. David Louis Schindler (Grand Rapids: Eerdmans, 1996). I am indebted here to conversations with Conor Cunningham. See his *Genealogy of Nihilism* (London: Routledge, 2002).

other domain, but from within a cloud.[12] And cloud, as both Paul and the writer of the Epistle to the Hebrews imply, is all we see. For this reason the Gospels, when read liturgically, are censed and veiled, as it were, with a kind of haze. It is therefore not the case that this haziness prevents apprehension of the truth, but rather that the mediation of the truth through the cloud is precisely the condition of its intelligibility. Yet this is a luminous darkness, a radiant fog, because if we now only see through a cloud, it is through a great cloud of witnesses.

12. Here there are affinities with Cunningham's account of the "nubility" of being (see *Genealogy of Nihilism*, pp. 194f., 220f.). He notes that the Latin *nubilis* (which means something like "marriageable") comes from *nubere*, "to veil." I would further add that *nubes* is Latin for "cloud."

Bibliography

Ackeren, Gerald van, S.J. "Is All Revelation in Scripture?" *Proceedings of the Sixth Annual Convention of the Catholic Theological Society of America,* 1951, pp. 249-61.

Agricola, Rudolph. *Three Books Concerning Dialectical Invention.* In *Renaissance Debates on Rhetoric,* edited and translated by Wayne Rebhorn. Ithaca, N.Y.: Cornell University Press, 2000.

Aristotle. *Ethics.* Translated by J. A. K. Thomson. London: Penguin, 1955.

Armstrong, Elizabeth. *Robert Estienne, Royal Printer: An Historical Study of the Elder Stephanus,* revised edition. Courtenay Studies in Reformation Theology 6. Abingdon: Sutton Courtenay, 1986.

Astell, Ann W. *The Song of Songs in the Middle Ages.* Ithaca, N.Y.: Cornell University Press, 1990.

Augustine. *Confessions.* Translated by Henry Chadwick. Oxford: Oxford University Press, 1991.

————. *Confessions.* 3 vols. Edited and translated by J. J. O'Donnell. Oxford: Oxford University Press, 1992.

————. *De Doctrina Christiana.* Edited and translated by R. P. H. Green. Oxford: Oxford University Press, 1995.

————. *On Free Choice of the Will.* Translated by Thomas Williams. Indianapolis: Hackett, 1993.

————. *On the Trinity.* Translated by Edmund Hill, O.P. Brooklyn: New City, 1991.

Backus, Irena Dorota, ed. *The Reception of the Church Fathers in the West.* Volume I: *From the Carolingians to the Maurists.* New York: Brill, 1997.

Baldovin, John F., S.J. *The Urban Character of Christian Worship: The Origins, Development, and Meaning of Stational Liturgy.* Orientalia Christiana Analecta 228. Rome: Pont. Institutum Studiorum Orientalium, 1987.

Balthasar, Hans Urs von. *Explorations in Theology,* Vol. IV: *Spirit and Institution.* Translated by Edward Oakes, S.J. San Francisco: Ignatius, 1995.

Basil the Great. *On the Holy Spirit.* Translated by David Anderson. Crestwood, N.Y.: St. Vladimir's, 1997.

Bazán, Bernardo C. *Les questions disputées, principalement dans les facultés de théologie.* Typologie des Sources du Moyen Âge Occidental, fasc. 44-45. Turnhout, Belgium: Brepols, 1985.

Benson, Robert L., and Giles Constable, eds. *Renaissance and Renewal in the Twelfth Century.* Cambridge, Mass.: Harvard University Press, 1982.

Bernard of Clairvaux. "Cistercians and Cluniacs: St. Bernard's *Apologia* to Abbot William." Translated by Michael Casey. In *The Works of Bernard Clairvaux,* Volume One: *Treatises I.* Cistercian Fathers Series 1. Spencer, Mass.: Cistercian Publications, 1970.

———. *On the Song of Songs,* vol. III. Translated by Killian Walsh, O.C.S.O. Cistercian Fathers Series 7. Kalamazoo, Mich.: Cistercian Publications, 1976.

Biblia Latina cum glossa ordinaria: facsimile reprint of the editio Princeps Adolph Rusch of Strassburg 1480/81. Introduction by Margaret T. Gibson and Karlfried Froehlich. Turnhout, Belgium: Brepols, 1992.

Bird, Otto. "How to Read an Article of the Summa." *The New Scholasticism* XXVII, 1953, 129-59.

Blanche, F. A. "Le vocabulaire de l'argumentation et la structure de l'article dans les ouvrages de saint Thomas." *Revue des sciences philosophiques et théologiques* XIV, 1925, 167-87.

Blanchette, Oliva. *The Perfection of the Universe According to Aquinas: A Teleological Cosmology.* University Park, Pa.: Penn State University Press, 1992.

Bonaventure. *The Soul's Journey into God, The Tree of Life, The Life of St. Francis.* Translated by Ewert Cousins. Classics of Western Spirituality. Mahwah, N.J.: Paulist, 1978.

Bossy, John. *Christianity in the West: 1400-1700.* Oxford: Oxford University Press, 1985.

Boyle, Leonard E., O.P.. *Facing History: A Different Thomas Aquinas.* Louvain-La-Neuve: Fédération Internationale des Instituts d'Etudes Médiévales, 2000.

———. "The Quodlibets of St. Thomas and Pastoral Care." *The Thomist* XXXVIII, 1 January 1974, 232-56.

———. *The Setting of the Summa Theologiae of Saint Thomas.* The Etienne Gilson Series 5. Toronto: Pontifical Institute of Mediaeval Studies, 1982.

Boyle, Marjorie O'Rourke. "Rhetorical Theology: Charity Seeking Charity." In *Rhetorical Invention and Religious Inquiry: New Perspectives,* edited by Walter Jost and Wendy Olmstead. New Haven: Yale University Press, 2000.

Brown, Peter. *Augustine of Hippo.* 2d ed. Berkeley: University of California Press, 1967, 2000.

Bruns, Gerald. *Hermeneutics Ancient and Modern.* New Haven: Yale University Press, 1992.

Burghardt, Walter J. "The Catholic Concept of Tradition in the Light of Modern Theological Thought." *Proceedings of the Seventeenth Annual Convention of the Catholic Theological Society of America,* 1962.

Busa, Roberto. *Clavis indicis Thomistici: in Indices Distributionis, Series I, vol. 1-8, et in Operum St. Thomae Concordantiam Primam, Series II, vol. 1-23.* Stuttgart: Frommann-Holzboog, 1979.

Bush, L. Russ. Review of *Summa Theologiae: A Concise Translation,* ed. Timothy S. McDermott. *Faith and Mission* VIII, Spring 1991, p. 108.

Caferro, William, and Duncan G. Fisher, eds. *The Unbounded Community: Papers in Christian Ecumenism in Honor of Jaroslav Pelikan.* New York: Garland, 1996.

Callahan, David J., Heiko A. Oberman, and Daniel J. O'Hanlon, eds. *Christianity Divided: Protestant and Roman Catholic Theological Issues.* New York: Sheed and Ward, 1961.

Calvin, John. *Institutes of the Christian Religion.* 2 vols. Edited by John T. McNeill and translated by Ford Lewis Battles. The Library of Christian Classics 21. Philadelphia: Westminster, 1960.

Cano, Melchior. *Opera.* 3 vols. Rome: Forzani et Soc., 1890.

Carruthers, Mary. *The Book of Memory: A Study of Memory in Medieval Culture.* Cambridge: Cambridge University Press, 1990.

———. *The Craft of Thought: Meditation, Rhetoric, and the Making of Images, 400-1200.* Cambridge: Cambridge University Press, 1998.

———. "Reading with Attitude, Remembering the Book." In *The Book and the Body,* edited by Dolores Warwick Frese and Katherine O'Brien O'Keefe. Ward-Phillips Lectures in English Language and Literature 14. Notre Dame, Ind.: University of Notre Dame Press, 1997.

Certeau, Michel de. *The Practice of Everyday Life.* Translated by Steven Rendall. Berkeley: University of California Press, 1984.

Cessario, Romanus. Review of *Summa Theologiae: A Concise Translation,* ed. Timothy S. McDermott. *Theological Studies* LII, March 1991, pp. 147-49.

Chemnitz, Martin. *Loci Theologici,* vol. I. Translated by J. A. O. Preus. St. Louis: Concordia, 1989.

Chenu, Marie-Dominique, O.P. *Toward Understanding St. Thomas.* Translated by Albert M. Landry, O.P., and Dominic Hughes, O.P. Chicago: Hugh Regnery, 1964.

Cicero. *Ad Herennium.* Translated by Harry Caplan. Loeb Classical Library 403. London: Harvard University Press, 1954.

———. *De Oratore.* Translated by H. Rackham. Loeb Classical Library 348. London: Harvard University Press, 1960.

Cobb, Peter G. "The Architectural Setting of the Liturgy." In *The Study of Liturgy,* 1st ed. Edited by Cheslyn Jones et al. London: SPCK, 1978.

Coffey, Brian. "The Notion of Order according to St. Thomas Aquinas." *The Modern Schoolman* XXVII, 1 November 1949, pp. 1-18.

Coleman, Janet. *Medieval Readers and Writers, 1350-1400.* New York: Columbia University Press, 1981.

Colish, Marcia. *Medieval Foundations of the Western Intellectual Tradition, 400-1400.* New Haven: Yale University Press, 1997.

Congar, Yves M. J., O.P. *Tradition and Traditions: An Historical and Theological Essay.* London: Burns & Oates, 1966.

Copeland, Rita. *Rhetoric, Hermeneutics, and Translation in the Middle Ages: Academic Traditions and Vernacular Texts.* Cambridge Studies in Medieval Literature 11. Cambridge: Cambridge University Press, 1991.

Corbin, Michel. *Le Chemin de la Théologie chez Thomas d'Aquin.* Paris: Beauchesne, 1974.

Crosby, Alfred W. *The Measure of Reality: Quantification and Western Society, 1250-1600.* Cambridge: Cambridge University Press, 1997.

Cuming, G. J. ed. *Studies in Church History V: The Church and Academic Learning.* Leiden: Brill, 1969.

Cunningham, Conor. *Genealogy of Nihilism.* London: Routledge, 2002.

Cunningham, David S. *Faithful Persuasion: In Aid of a Rhetoric of Christian Theology.* Notre Dame, Ind.: University of Notre Dame Press, 1990.

Cunningham, Lawrence S. Review of *Summa Theologiae: A Concise Translation,* ed. Timothy S. McDermott. *Commonweal* CXVII.2, 26 January 1990, p. 61.

Curtius, Ernst Robert. *European Literature in the Latin Middle Ages.* Translated by Willard R. Trask. Princeton: Princeton University Press, 1953, 1990.

Deferrari, Roy J., and M. Inviolata Barry. *A Complete Index of the* Summa Theologica *of St. Thomas Aquinas.* Baltimore: Catholic University of America Press, 1956.

Derrida, Jacques. *Of Grammatology.* Translated by Gayatri Chakravorty Spivak. London: Johns Hopkins University Press, 1976.

Deusen, Nancy van. *Theology and Music at the Early University: The Case of Robert Grosseteste and Anonymous IV.* Brill Studies in Intellectual History 57. Leiden: Brill, 1994.

Dodaro, Robert, and George Lawless, eds. *Augustine and His Critics.* London: Routledge, 2000.

Dondaine, Hyacinthe François. *Codices Manuscripti Operum Thomae de Aquino.* Recensuerunt H. F. Dondaine et H. V. Shooner, cooperantibus sociis Commissionis Leoninae. Rome: Leonine Commission, 1967-.

Duffy, Eamon. *The Stripping of the Altars: Traditional Religion in England, 1400-1580.* New Haven: Yale University Press, 1992.

Elders, Leo J. *The Metaphysics of Being of St. Thomas in a Historical Perspective.* Studien und Texte zur Geistesgeschichte des Mittelalters 34. Leiden: Brill, 1993.

Eliot, T. S. *Collected Poems, 1909-1962.* London: Faber and Faber, 1963.

Estienne, Robert. *In Evangelium secundum Matthaeum, Marcum, et Lucam Commentarii ex Ecclesiasticis Scriptoribus Collecti, Novae Glossae Ordinariae specimen, donec Meliora Dominus.* Geneva: Oliva Roberti Stephani, 1553.

Evans, G. R. *The Language and Logic of the Bible: The Earlier Middle Ages.* Cambridge: Cambridge University Press, 1984.

———. *The Medieval Theologians.* Oxford: Basil Blackwell, 2000.

———. *Old Arts and New Theology: The Beginnings of Theology as an Academic Discipline.* Oxford: Oxford University Press, 1980.

Fassler, Margot E., and Rebecca A. Balzer, eds. *The Divine Office in the Latin Middle Ages: Methodology and Source Studies, Regional Developments, Hagiography.* Oxford: Oxford University Press, 2000.

Ferruolo, Stephen. *The Origins of the University: The Schools of Paris and Their Critics, 1100-1215.* Stanford: Stanford University Press, 1985.

Foucault, Michel. *The Order of Things: An Archaeology of the Human Sciences.* New York: Random House, 1970.

Frese, Dolores Warwick, and Katherine O'Brien O'Keefe, eds. *The Book and the Body.*

Ward-Phillips Lectures in English Language and Literature 14. Notre Dame, Ind.: University of Notre Dame Press, 1997.

Froehlich, Karlfried. "The Printed Gloss." In *Biblia Latina cum glossa ordinaria: facsimile reprint of the editio Princeps Adolph Rusch of Strassburg 1480/81.* Introduction by Margaret T. Gibson and Karlfried Froehlich. Turnhout, Belgium: Brepols, 1992.

———. "Walafrid Strabo and the *Glossa Ordinaria:* The Making of a Myth." *Studia Patristica* XXIII, 1969, pp. 192-96.

Gadamer, Hans-Georg. *Truth and Method.* 2nd ed. Translated and revised by Joel Weinsheimer and Donald G. Marshall. New York: Continuum, 1975, 1989.

Galavaris, George. *Bread and the Liturgy: The Symbolism of Early Christian and Byzantine Bread Stamps.* Madison: University of Wisconsin Press, 1970.

Geenan, G., O.P. "The Place of Tradition in the Theology of St. Thomas." *The Thomist* XV, 1952, pp. 110-35.

Geiselmann, Josef Rupert. "Scripture, Tradition, and the Church: An Ecumenical Problem." In *Christianity Divided: Protestant and Roman Catholic Theological Issues,* edited by David Callahan et al. New York: Sheed and Ward, 1961.

Gellrich, Jesse M. *The Idea of the Book in the Middle Ages: Language Theory, Mythology, and Fiction.* Ithaca, N.Y.: Cornell University Press, 1985.

George, Marie I. "Mind Forming and Manuductio in Aquinas." *The Thomist* LVII, 2 April 1993, pp. 201-13.

Gibson, Margaret T. "The Place of the *Glossa Ordinaria* in Medieval Exegesis." In *Ad Litteram: Medieval Texts and Their Readers,* edited by Mark D. Jordan. Notre Dame, Ind.: University of Notre Dame Press, 1992, pp. 5-27.

———. "The Twelfth-Century Glossed Bible." *Studia Patristica* XXIII, 1969, pp. 232-44.

———, ed. *The Bible in the Latin West.* The Medieval Book 1. Notre Dame, Ind.: University of Notre Dame Press, 1993.

Gilby, Thomas, O.P. "Structure of the *Summa,*" Appendix I. In St. Thomas Aquinas, *Summa Theologiae: Latin Text and English Translation, Introductions, Notes, Appendices and Glossaries,* Vol. I. London: Blackfriars, 1963, pp. 43-46.

Gilson, Etienne. *The Christian Philosophy of St. Thomas Aquinas.* Translated by L. K. Shook, C.S.B. Notre Dame, Ind.: University of Notre Dame Press, 1956, 1994.

Glossa Ordinaria, Pars 22: In Canticvm Canticorvm. Corpus Christianorum: Continuatio Mediaevalis 170. Turnhout, Belgium: Brepols, 1997.

Grabmann, Martin. *Introduction to the Theological Summa of St. Thomas.* Translated by John S. Zybura. St. Louis: Herder, 1930.

Graham, William A. *Beyond the Written Word: Oral Aspects of Scripture in the History of Religion.* Cambridge: Cambridge University Press, 1987.

Greenslade, S. L., ed. *The Cambridge History of the Bible,* Volume III: *The West from the Reformation to the Present Day.* Cambridge: Cambridge University Press, 1963.

Grossmann, Maria. "Wittenberg Printing, Early Sixteenth Century." *Sixteenth Century Essays and Studies* I, 1970, pp. 53-74.

Hadot, Pierre. *Philosophy as a Way of Life: Spiritual Exercises from Socrates to Foucault.* Edited by Arnold Davidson and translated by Michael Chase. Oxford: Basil Blackwell, 1995.

Hagen, Kenneth, ed. *The Quadrilog: Tradition and the Future of Ecumenism. Essays in Honor of George H. Tavard.* Collegeville, Minn.: The Liturgical Press, 1994.

Hall, Basil. "The Trilingual College of San Ildefonso and the Making of the Complutensian Polyglot Bible." In *Studies in Church History V: The Church and Academic Learning,* edited by G. J. Cuming. Leiden: Brill, 1969.

Hamel, C. F. R. de. *Glossed Books of the Bible and the Origins of the Paris Booktrade.* Woodbridge, Suffolk: D. S. Brewer, 1984.

Hankey, Wayne J. *God in Himself: Aquinas' Doctrine of God as Expounded in the* Summa Theologiae. Oxford: Oxford University Press, 1987.

Harley, J. B. "Silences and Secrecy: The Hidden Agenda of Cartography in Early Modern Europe." *Imago Mundi* XL, 1988, pp. 57-76.

Harley, J. B., and David Woodward, eds. *The History of Cartography,* Volume I: *Cartography in Prehistoric, Ancient, and Medieval Europe and the Mediterranean.* Chicago: University of Chicago Press, 1987.

Harrison, Carol. "The Rhetoric of Scripture and Preaching: Classical Decadence or Christian Aesthetic?" In *Augustine and His Critics,* edited by Robert Dodaro and George Lawless. London: Routledge, 2000, pp. 214-30.

Harrison, Peter. *The Bible, Protestantism, and the Rise of Natural Science.* Cambridge: Cambridge University Press, 1998.

Hawkins, Peter S. *Dante's Testaments: Essays in Scriptural Imagination.* Stanford: Stanford University Press, 1999.

Hayen, André. *Saint Thomas d'Aquin et la vie de l'Eglise.* Louvain: Publications universitaires de Louvain, 1952.

Henry, Michel. *I Am the Truth: Toward a Philosophy of Christianity.* Translated by Susan Emanuel. Stanford: Stanford University Press, 2003.

Hillgarth, J. N. *Who Read Thomas Aquinas?* The Etienne Gilson Series 13. Toronto: Pontifical Institute of Mediaeval Studies, 1992.

Hollier, Denis. *Against Architecture: The Writings of Georges Bataille.* Translated by Betsy Wing. Cambridge, Mass.: MIT Press, 1989.

Hugh of St. Victor. *The* Didascalicon *of Hugh of St. Victor.* Translated by Jerome Taylor. Chicago: University of Chicago Press, 1961.

————. *The Divine Love: The Two Treatises* De Laude Caritatis *and* De Amore Sponsi ad Sponsam. Translated by a Religious of C.S.M.V. Oxford: A. R. Mowbray & Co., 1956.

Huizinga, Johan. *The Autumn of the Middle Ages.* Translated by Rodney J. Payton and Ulrich Mammitzsch. Chicago: University of Chicago Press, 1996.

Illich, Ivan. *In the Vineyard of the Text: A Commentary to Hugh's* Didascalicon. Chicago: University of Chicago Press, 1993.

Jardine, Lisa. *Erasmus, Man of Letters.* Princeton: Princeton University Press, 1993.

Jenkins, John I., CSC. *Knowledge and Faith in Thomas Aquinas.* Cambridge: Cambridge University Press, 1997.

John Climacus. *The Ladder of Divine Ascent.* Translated by Colm Luibheid and Norman Russell. Mahwah, N.J.: Paulist, 1982.

Jones, Cheslyn, Geoffrey Wainwright, and Edward Yarnold, S.J., eds. *The Study of Liturgy,* 1st ed. London: SPCK, 1978.

Jones, Lindsay. *The Hermeneutics of Sacred Architecture: Experience, Interpretation, Comparison*. Volume I: *Monumental Occasions: Reflections on the Eventfulness of Religious Architecture*. Cambridge, Mass.: Harvard University Press, 2000.

Jordan, Mark D. *The Alleged Aristotelianism of Thomas Aquinas*. The Etienne Gilson Series 15. Toronto: Pontifical Institute of Mediaeval Studies 1992.

———. "The *Summa*'s Reform of Moral Teaching — and Its Failures." In *Contemplating Aquinas: On the Varieties of Interpretation*, edited by Fergus Kerr. London: SCM, 2003.

———. "The Competition of Authoritative Languages and Aquinas's Theological Rhetoric." *Medieval Philosophy and Theology* IV, 1994, pp. 71-90.

———. *Ordering Wisdom: The Hierarchy of Philosophical Discourses in Aquinas*. Notre Dame, Ind.: University of Notre Dame Press, 1986.

———. "Theological Exegesis and Aquinas' Treatise 'Against the Greeks.'" *Church History* LVI, December 1987, pp. 445-56.

———. "Thomas Aquinas on Bernard and the Life of Contemplation." In *Bernardus Magister: In Celebration of the Nonacentenary of the Birth of Saint Bernard of Clairvaux: 1090-1990*, edited by John R. Sommerfeldt. Cistercian Studies 135. Kalamazoo, Mich.: Cistercian Publications, 1992.

———, ed. *Ad Litteram: Medieval Texts and Their Readers*. Notre Dame: University of Notre Dame Press, 1992.

Jost, Walter, and Wendy Olmstead, eds. *Rhetorical Invention and Religious Inquiry: New Perspectives*. New Haven: Yale University Press, 2000.

Jungmann, Josef A., S.J. *The Mass: An Historical, Theological, and Pastoral Survey*. Translated by Julian Fernandes, S.J. Collegeville, Minn.: The Liturgical Press, 1976.

———. *The Mass of the Roman Rite: Its Origins and Development*. 2 vols. Translated by Francis Brunner. Allen, Texas: Christian Classics, 1986, 1949.

Kaczor, Christopher. "Thomas Aquinas on the Development of Doctrine." *Theological Studies* LXII, 2001, pp. 283-302.

Kaufmann, Walter, ed. *The Basic Writings of Nietzsche*. New York: Modern Library, 1992.

Kennedy, George A. *Classical Rhetoric and Its Christian and Secular Tradition from Ancient to Modern Times*, 2d ed. Chapel Hill, N.C.: University of North Carolina Press, 1999.

Kerr, Fergus. *Contemplating Aquinas: On the Varieties of Interpretation*. London: SCM, 2003.

Kierkegaard, Søren. *Fear and Trembling; Repetition*. Edited by Howard V. and Edna H. Hong. Princeton: Princeton University Press, 1983.

Knowles, David. *The Evolution of Medieval Thought*, 1st ed. London: Longmans, 1962.

Kolb, Robert. "The Ordering of the *Loci Communes Theologici*: The Structuring of the Melanchthonian Dogmatic Tradition." *Concordia Journal* XXIII, 4 October 1997, pp. 317-37.

———. "Teaching the Text: The Commonplace Method in Sixteenth Century Lutheran Biblical Commentary." *Bibliothèque d'Humanisme et Renaissance* XLIX.3, 1987, pp. 571-85.

Kristeller, Paul Oskar. *Medieval Aspects of Renaissance Learning*. Edited and translated by Edward P. Mahoney. New York: Columbia University Press, 1992.

Lash, Nicholas. *The Beginning and the End of 'Religion'.* Cambridge: Cambridge University Press, 1996.

———. *Theology on the Way to Emmaus.* London: SCM, 1986.

Loughlin, Gerard. *Telling God's Story: Bible, Church, and Narrative Theology.* Cambridge: Cambridge University Press, 1996.

Lubac, Henri de. *Catholicism: Christ and the Common Destiny of Man.* Translated by Lancelot C. Sheppard and Sister Elizabeth Englund, O.C.D. San Francisco: Ignatius, 1988.

———. *Medieval Exegesis,* Volume One: *The Four Senses of Scripture.* Translated by Mark Sebanc. Grand Rapids: Eerdmans, 1997.

———. *Medieval Exegesis,* Volume Two: *The Four Senses of Scripture.* Translated by E. M. Macierowski. Grand Rapids: Eerdmans, 2000.

———. *Theology in History.* Translated by Anne Englund Nash. San Francisco: Ignatius, 1996.

Luther, Martin. *First Lectures on the Psalms.* Volume I: *Psalms 1-75.* Edited by Hilton C. Oswald. Luther's Works 10. St. Louis: Concordia, 1974.

McDermott, Timothy S., ed. *Summa Theologiae: A Concise Translation.* Westminster, Md.: Christian Classics, 1989.

MacIntyre, Alasdair. *Three Rival Versions of Moral Enquiry: Encyclopaedia, Genealogy, and Tradition.* London: Duckworth, 1990.

———. *Whose Justice? Which Rationality?* Notre Dame, Ind.: University of Notre Dame Press, 1988.

Mack, Peter. *Renaissance Argument: Valla and Agricola in the Traditions of Rhetoric and Dialectic.* Leiden: Brill, 1993.

McKeon, Richard. *Rhetoric: Essays in Invention and Discovery.* Woodbridge, Conn.: Ox Bow, 1987.

McLelland, Joseph C., ed. *Peter Martyr Vermigli and Italian Reform.* Waterloo, Ontario: Wilfrid Laurier University Press, 1980.

McNally, J. R. "Rudolph Agricola's *De Inventione Dialectica Libri Tres:* A Translation of Selected Chapters." *Speech Monographs* 34, 1967, 393-422.

McWilliam, Joanne, ed. *Augustine: From Rhetor to Theologian.* Waterloo, Ontario: Wilfrid Laurier University Press, 1992.

Mâle, Emile. *The Gothic Image: Religious Art in France of the Thirteenth Century.* Translated by Dora Nussey. New York: Harper and Row, 1972.

Marenbon, John. *Later Medieval Philosophy, 1150-1350.* London: Routledge & Kegan Paul, 1987.

Marion, Jean-Luc. *God without Being: Hors-Texte.* Translated by Thomas A. Carlson. Chicago: University of Chicago Press, 1991.

Martin, Thomas F., O.S.A. "Augustine's *Confessions* as Pedagogy: Exercises in Transformation." In *Augustine and Liberal Education,* edited by Kim Paffenroth and Kevin L. Hughes. Aldershot: Ashgate, 2000.

Matter, E. Ann. "The Bible in the Center: The *Glossa Ordinaria.*" In *The Unbounded Community: Papers in Christian Ecumenism in Honor of Jaroslav Pelikan,* edited by William Caferro and Duncan G. Fisher. New York: Garland, 1996.

———. "The Church Fathers and the *Glossa Ordinaria.*" In *The Reception of the Church*

Fathers in the West, Volume I: *From the Carolingians to the Maurists,* edited by Irena Dorota Backus. New York: Brill, 1997.

————. *The Voice of My Beloved: The Song of Songs in Western Medieval Christianity.* Philadelphia: University of Pennsylvania Press, 1990.

Melanchthon, Philipp. *Melanchthon on Christian Doctrine. Loci Communes 1555.* Edited by Clyde L. Manschreck. Oxford: Oxford University Press, 1965.

————. *Orations on Philosophy and Education.* Edited by Sachiko Kusukawa and translated by Christine F. Salazar. Cambridge: Cambridge University Press, 1999.

Milbank, John. *Theology and Social Theory: Beyond Secular Reason.* Oxford: Basil Blackwell, 1990.

————. *The Word Made Strange: Theology, Language, Culture.* Oxford: Basil Blackwell, 1997.

Milbank, John, and Catherine Pickstock. *Truth in Aquinas.* London: Routledge, 2001.

Moss, Ann. *Printed Commonplace-Books and the Structuring of Renaissance Thought.* Oxford: Clarendon, 1996.

Mulchahey, M. Michèle. *"First the Bow Is Bent in Study . . .": Dominican Education Before 1350.* Toronto: Pontifical Institute of Mediaeval Studies, 1998.

Murphy, James J. *Rhetoric in the Middle Ages: A History of the Rhetorical Theory from Saint Augustine to the Renaissance.* Medieval and Renaissance Texts and Studies 227. Tempe: Arizona Center for Medieval and Renaissance Studies, 1974, 2001.

New Catholic Encyclopedia. Vol. V. New York: McGraw-Hill, 1967.

Nietzsche, Friedrich. *Daybreak.* Translated by R. J. Hollingdale. Texts in German Philosophy. Cambridge: Cambridge University Press, 1982.

Oberman, Heiko A. *The Harvest of Medieval Theology: Gabriel Biel and Late Medieval Nominalism.* 3d ed. Grand Rapids: Baker, 2000.

O'Connor, Flannery. *The Habit of Being.* Edited by Sally Fitzgerald. New York: Farrar, Straus, and Giroux, 1979.

Oliver, Simon. "The Eucharist before Nature and Culture." *Modern Theology* XV.3, July 1999, pp. 331-53.

Ong, Walter J., S.J. *Orality and Literacy: The Technologization of the Word.* London: Routledge, 1982.

————. *The Presence of the Word: Some Prolegomena for Cultural and Religious History* New Haven: Yale University Press, 1967.

————. *Ramus, Method, and the Decay of Dialogue: From the Art of Discourse to the Art of Reason.* Cambridge: Harvard University Press, 1958, 1983.

Origen. *Commentary on John,* Book 13.3-192. In *Origen,* edited by Joseph W. Trigg. London: Routledge, 1998.

————. *Commentary on the Song of Songs.* Translated by R. P. Lawson. Ancient Christian Writers 26. New York: Newman, 1957.

Paetow, Louis John. *The Arts Course at Medieval Universities with Special Reference to Grammar and Rhetoric.* Champaign-Urbana: University of Illinois Press, 1910.

Paffenroth, Kim, and Kevin L. Hughes, eds. *Augustine and Liberal Education.* Aldershot: Ashgate, 2000.

Panofsky, Erwin. *Gothic Architecture and Scholasticism.* New York: Meridian, 1957.

————, ed. *Abbot Suger: On the Abbey Church of St.-Denis and Its Art Treasures*. 2d ed. Princeton: Princeton University Press, 1979.

Péguy, Charles. *The Portal of the Mystery of Hope*. Translated by David Louis Schindler. Grand Rapids: Eerdmans, 1996.

Persson, Per Erik. *Sacra Doctrina: Reason and Revelation in Aquinas*. Translated by Ross Mackenzie. Philadelphia: Fortress, 1970.

Petroski, Henry. *The Book on the Bookshelf*. New York: Alfred A. Knopf, 1999.

Pickstock, Catherine. *After Writing: On the Liturgical Consummation of Philosophy*. Oxford: Basil Blackwell, 1997.

Pieper, Josef. *The Four Cardinal Virtues: Prudence, Justice, Fortitude, Temperance*. New York: Harcourt, Brace & World, 1965.

————. *Leisure, the Basis of Culture*. Translated by Gerald Malsbary. South Bend, Ind.: St. Augustine's, 1998.

Plato. *Timaeus and Critias*. Translated by Desmond Lee. London: Penguin, 1965, 1971.

Poovey, Mary. *A History of the Modern Fact: Problems of Knowledge in the Sciences of Wealth and Society*. Chicago: University of Chicago Press, 1998.

Principe, Walter H., C.S.B. "'Tradition' in Thomas Aquinas' Scriptural Commentaries." In *The Quadrilog: Tradition and the Future of Ecumenism. Essays in Honor of George H. Tavard*, edited by Kenneth Hagen. Collegeville, Minn.: The Liturgical Press, 1994, pp. 43-60.

Rand, E. K. *Cicero in the Courtroom of St. Thomas Aquinas*. The Aquinas Lecture 1945. Milwaukee: Marquette University Press, 1946.

Rebhorn, Wayne, ed. and tr. *Renaissance Debates on Rhetoric*. Ithaca, N.Y.: Cornell University Press, 2000.

Robertson, Anne Walters. "From Office to Mass: The Antiphons of Vespers and Lauds and the Antiphons before the Gospel in Northern France." In *The Divine Office in the Latin Middle Ages: Methodology and Source Studies, Regional Developments, Hagiography*, edited by Margot E. Fassler and Rebecca A. Balzer. Oxford: Oxford University Press, 2000.

Roover, Florence Edler de. "The Scriptorium." In *The Medieval Library*, edited by James Westfall Thompson. Chicago: University of Chicago Press, 1939.

Rosemann, Philipp W. *Understanding Scholastic Thought with Foucault*. New York: St. Martin's, 1999.

Rouse, Richard H., and Mary A. Rouse. "*Statim invenire:* Schools, Preachers, and New Attitudes to the Page." In *Renaissance and Renewal in the Twelfth Century*, edited by Robert L. Benson and Giles Constable. Cambridge, Massachusetts: Harvard University Press, 1982.

Schroeder, H. J., O.P. *The Canons and Decrees of the Council of Trent*. Rockford, Ill.: TAN, 1978.

Shuger, Debra K. *Sacred Rhetoric: The Christian Grand Style in the English Renaissance*. Princeton: Princeton University Press, 1988.

Smalley, Beryl. "Glossa Ordinaria." In *Theologische Realenzyklopädie*, Volume XIII. Berlin: Walter de Gruyter, 1984.

———. *The Study of the Bible in the Middle Ages*. South Bend: University of Notre Dame Press, 1964.

Sommerfeldt, John R., ed. *Bernardus Magister: In Celebration of the Nonacentenary of the Birth of Saint Bernard of Clairvaux, 1090-1990*. Cistercian Studies 135. Kalamazoo, Mich.: Cistercian Publications, 1992.

Spijker, Willem van't, ed. *Calvin: Erbe und Auftrag: Festschrift für Wilhelm Heinrich Neuser zum 65. Geburtstag*. Kampen, The Netherlands: Kok Pharos, 1991.

Steinhauser, Kenneth B. "The Literary Unity of the *Confessions*." In *Augustine: From Rhetor to Theologian*. edited by Joanne McWilliam. Waterloo, Ont.: Wilfrid Laurier University Press, 1992, pp. 15-30.

Stock, Brian. *After Augustine: The Meditative Reader and the Text*. Philadelphia: University of Pennsylvania Press, 2001.

———. *Augustine the Reader: Meditation, Self-Knowledge, and the Ethics of Interpretation*. Cambridge, Mass.: Harvard University Press, 1996.

Stone, Jon R. "The Medieval Mappaemundi: Toward an Archaeology of Sacred Cartography." *Religion* XXIII, 1993, pp. 197-216.

Sullivan, Francis A., S.J. *Magisterium: Teaching Authority in the Catholic Church*. New York: Paulist, 1983.

Swanson, Jenny. "The *Glossa Ordinaria*." In *The Medieval Theologians*, edited by G. R. Evans. Oxford: Basil Blackwell, 2000.

Tavard, George. *Holy Writ or Holy Church: The Crisis of the Protestant Reformation*. New York: Harper & Bros., 1959.

———. "Tradition in Early Post-Tridentine Theology." *Theological Studies* XXIII.3, September 1962, pp. 377-405.

Thomas Aquinas. *On Truth* [*Quaestiones disputatae de veritate*]. 3 vols. Translated by Robert W. Mulligan et al. Indianapolis: Hackett, 1994.

———. *Summa Theologiae*. 61 vols. Cambridge: Blackfriars, 1964-81.

———. *Summa Theologica*. Translated by Fathers of the English Dominican Province. Allen, Texas: Christian Classics, 1948.

Thompson, James Westfall, ed. *The Medieval Library*. Chicago: University of Chicago Press, 1939.

Torrell, Jean-Pierre, O.P. *Saint Thomas Aquinas,* Volume One: *The Person and His Work*. Translated by Robert Royal. Washington, D.C.: Catholic University of America Press, 1993.

———. *Saint Thomas Aquinas,* Volume Two: *Spiritual Master*. Translated by Robert Royal. Washington, D.C.: Catholic University of America Press, 2003.

Toulmin, Stephen. *Cosmopolis: The Hidden Agenda of Modernity*. Chicago: University of Chicago Press, 1990.

Trigg, Joseph W. *Origen*. London: Routledge, 1998.

Vasoli, Cesare. "*Loci Communes* and the Rhetorical and Dialectical Traditions." In *Peter Martyr Vermigli and Italian Reform*, edited by Joseph C. McLelland. Waterloo, Ont.: Wilfrid Laurier University Press, 1980.

Velde, Rudi A. te. *Participation and Substantiality in Thomas Aquinas*. Studien und Texte zur Geistesgeschichte des Mittelalters 46. Leiden: Brill, 1995.

Wagner, David L., ed. *The Seven Liberal Arts in the Middle Ages*. Bloomington: Indiana University Press, 1983.

Ward, Graham, ed. *The Certeau Reader*. Oxford: Basil Blackwell, 2000.

Weisheipl, James, O.P. *Friar Thomas d'Aquino: His Life, Thought, and Works*. Washington, D.C.: Catholic University of America Press, 1974, 1983.

White, Victor, O.P. *Holy Teaching: The Idea of Theology according to St. Thomas Aquinas*. London: Blackfriars, 1958.

Williams, A. N. "Deification in the *Summa Theologiae:* A Structural Interpretation of the *Prima Pars*." *The Thomist* LXI.2, April 1997, pp. 219-55.

———. *The Ground of Union: Deification in Aquinas and Palamas*. Oxford: Oxford University Press, 1999.

———. "Mystical Theology Redux: The Pattern of Aquinas' *Summa Theologiae*." *Modern Theology* XIII.1, January 1997, pp. 53-74.

Williams, Rowan. "Language, Reality and Desire in Augustine's *De Doctrina*." *Journal of Literature & Theology* III.2, July 1989, pp. 138-50.

———. "What Does Love Know? St. Thomas on the Trinity." *New Blackfriars* LXXXII.964, June 2001, pp. 260-72.

Wippel, John F. "Quodlibetal Questions Chiefly in Theology Faculties." In *Les Questions Disputées et les Questions Quodlibétiques dans les Facultés de Théologie, de Droit et de Médecine,* edited by Bernardo C. Bazan. Typologie des Sources du Moyen Âge Occidental 44-45. Turnhout, Belgium: Brepols, 1985.

Woodward, David. "Reality, Symbolism, Time, and Space in Medieval World Maps." *Annals of the Association of American Geographers* LXXV.4, 1985, pp. 510-21.

Wright, D. F. "Robert Estienne's *Nova Glossa Ordinaria:* A Protestant Quest for a Standard Bible Commentary." In *Calvin: Erbe und Auftrag: Festschrift für Wilhelm Heinrich Neuser zum 65. Geburtstag,* edited by Willem van't Spijker. Kampen, The Netherlands: Kok Pharos, 1991, pp. 40-51.

Yates, Frances. *The Art of Memory*. London: Routledge & Kegan Paul, 1966; Pimlico, 1992.

Index

Benedict, 7

Bernard of Clairvaux, 7, 83n.30, 87, 155n.51, 156

Bible, 82-83; glossed, 33-34, 49, 69, 72, 75n.12, 79n.21; glossless, 14, 32n.37, 75; as a physical thing, 15, 18, 119; and *sola scriptura*, 14, 18, 74. See also *traditio;* Word of God

Biel, Gabriel, 119

Bird, Otto, 106

Blanchette, Olivia, 109n.7, 113

Blessed Virgin. *See* Mary, the Blessed Virgin

Body of Christ, 13-14, 77; church as, 14, 50, 57; and the Eucharist, 78, 86, 161; the *Glossa* as textual figure of, 19, 89; participation in, 61, 141, 143. *See also* Jesus Christ

Boethius, 32

Bonaventure, 41n.1, 44-47, 83, 107n.47, 121

book, 11-12, 28, 32; Bible as, 18, 76, 79; as container of truth, 27, 70n.2; shift in production of, 13, 23, 33. *See also* moveable type

Book of Kells, 10

"borrowing," 51; of language, 19, 38; of speech, and Augustine, 52-69; and Thomas, 128

Bossy, John, 16n.34, 50n.24

Boyle, Leonard E., 90-91, 126n.65

Brown, Peter, 67n.53

Bruns, Gerald, 74-75

Burghardt, Walter J., 28n.22

Bush, L. Russ, 94n.17, 97

Calvin, John, 13n.27, 14, 16, 17n.37, 22

Camargo, Martin, 147n.23

Cano, Melchior, 18, 28-29, 97

caritas, 57, 68

Carruthers, Mary, 6n.13, 9, 18, 37n.51, 43n.6, 44, 45n.8, 46n.12, 49, 50n.23, 64n.43, 80n.24, 83, 85n.38, 112n.16, 113n.21, 114nn.22-23, 153n.44, 155nn.51-52, 157

Cartesian "revolution," and representation, 22, 79n.23

cartography, 42-43

Catena Aurea (Thomas), 48

catholicae veritatis doctor (Thomas), 99, 125-26

Celestine I, 52

Certeau, Michel de, 2n.3, 9-10, 18, 30-31, 36-40, 42-43, 71, 73-75, 82, 129n.73, 149

Cessario, Romanus, 93n.13

Chaucer, 64n.43

Chemnitz, Martin, 27n.18

Chenu, Marie-Dominique, 47, 139, 141

Christ. *See* Jesus Christ

Christianity, pedagogical project of, 15, 45, 60-61

Christmas Day, masses said on, 152

Church, as coming into existence by liturgy, 81, 117-18, 123, 163

Church Dogmatics (Barth), 21

Cicero, 26, 55, 56n.10, 58-59, 148, 150

city, as *locus* of liturgy, 157. *See also* pilgrim city

cloud of witnesses, 49, 167-68

Cobb, Peter G., 17n.38

Coffey, Brian, 128n.72

Coleman, Janet, 49

collect, in the Mass, 159

Commentary on the Psalms (Gilbert of Poitier), 8

Commentary on the Sentences (Henry of Ghent), 117

communication: and the scriptural economy, 14; and the Eucharist, 14, 161; of the sermon, 17

Complutensian Polygot, 33

Confessions (Augustine), 17-19, 53-54, 63-69, 141

Congar, Yves M. J., 117, 119

contemplation, 110-12, 115-16, 135-38

Copeland, Rita, 59, 60n.25

Corbin, Michel, 141

Council of Trent, 28-29, 70-72, 76, 118n.40

counter-Reformation, 71